HTML

VIRTUAL CLASSROOM

MW01015628

2 8⁰⁰

About the Author

Robert Fuller is a web developer, author, and instructor. He is currently "Web Guru" at Philadelphia's Limehat & Company (which means he drinks a lot of coffee and pushes his responsibilities off on interns). A veteran of New York's Silicon Alley, it's been his great pleasure to take that experience into the classroom. He's trained thousands of students from such schools as Pratt Institute in his native Brooklyn to Temple University in his adopted Philadelphia (though his corporate clients at Bell Atlantic Digital Graphics are still his favorites).

Robert has developed online courses in web design, and has been published on other related topics that include web programming and graphic design for the web. He is the author of another book in this series, *Dreamweaver® 4 Virtual Classroom*.

About the Technical Editor

Merlyn Holmes is a founder and partner of Hot Tea Productions: a fine brew of print, video, web, and other media. Lately, she has focused on web courseware design and has taught classes and conducted Train-the-Trainers across the United States and Europe. She has been a Subject Matter Expert and the lead author on two five-day courses called "Web Design" and "Web Production," which are currently being offered at training centers internationally.

In between such commitments, Merlyn has also been the Gallery Director and/or judge for the Macromedia People's Choice Awards and the NewMedia Invision Awards since 1996; as such, she has—sometimes with delight and sometimes with despondency—reviewed over 3500 web and multimedia entries. She is propelled by those moments when, while reviewing piles and piles of entries, she finds herself looking at her monitor and seeing an absolute gem, an example of a web site or CD-ROM or some other new media that takes its medium to a higher level.

HTML

VIRTUAL CLASSROOM

Robert Fuller

 OSBORNE

New York   Chicago   San Francisco
Lisbon   London   Madrid   Mexico City
Milan   New Delhi   San Juan
Seoul   Singapore   Sydney   Toronto

McGraw-Hill/Osborne
2600 Tenth Street
Berkeley, California 94710
U.S.A.

To arrange bulk purchase discounts for sales promotions, premiums, or fund-raisers, please contact McGraw-Hill/Osborne at the above address. For information on translations or book distributors outside the U.S.A., please see the International Contact Information page immediately following the index of this book.

HTML Virtual Classroom

Copyright © 2002 by The McGraw-Hill Companies. All rights reserved. Printed in the United States of America. Except as permitted under the Copyright Act of 1976, no part of this publication may be reproduced or distributed in any form or by any means, or stored in a database or retrieval system, without the prior written permission of the publisher, with the exception that the program listings may be entered, stored, and executed in a computer system, but they may not be reproduced for publication.

Brainsville.com™
The better way to learn.

CD-ROM Portions Copyright © 2002 The McGraw-Hill Companies, Inc., and Portions Copyright © 2002 Brainsville.com. The exact portions on the Work owned by each of the parties has been recorded with the U.S. Copyright Office.

1234567890   QPD QPD 0198765432

Book p/n 0-07-219257-7 and CD p/n 0-07-219258-5
parts of
ISBN 0-07-219256-9

Publisher	**Project Manager**	**Design and Production**
Brandon A. Nordin	Jenn Tust	epic
Vice President &	**Acquisitions Coordinator**	**Cover Design**
Associate Publisher	Tana Diminyatz	Ted Holladay
Scott Rogers		
	Technical Editor	
Acquisitions Editor	Merlyn Holmes	
Gretchen Campbell		

This book was composed with QuarkXPress™.

Information has been obtained by McGraw-Hill/Osborne from sources believed to be reliable. However, because of the possibility of human or mechanical error by our sources, McGraw-Hill/Osborne, or others, McGraw-Hill/Osborne does not guarantee the accuracy, adequacy, or completeness of any information and is not responsible for any errors or omissions or the results obtained from use of such information.

Dedication

Because HTML is essentially the beginning for web-based media, I thought
I'd dedicate this to the people responsible for my beginnings—my folks.

Mom, I miss you every damn day.

Dad, I miss you too. I realize with each passing day, we have more and more in
common. When I stop and think about that, I find I'm rather pleased.

Acknowledgments

Roger, thank you again for giving me the opportunity to write a second book for
this series. If I develop one umpteenth of your wisdom and patience before my
time is done, I will consider myself enlightened.

A book is never the result of just one person's efforts. There isn't enough space
here to adequately thank Chrisa Hotchkiss and Eric Houts who've managed to
make me look in print much more sophisticated than I do in person.

Many thanks to my technical editor, Merlyn Holmes, who really came through
in a pinch contributing material throughout the appendixes.

Finally, I thank Gretchen Campbell for making me smile!

Contents at a Glance

Introduction   xvii

1   The Internet and HTML   1

2   The HTML Document   11

3   Formatting Text   19

4   Working with Images and Rules   41

5   Hyperlinks   59

6   Creating Lists   71

7   Tables   85

8   Forms   107

9   Frames   129

10 Cascading Style Sheets   145

11 Layers   171

12 The Future of HTML   185

A   HTML Tag and Special Character Reference   195

B   Coloring the Web   211

C   Planning Your Web Site   227

D   Uploading and Testing   237

Index   259

Contents

Introduction xvii

1 The Internet and HTML 1

A BRIEF HISTORY OF THE INTERNET 2

THE BIRTH OF THE WEB 2

UNDERSTANDING MARKUP AND MARKUP LANGUAGES 4

THE BROWSER 5

HOW YOUR BROWSER WORKS 6

TOOLS OF THE TRADE 7

HOW MANY BROWSERS ARE TOO MANY? 7

TEXT EDITORS 8

A WORD ABOUT WYSIWYG EDITORS 10

FINAL THOUGHTS 10

2 The HTML Document 11

A SIMPLE HTML DOCUMENT 12

THE <html> TAGS 13

THE HEAD ELEMENT 13

THE BODY ELEMENT 14

HTML SYNTAX 14

   TAGS AND THEIR ATTRIBUTES 15

   CLOSING TAGS 16

   CASE SENSITIVITY 16

   COMMENT TAGS 16

MOVING FORWARD 18

   ON THE VIRTUAL CLASSROOM CD-ROM:
   LESSON 1 18

3 Formatting Text 19

HTML TEXT FORMATTING AND
CASCADING STYLE SHEETS 20

PARAGRAPHS, LINE BREAKS, AND HEADINGS 20

   PARAGRAPHS 22

   LINE BREAKS 24

   HEADINGS 25

FONTS, SIZES, AND COLOR 27

   THE <font> TAG 27

   FONT COLOR 31

PHYSICAL AND LOGICAL STYLES 32

NESTING TAGS 34

PREFORMATTED TEXT 35

BLOCK QUOTES 36

SPECIAL CHARACTERS 38

   ON THE VIRTUAL CLASSROOM CD-ROM:
   LESSON 2 39

4 Working with Images and Rules 41

IMAGE FORMATS 42

   GIF AND JPEG USAGE 42

INSERTING IMAGES 43

   DEFINING THE SOURCE OF AN IMAGE 44

   SETTING IMAGE DIMENSIONS 45

SPECIFYING A BORDER WIDTH 46

ALIGNING AN IMAGE 46

VERTICAL AND HORIZONTAL SPACING 50

USING ALTERNATIVE TEXT 51

HORIZONTAL RULES 53

THE <hr> TAG 53

ON THE VIRTUAL CLASSROOM CD-ROM:
LESSON 3 57

5 Hyperlinks 59

WHAT'S IN A LINK? 60

THE <a> TAG 60

THE URL 61

PATHNAMES REVISITED 62

ABSOLUTE PATHNAMES 62

RELATIVE PATHNAMES 63

FORMATTING HYPERLINKS 65

SETTING LINK COLORS 66

CONTROLLING IMAGE-LINK BORDERS 66

NAMED ANCHORS 67

CREATING NAMED ANCHORS 67

LINKING TO NAMED ANCHORS 68

USING THE id ATTRIBUTE 68

CREATING E-MAIL LINKS 69

ON THE VIRTUAL CLASSROOM CD-ROM:
LESSON 4 69

6 Creating Lists 71

UNORDERED LISTS 72

MODIFYING THE BULLET STYLE 73

ORDERED LISTS 74

MODIFYING THE NUMBERING STYLE 74

THE start ATTRIBUTE 76

THE value ATTRIBUTE 78

NESTING LISTS 79

   NESTING UNORDERED LISTS 79

   NESTING ORDERED LISTS 80

DEFINITION LISTS 81

   ON THE VIRTUAL CLASSROOM CD-ROM:
   LESSON 5 83

7 Tables 85

THE TABLE TAGS 86

FORMATTING TABLE PROPERTIES 87

   TABLE BORDERS 87

   TABLE ALIGNMENT 88

   TABLE DIMENSIONS 90

   CELL PADDING AND CELL SPACING 91

   BACKGROUND COLORS AND IMAGES 93

FORMATTING ROW AND CELL PROPERTIES 94

   TABLE HEADERS 94

   ROW AND CELL ALIGNMENT 95

   WIDTH AND HEIGHT 97

   SPANNING ROWS AND COLUMNS 98

NESTING TABLES 99

   ON THE VIRTUAL CLASSROOM CD-ROM:
   LESSON 6 105

8 Forms 107

DISSECTING A FORM 108

   THE <form> TAG 113

   FORM CONTROLS 114

FORMATTING TEXT BOXES 116

   TEXT FIELDS 117

   PASSWORD FIELDS 119

   TEXT AREAS 119

FORMATTING CHECK BOXES 121

FORMATTING RADIO BUTTONS 121

FORMATTING MENUS AND LISTS 122

FORMATTING FILE FIELDS 124

FORMATTING HIDDEN FIELDS 125

FORMATTING SUBMIT AND RESET BUTTONS 126

USING GRAPHIC IMAGES FOR SUBMIT BUTTONS ... 126

ON THE VIRTUAL CLASSROOM CD-ROM:
LESSON 7 127

9 Frames 129

UNDERSTANDING FRAMES-BASED WEB PAGES 130

THE FRAMESET DOCUMENT 130

DEFINING COLUMNS AND ROWS 132

NESTING FRAMESETS 134

FORMATTING BORDER PROPERTIES 135

SETTING SCROLL BAR PROPERTIES 138

SETTING FRAME MARGINS 138

LINKING BETWEEN FRAMES 140

SPECIAL TARGET NAMES 141

SETTING A BASE TARGET 141

ACCOMMODATING OLDER BROWSERS 141

THE PROS AND CONS OF FRAMES 142

ON THE VIRTUAL CLASSROOM CD-ROM:
LESSON 8 143

10 Cascading Style Sheets 145

INTRODUCTION TO STYLE SHEETS 146

CSS SYNTAX 147

STYLE RULES 147

DECLARATIONS 147

CONTEXTUAL SELECTORS 148

STYLE CLASSES 148

SELECTOR CLASSES 149

STANDARD CLASSES 149

ID CLASSES 149

STYLE SHEET TYPES 150

    INLINE STYLES 151

    EMBEDDED STYLE SHEETS 151

    LINKED STYLE SHEETS 152

    IMPORTED STYLE SHEETS 153

STYLE PROPERTIES 153

    UNITS OF MEASURE 153

    PARENTS AND CHILDREN 156

FONT PROPERTIES 157

    THE font-family PROPERTY 157

    THE font-size PROPERTY 158

    THE font-style PROPERTY 158

    THE font-weight PROPERTY 159

    THE font-variant PROPERTY 159

COLOR AND BACKGROUND PROPERTIES 159

    THE color PROPERTY 159

    THE background-color PROPERTY 160

    THE background-image PROPERTY 160

    THE background-repeat PROPERTY 160

    THE background-attachment PROPERTY 161

    THE background-position PROPERTY 161

TEXT PROPERTIES 162

    THE word-spacing PROPERTY 162

    THE letter-spacing PROPERTY 163

    THE text-decoration PROPERTY 163

    THE vertical-align PROPERTY 163

    THE text-transform PROPERTY 164

    THE text-align PROPERTY 164

    THE text-indent PROPERTY 164

    THE line-height PROPERTY 165

BOX PROPERTIES 165

    PADDING PROPERTIES 166

    BORDER PROPERTIES 166

    UNIQUE BOX PROPERTIES 167

    MARGIN PROPERTIES 169

CLASSIFICATION PROPERTIES 169

THE white-space PROPERTY 169

THE display PROPERTY 169

THE list-style-type PROPERTY 170

THE list-style-image PROPERTY 170

THE list-style-position PROPERTY 170

ON THE VIRTUAL CLASSROOM CD-ROM:
LESSON 9 170

11 Layers 171

UNDERSTANDING CSS-POSITIONING 172

THE <div> AND <span> TAGS 174

HOW CSS CREATES LAYERED CONTENT 174

UNDERSTANDING CSS-POSITIONING
PROPERTIES 175

THE position PROPERTY 175

THE COORDINATE PROPERTIES 177

DEFINING LAYER DIMENSIONS 180

THE visibility PROPERTY 181

THE z-index PROPERTY 181

CONTROLLING LAYER OVERFLOW 182

DEFINING A CLIPPING AREA 183

ON THE VIRTUAL CLASSROOM CD-ROM:
LESSON 10 183

12 The Future of HTML 185

THE DEATH OF HTML 186

XML 186

XML + HTML = XHTML 190

SYNTAX: XHTML VS. HTML 190

CASE SENSITIVITY 190

CLOSING TAGS 191

EMPTY TAGS 191

ATTRIBUTE QUOTATION MARKS 191

SINGLE-WORD ATTRIBUTE VALUES 192

SPECIAL CHARACTERS 192

THE id ATTRIBUTE 193

SUGGESTED READING AND RESOURCES 193

A   HTML Tag and Special Character Reference 195

HTML TAGS AND ATTRIBUTES 196

HTML SPECIAL CHARACTERS 206

B   Coloring the Web 211

HEXADECIWHAT? LEARNING HOW TO
SPEAK COLOR FOR THE WEB 212

RGB 212

HEXADECIMAL VALUES 213

COMMON COLOR NAMES 216

WHICH COLORS CAN YOU USE?
DEFINING WEBSAFE COLORS 218

THE MYTHICAL WEBSAFE PALETTE 218

THE TRUE WEBSAFE PALETTE 219

HYBRID WEBSAFE COLORS 221

IN PRACTICE: USABILITY GUIDELINES FOR
COLOR ON THE WEB 221

USE APPROPRIATE COLORS FOR THE AUDIENCE
AND THE SITE GOALS 222

USE COLORS WITHIN THE NAVIGATION TO SUPPORT
THE ORGANIZATION OF YOUR CONTENT 224

DON'T OVERUSE COLOR 225

DON'T RELY EXCLUSIVELY ON COLOR 226

C   Planning Your Web Site 227

GROUNDWORK 228

WHAT IS YOUR OBJECTIVE? 228

WHO IS YOUR AUDIENCE? 228

WHICH HARDWARE AND SOFTWARE WILL
YOUR VISITORS BE USING? 229

How Do You Want Visitors to Navigate
Your Site? 230

How Will Your Site Look? 230

STORYBOARDING YOUR SITE 230

Sketching Your Ideas 231

Choosing a Storyboarding Medium 232

Building the Level of Storyboard Detail 233

GATHERING YOUR ASSETS 234

STRUCTURING YOUR LOCAL SITE FILES 235

D   Uploading and Testing 237

POSTING PAGES TO THE WEB 238

Using FTP Software 238

Organizing Your Files on the Web Server 241

TESTING YOUR WEB SITE 242

TESTING EQUIPMENT 243

TESTING TOOLS 243

SITEWIDE TESTING ISSUES 244

Does the Site Appear Consistently in Target
Browsers and Operating Systems? 244

Is the Navigation Consistent
Throughout the Site? 245

Is the Look and Feel Consistent and
Appropriate for the Audience? 246

Is the Background Color Consistent? 247

Does Each Section Contain the
Correct Content? 247

Does the Site Map Correctly Reflect
the Structure of the Site? 248

Do All Pages Load? 248

SPECIFIC PAGE TESTING 248

Do the Titles Appear Correctly at the
Top of the Browser? 248

Are the meta Tags Complete? 249

Does the Page Download Quickly? 249

ARE THE MOST IMPORTANT ELEMENTS ON
EACH PAGE VISIBLE BEFORE SCROLLING? 250

DOES RESIZING THE BROWSER WINDOW ADVERSELY
AFFECT THE PAGE OR INDIVIDUAL ELEMENTS? 250

DOES THE CORRECT VERSION OF THE PAGE
DISPLAY IN THE BROWSER? 250

DOES UNWANTED CONTENT (SUCH AS CODE)
APPEAR ON ANY PAGE? 251

IS THE SOURCE CODE WELL COMMENTED IN
PREPARATION FOR MAINTENANCE? 251

IS THE TEXT CONTENT READABLE? 252

DOES TEXT APPEAR IN THE DESIRED FONT? 253

DO ALL SPECIAL CHARACTERS APPEAR? 253

DO ANY UNWANTED CHARACTERS APPEAR
IN THE TEXT? 253

DO ALL PAGE ELEMENTS LOAD? 254

DO PAGE ELEMENTS LOAD IN THE
APPROPRIATE ORDER? 254

DO UNWANTED DASHES APPEAR BY
LINKED IMAGES? 254

ARE THE alt ATTRIBUTES FOR EACH
ELEMENT WORKING? 254

ARE ALL THE LINKS WORKING PROPERLY? 255

DO ALL SCRIPTS WORK? 255

TESTING CHECKLIST 256

Index 259

Introduction

WHO WILL ENJOY THIS BOOK?

Hopefully, you will. It's my desire to share with you how simple HTML can be. A number of web design packages generate HTML code for you as you build documents and sites, in the same manner as a word processor or layout program. Some might argue that this convenience eliminates any need to ever learn the Hypertext Markup Language itself, but even the best web design applications provide quick and easy access to the source code. Why? Because no matter how good a product may be, sometimes, you just have to get at the code to make something work. I think that by the time you've read this book and watched the CD lessons, you'll agree that HTML was never anything to be intimidated by.

WHAT MAKES THIS A VIRTUAL CLASSROOM?

The accompanying CD makes this book a *virtual classroom*. Instead of just reading about HTML, you can watch and listen as the author discusses the different topics examined in each chapter while helpful visuals appear on screen, demonstrating various features and techniques.

However, the CD is not a visual repetition of the book—not everything discussed in the book is covered on the CD, and some topics broached on the CD are covered in more detail there than in the book. The goal for the CD is to give you the experience of sitting in on one of my classes, allowing me to elaborate on certain topics that can be better expressed and explained in a full-color, moving medium. Topics in the book that wouldn't be any better explained through sound, color, and motion are not found on the CD, whereas topics that couldn't be effectively explained through text and black-and-white images *are* found on the CD.

You can learn a great deal from the book without ever watching the CD. I hope, however, that you'll read the book *and* watch the CD to enhance what you've absorbed through your reading. This approach is the closest match to hands-on classroom training experience, because I typically discuss a topic and then show it to or demonstrate it for the class, inviting the students to work along with me on their computers so that the skills become part of each student's personal experience.

HOW THIS BOOK WORKS

Of course you know how a book *works*: you open it and start reading, turning pages as you go. Not too difficult, right? This book, however, has some useful features that you should be aware of:

► **Figures and illustrations** Figures are referred to by number in the text, and those numbers appear next to the figures themselves to help you associate them. When I think you will be helped by looking at a picture of what I'm describing in the text, you'll see "as shown in Figure…" or "see Figure…" and a reference to a particular figure by its number. Illustrations are not numbered, but each illustration appears directly below or next to the text that refers to it.

▶ **Tips and sidebars** Whenever I thought of something that I'd present as a quick aside during class, I turned it into a tip. Tips relate to the main topic in the nearby text, but they are extra bits of helpful information rather than entire topics unto themselves. Sidebars delve a little deeper, discussing larger topics that relate to nearby text.

▶ **CD references** At the end of chapters containing topics covered on the CD, an "On the Virtual Classroom CD-ROM" notation appears, directing you to the specific CD lesson that relates to the chapter you've just read.

I hope you enjoy this book, and if you have any specific design questions or quandaries, I invite you to contact me via e-mail at robert@highstrungproductions.com. I answer all reader mail, attempting to do so within 24 to 48 hours of receiving it. I look forward to hearing from you!

 # HTML VIRTUAL CLASSROOM CD

This CD contains an exciting new kind of video-based instruction to help you learn HTML faster. We believe this learning tool is a unique development in the area of computer-based training. The author actually talks to you, right from your computer screen, demonstrating topics he wrote about in the book. Moving "screencams" and slides accompany his presentation, reinforcing what you're learning.

The technology and design of the presentation were developed by Brainsville.com. The content on the CD-ROM was developed by Osborne/McGraw-Hill, Robert Fuller, and Brainsville.com. Patents (pending), copyright, and trademark protections apply to this technology and the name *Brainsville.com*.

Please read the following directions for usage of the CD-ROM, to ensure that the lessons play as smoothly as possible.

GETTING STARTED

The CD-ROM is optimized to run under Windows 95/98/ME/NT/2000 or a Mac, using the QuickTime player version 5 (or greater), from Apple. If you don't have the QuickTime 5 player installed, you must install it, either by downloading it from the Internet at http://www.quicktime.com, or running the Setup program from the CD-ROM. If you install from the Web, it's fine to use the free version of the QuickTime player. You don't need to purchase the full version. If you can't install the QuickTime player, or you prefer to use Windows Media Player, we have provided the lessons in that format as well, primarily as a backup plan. See the Troubleshooting section for details.

Note: If you have QuickTime Player 4 or earlier, individual lessons will still play, but you will not be able to switch between lessons using the navigation links in the lessons. In order to use these links, be sure to install QuickTime Player version 5, which is included on this CD.

To install the QuickTime player from the CD-ROM follow these steps:

On a Windows PC

1. Insert the CD-ROM in the drive.
2. Use Explorer or My Computer to browse to the CD-ROM.
3. Open the QuickTime folder.
4. Open the Windows folder.
5. Double-click on the QuickTime Installer program there.
6. Follow the setup instructions on screen.

On a Mac

1. Insert the CD-ROM in the drive.
2. Open the QuickTime folder.
3. Open the Mac folder.
4. Run the QuickTime installer file there.

RUNNING THE CD IN WINDOWS 95/98/ME/NT/2000

Minimum Requirements

▶ QuickTime 5 player

▶ Pentium II P300 (or equivalent)

▶ 64MB of RAM

▶ 8X CD-ROM

▶ Windows 95, Windows 98, Windows 2000, Windows ME, or Windows NT 4.0 with at least Service Pack 4

▶ 16-bit sound card and speakers

The HTML Virtual Classroom CD-ROM can run directly from the CD (see below for running it from the hard drive for better performance if necessary) and should start automatically when you insert the CD in the drive. If the program does not start automatically, your system may not be set up to automatically detect CDs. To change this, you can do the following:

1. Choose Settings, Control Panel, and click the System icon.
2. Click the Device Manager tab in the System Properties dialog box.
3. Double-click the Disk drives icon and locate your CD-ROM drive.
4. Double-click the CD-ROM drive icon and then click the Settings tab in the CD-ROM Properties dialog box. Make sure the "Auto insert notification" box is checked. This specifies that Windows will be notified when you insert a compact disc into the drive.

If you don't care about the auto-start setting for your CD-ROM, and don't mind the manual approach, you can start the lessons manually, this way:

1. Insert the CD-ROM.
2. Double-click the My Computer icon on your Windows desktop.
3. Open the CD-ROM folder.
4. Double-click the startnow.exe icon in the folder.
5. Follow instructions on the screen to start.

RUNNING THE CD ON A MAC

Minimum Requirements

▶ A PowerPC processor–based Macintosh computer.

▶ At least 64MB of RAM

▶ Mac OS 7.5.5 or later (but not OS X)

As of this writing QuickTime 5 is not compatible with OS X. However, this issue should soon be fixed by Apple, and you can download a free copy of the updated version of QuickTime from www.quicktime.com.

To run the CD

1. Insert the CD-ROM.
2. Double-click on the file "INlesson" to start the introduction.

THE OPENING SCREEN

When the program autostarts, you'll see a small window in the middle of your screen with an image of the book. Simply click the book to launch the QuickTime player and start the lessons.

The QuickTime player window should soon open and the Virtual Classroom introduction should begin running. On some computers, after the lesson loads you must click the Play button to begin. The Play button is the big round button with an arrow on it at the bottom center of the QuickTime player window. It looks like the play button on a VCR. You can click on the links in the lower left region of the QuickTime window to jump to a given lesson. The author will explain how to use the interface.

The QuickTime player will completely fill a screen that is running at 800×600 resolution. (This is the minimum resolution required to play the lessons.) For screens with higher resolution, you can adjust the position of the player on screen, as you like.

If you are online, you can click on the Brainsville.com logo under the index marks to jump directly to the Brainsville.com web site for information about additional video lessons from Brainsville.com.

IMPROVING PLAYBACK

Your Virtual Classroom CD-ROM employs some cutting-edge technologies, requiring that your computer be pretty fast to run the lessons smoothly. Many variables determine a computer's video performance, so we can't give you specific requirements for running the lessons. CPU speed, internal bus speed, amount of

RAM, CD-ROM drive transfer rate, video display performance, CD-ROM cache
settings, and other variables will determine how well the lessons will play. Our
advice is to simply try the CD. The disc has been tested on laptops and desktops
of various speeds, and in general, we have determined that you'll need at least a
Pentium II-class computer running in excess of 300MHz for decent performance. (If
you're doing serious web-design work, it's likely your machine is at least this fast.)

CLOSE OTHER PROGRAMS

For best performance, make sure you are not running other programs in the background while viewing the CD-based lessons. Rendering the video on your screen
takes a lot of computing power, and background programs such as automatic
e-mail checking, web-site updating, or Active Desktop applets (such as scrolling
stock tickers) can tax the CPU to the point of slowing the videos.

ADJUST THE SCREEN COLOR DEPTH
TO SPEED UP PERFORMANCE

It's possible the author's lips will be out of synch with his or her voice, just like
web-based videos often look. There are a couple solutions. Start with this one.
Lowering the color depth to 16 bit color makes a world of difference with many
computers, laptops included. Rarely do people need 24-bit or 32-bit color for
their work anyway, and it makes scrolling your screen (in any program) that
much slower when running in those higher color depths. Try this:

1. Right-click on the desktop and choose Properties.
2. Click the Settings tab.
3. In the Colors section, open the drop-down list box and choose a lower setting. If
   you are currently running at 24-bit (True Color) color, for example, try 16-bit
   (High Color). Don't use 256 colors, since video will appear very funky if you do.
4. OK the box. With most computers these days, you don't have to restart the
   computer after making this change. The video should run more smoothly now,
   since your computer's CPU doesn't have to work as hard to paint the video pictures on your screen.

If adjusting the color depth didn't help the synch problem, see the section on the
next page about copying the CD's files to the hard disk.

TURN OFF SCREEN SAVERS, SCREEN BLANKERS, AND STANDBY OPTIONS

When lessons are playing, you're not likely to interact with the keyboard or mouse. Because of this, your computer screen might blank, and in some cases (such as with laptops) the computer might even go into a standby mode. You'll want to prevent these annoyances by turning off your screen saver and by checking the power options settings to ensure they don't kick in while you're viewing the lessons. You make settings for both of these parameters from the Control Panel.

1. Open Control Panel, choose Display, and click on the Screen Saver tab. Choose "None" for the screen saver.
2. Open Control Panel, choose Power Management, and set System Standby, Turn Off Monitor, and Turn Off Hard Disks to Never. Then click Save As and save this power setting as *Brainsville Courses*.

You can return your power settings to their previous state if you like, after you are finished viewing the lessons. Just use the Power Schemes drop-down list and choose one of the factory-supplied settings, such as Home/Office Desk.

COPY THE CD FILES TO THE HARD DISK TO SPEED UP PERFORMANCE

The CD-ROM drive will whir quite a bit when running the lessons from the CD. If your computer or CD-ROM drive is a bit slow, it's possible the author's lips will be out of synch with his or her voice, just like web-based videos often look. The video might freeze or slow down occasionally, though the audio will typically keep going along just fine. If you don't like the CD constantly whirring, or you are annoyed by out-of-synch video, you may be able to solve either or both problems by copying the CD-ROM's contents to your hard disk and running the lessons from there. To do so:

1. Using My Computer or Explorer, check to see that you have at least 650MB free space on your hard disk.
2. Create a new folder on your hard disk (the name doesn't matter) and copy all the contents of the CD-ROM to the new folder (you must preserve the subfolder names and folder organization as it is on the CD-ROM).

3. Once this is done, you can start the program by opening the new folder and double-clicking on the file startnow.exe. This will automatically start the lessons and run them from the hard disk.

(Optional) For convenience, you can create a shortcut to the startnow.exe file and place it on your desktop. You will then be able to start the program by clicking on the shortcut.

UPDATE YOUR QUICKTIME PLAYER

The QuickTime software is updated frequently and posted on the Apple QuickTime Web site, www.quicktime.com. You can update your software by clicking Update Existing Software, from the Help menu in the QuickTime player. We strongly suggest you do this from time to time.

MAKE SURE YOUR CD-ROM DRIVE IS SET FOR OPTIMUM PERFORMANCE

CD-ROM drives on IBM PCs can be set to transfer data using the DMA (Direct Memory Access) mode, assuming the drive supports this faster mode. If you are experiencing slow performance and out-of-synch problems, check this setting. These steps are for Windows 98 and Windows ME.

1. Open Control Panel, choose System.
2. Click on the Device Manager tab
3. Click on the + sign to the left of the CD-ROM drive.
4. Right-click on the CD-ROM drive.
5. Choose Properties.
6. Click the Settings tab.
7. Look to see if the DMA check box is turned on (has a checkmark in it).

If selected, this increases the CD-ROM drive access speed. Some drives do not support this option. If the DMA check box remains selected after you restart Windows, then this option is supported by the device.

In Windows 2000, the approach is a little different. You access the drive's settings via Device Manager as above, but click on IDE/ATAPI Controllers. Right-click the IDE channel that your CD-ROM drive is on, choose Properties, and make the settings as appropriate. Choose the device number, 0 or 1, and check the settings. Typically it's set to "DMA if available," which is fine. It's not recommended that you change these settings unless you know what you are doing.

TROUBLESHOOTING

This section offers solutions to common problems. Check www.quicktime.com for much more information about the QuickTime player, which is the software the Virtual Classroom CDs use to play.

THE CD WILL NOT RUN

If you have followed the instructions above and the program will not work, you may have a defective drive or a defective CD. Be sure the CD is inserted properly in the drive. (Test the drive with other CDs, to see if they run.)

THE SCREENCAM MOVIE IN A LESSON HANGS

If the author continues to talk, but the accompanying screencam seems to be stuck, just click on the lesson index in the lower left region of the QuickTime window to begin your specific lesson again. If this doesn't help, close the QuickTime window, then start the Virtual Classroom again.

VOLUME IS TOO LOW OR IS TOTALLY SILENT

1. Check your system volume first. Click on the little speaker icon next to the clock, down in the lower right-hand corner of the screen. A little slider pops up. Adjust the slider, and make sure the Mute check box is not checked.

2. Next, if you have external speakers on your computer, make sure your speakers are turned on, plugged in, wired up properly, and the volume control on the speakers themselves is turned up.

3. Note that the QuickTime player also has a volume control setting. The setting is a slider control in the lower left of the QuickTime player window.

4. The next place to look, if you're still having trouble, is in the Windows volume controls. Double-click on the little speaker by the clock, and it will bring up the Windows Volume Control sliders. Make sure the slider for "Wave" is not muted, and it's positioned near the top.

BACKUP LESSONS This CD includes alternate files for all of the lessons, in the Windows Media format, for playing in the Windows Media Player. We've supplied these extra files in case you have trouble running the lessons in the QuickTime player. These files, though of a somewhat lower-quality appearance than the QuickTime files, may still be useful if you have trouble running the QuickTime files. Note also that the navigation links that appear beneath the author's face will not work in the Windows Media Player files. This is due to limitations in the Windows Media player.

To view the backup lessons:

Windows users can click on the Windows Media Files link on the normal startup screen for this CD. (If the startup screen didn't appear when you inserted the CD, double-click the startnow.exe icon.) Use the resulting browser window for starting your lessons. When a lesson ends, return to the browser window and click on the next lesson you want to run.

Mac users can double-click the HTML file called WMfiles.html. Use the resulting browser window for starting your lessons. When a lesson ends, return to the browser window and click on the next lesson you want to run.

In Media Player, we suggest you set the skin to Classic, and then switch to "compact mode," then set the view to 100%. The picture will be much clearer that way.

As an alternative approach to running the Windows Media files, you can simply use Windows Explorer or the Mac Finder to navigate to the Windows Media folder on the CD. Then open the Windows Media folder and double-click on the lesson name you want to see. For example, 01lesson.wmv is lesson 1.

To view the Windows Media files, you will need the Windows Media Player. (This player is available for both the PC and Mac platforms.) It is likely to be installed on your Windows PC already. If you're on a Mac, or if you don't have the latest Windows Media Player (you'll need version 6.4 or later), you can download the latest Windows Media Player for free from www.microsoft.com/windowsmedia.

FOR TECHNICAL SUPPORT

▶ Phone Hudson Software at (800) 217-0059

▶ Visit www.quicktime.com

▶ Visit www.brainsville.com

© 2002 The McGraw-Hill Companies

© 2002 Brainsville.com Patents pending

1

The Internet and HTML

So you want to learn HTML? This is good—HTML is the underlying markup language of every web page you've ever seen. If you've never heard the terms "markup language" before, don't worry; you'll learn about that in a moment. Before delving into the specifics of HTML, however, it's important to get a little of the back-story first: for example, where HTML comes from and what HTML has to do with the World Wide Web and the Internet.

A BRIEF HISTORY OF THE INTERNET

Like so many "modern conveniences," the Internet has its origins in military research. Throughout the '60s, researchers at different institutions both in the United States and abroad were theorizing about large-scale computer networks and developing technologies by which computers of the time could be connected and communicate with one another seamlessly. The end result was called ARPANET, which came online in 1969 under the auspices of the U.S. Defense Advanced Research Projects Agency (DARPA).

ARPANET initially connected four large computers at UCLA, UC Santa Barbara, Stanford, and the University of Utah. Within a year, both MIT and Harvard were added. The next year, Carnegie-Mellon and Case-Western came on board, followed quickly by the NASA Ames Research Center and the University of Illinois. Other research institutions also swelled the ranks during this period, and by 1972, more computers were connected to ARPANET than space here allows me to mention.

At this stage in the game, no one was thinking about commercial applications for this system. The research community, benefiting from the linked resources of all those universities and institutes, was concerned with opening new vistas in computer science, while the Defense Department was interested in the feasibility of maintaining a series of linked computer networks that could survive a nuclear strike. In fact, commercial use of ARPANET was prohibited unless it directly served the goals of research and education.

This policy continued until 1990, when ARPANET officially ceased to be an independent entity and simply became another part of the Internet, which by then had become a global entity containing networks created in Europe, Australia, South America, and elsewhere. But I'm getting ahead of myself. You see, just a few years prior to that, something really amazing happened.

THE BIRTH OF THE WEB

Up to this point, using the "Internet" was far from what you're used to today. Web browsers didn't exist yet; in fact, there was no "Web" to browse. Computers with graphical user interfaces—the likes of which you use today on a Windows or Macintosh system—were not mainstream. Most folks who actually had access to the early Internet accomplished tasks through *terminal interfaces*: black screen, white text (OK, green and tan, too).

In 1989, Tim Berners-Lee and other members of the European Laboratory for Particle Physics, or CERN, as it is more commonly called, developed a new protocol for distributing information across the Internet. Known as the Hypertext Transfer Protocol (http://), it relied on a browser program that read documents laid out with their other invention, the Hypertext Markup Language (HTML). HTML allowed for the creation of embedded text links, tying one document to another—creating a web of linked documents that resided on servers across the Internet. This was brought online in 1991, and thus, the Web was born.

Sometimes the terms "Internet" and "Web" are used interchangeably. However, one is actually a part of the other. Think of them in terms of hardware and software. There's the physical network of computers (the hardware), and the software (Hypertext Transfer Protocol and Hypertext Markup Language, to name only a fraction), which, when all combined, create the thing we call the Internet. The Web is simply a part of this greater whole. The Internet is the hardware (phone lines and computers), while the World Wide Web is the result of software (the Hypertext Transfer Protocol and Hypertext Markup Language) running on computers that are part of the Internet.

Dif. between web + Net

With the dissolution of ARPANET and the development of independent commercial networks like Prodigy, CompuServe, and America Online (AOL), the early '90s saw the dawning of the Internet and World Wide Web we know today. By 1993, Marc Andreessen had developed the first graphical web browser for mass consumption at the National Center for Supercomputing Applications (NCSA), called Mosaic. Shortly thereafter, he founded the Netscape Corporation, whose famous web browser and server software soon became the commercial standard. Of course, Microsoft was soon to follow with Internet Explorer, and the browser wars began.

Browsers

Today, Netscape is a subsidiary of AOL/Time Warner, the largest media conglomerate in history, and is no longer the major player it once was. Microsoft has been brought to court for, among other infractions, tying their web browser into their operating system, making it difficult to use a competitor's browser software as the primary browser on a Windows system.

So there you have it. When ARPANET went online, computers were large machines that occupied whole rooms and buildings, and they were the private province of the government, corporations, universities, and research institutes. The number of

ARPANET users could probably have fit in a lecture hall. Today, laptop PCs that would make an old IBM mainframe blush can fit in a backpack and are as much a part of mainstream life as cars and television sets. In the United States alone, there are over 100 million people online, and with an estimated 55 thousand new users every day, that number is growing every minute.

To quote from the UCLA Center for Communication Policy's *2000 Internet Report* (http://www.ccp.ucla.edu):

"The Internet has become the fastest growing electronic technology in world history. In the United States, for example, after electricity became publicly available, 46 years passed before 30 percent of American homes were wired; 38 years passed before the telephone reached 30 percent of U.S. households, and 17 years for television. The Internet required only seven years to reach 30 percent of American households."

UNDERSTANDING MARKUP AND MARKUP LANGUAGES

OK, the invention of the Hypertext Markup Language made the Web possible, but what exactly is a markup language in the first place? Well, the term "markup" has been around for quite some time. Traditionally, *markup* referred to the process of laying out manuscript pages for typesetting. It consisted of instructions for which type faces and sizes should be used, the word and character spacing, indentation, etc. A manuscript page would be written on, or "marked up," with all these various instructions and given to the typesetter who would then set the type and print the manuscript. HTML is not much different in its scope. You use it to mark up a standard electronic text file in such a way that a web browser can understand and display it.

Obviously, you can't scribble on an electronic text document, so you need another method for marking it up. Enter the HTML *tag*. Generally, an HTML tag is a character or abbreviation bracketed between greater-than and less-than symbols, like so: <p>. This is the tag for marking up a paragraph. In most cases, tags have both an opening and closing form to signify the starting and ending points of the page element they define. The closing tag simply repeats the opening tag with the addition of a forward slash in front of the character or abbreviation, so in this example, the closing paragraph tag looks like this: `</p>`. These two tags together create a container (`<p></p>`). The browser reads the document, sees the tags, and displays what falls between them as a paragraph.

THE BROWSER

Because the browser makes viewing a web page possible, you need to understand its past as well. You see, the development of both the web browser and HTML walk hand in hand. As previously mentioned, Marc Andreessen's work on Mosaic spawned Netscape's Navigator browser. This was in 1994, by which time, HTML had been around for five years and had a developed standard. Netscape was creating a name for itself, not only for being the first commercial browser in existence, but by expanding on the HTML standard with proprietary tags of its own.

By the time Netscape released version 2.0 of its browser software, it supported objects called *applets* written in the Java programming language, as well as having its own scripting language called Live Script. Netscape soon changed the name to JavaScript in collaboration with Sun Microsystems, to capitalize on the popularity of Sun's previously mentioned Java programming language, although the two have little in common. Much of the functionality that Netscape pioneered found its way into the HTML standard, at which point, the standard was simply trying to keep up with market innovation instead of the other way around.

After the release of their Windows 95 operating system, Microsoft began to realize the importance of the Internet and started to seriously develop their Internet strategy. It took a few attempts, but by version 3.0 of their Internet Explorer browser, they were on a competitive footing with Netscape and were also creating their own proprietary tags. Microsoft, of course, had one serious advantage over Netscape. They could afford to bundle their browser with the Windows operating system, effectively giving it away for free and capitalizing on the likelihood that people wouldn't feel the need to go download another browser if they already had one in hand. Netscape could not compete on an equal footing. This simple fact was what drove Netscape into decline, and it was a compelling part of the Justice Department's antitrust claims against Microsoft.

Although a number of other browsers exist on the market, Internet Explorer and Netscape Navigator are and have been the two leading forces. As of this writing,

Netscape has released version 6.0 of their browser, having jumped there directly from version 4.76. Internet Explorer is currently in version 5.5, with 6.0 right around the corner. Both still possess a number of proprietary tags not found in the current HTML 4.01 standard, both support different implementations of JavaScript (called JScript in Internet Explorer), and both display various web page elements in a slightly different fashion. What's more, with each successive release of a browser, new functionality ensures that the older versions are not capable of all the tricks the new versions are. And because there is no guarantee that web site visitors are all using the latest and greatest web browsers, web designers and developers are in a constant struggle to deliver content that is both cutting-edge and backward compatible.

HOW YOUR BROWSER WORKS

When you open your browser and go to a web site, what's happening? In effect, you are initiating a kind of conversation. You are sending a request via your browser out to the computer on which the web page is stored. This computer is called the *web server*. Once the web server receives your request to see that particular page, it checks to see if that page is in fact there. If it locates the page within its stock of files, it bundles up the HTML information and returns it to your browser via the Hypertext Transfer Protocol (http://). If the web server can't locate the page you requested, it returns an error message, informing you that the file wasn't found.

This little conversation between your browser and the web server reflects what is known in computer parlance as a *client/server relationship*. You can probably guess that the web server fulfills the server side of this relationship, so that would mean that the browser functions as the client. Anything that takes place on the server side of the "conversation" is referred to as just that: *server side*. Anything that needs to take place on your computer is called *client side*.

In this client/server relationship, it is the client (you and your browser) who initiates all interaction. You make the request to the web server to view a page, and then the web server "serves it up" to you. In most cases, the web server keeps a log of all the requests clients make, noting the client computer, the time, and the document requested. It's important to point out another Internet/Web difference here. To view an HTML document in your browser, it isn't necessary to be connected to the Internet at all. A web browser reads an HTML document wherever it's located, whether it's on a web server out on the Internet, stored on a local network, or sitting in a folder on your hard disk. As long as it's HTML, you browser can handle it.

TOOLS OF THE TRADE

What do you need to create HTML documents? Not a whole lot, really. Just some kind of text editor that allows you to save your files with an .htm or .html extension and a browser to view them in. That's it. With these rather minor restrictions, what follows is a discussion of the tools available to you and some advice on making choices that will benefit your work style.

HOW MANY BROWSERS ARE TOO MANY?

In terms of web browsers, at the very least, you should have the most recent versions of both Internet Explorer and Netscape Navigator. They are both available for download from their respective web sites, free of charge. If you plan on doing serious web development, however, you will want more browsers in your toolkit. Why? To test the pages you design across the widest spectrum possible to ensure that what you create looks as good as possible to as many potential viewers as possible. If your creation looks good in one browser, but it is virtually unusable in a number of others, you need to rethink your design strategy.

So how should you round out your browser collection? Have a number of the older versions, at least back to version 4.0 of a given browser. Be aware that Windows will not allow you to have more than one version of Internet Explorer installed at a time. You can have multiple versions of Netscape on a computer, but you usually can't have two different versions open at the same time. In a perfect world, you'd have a number of operating system, browser, and monitor configurations set up across which to test your work. This is what professional web developers do, but this is not always feasible for the home hobbyist, and I'm not about to suggest that you go buy two or three computers to learn HTML—unless you really want to. Of course, you will need at least one.

The following are three sites that, as of this writing, provide downloads of old and exotic browsers. The Netscape FTP site listed here can be accessed via your browser, while the Interlog FTP site requires you to use FTP software.

▶ http://browsers.evolt.org

This site is an archive representing over 100 different browsers, both common and exotic, from their earliest beta versions up through their most recent releases for all applicable operating systems.

▶ ftp://archive:oldies@archive.netscape.com/archive/index.html

This is the Netscape archive, which has all versions of their browsers for both Mac and PC.

▶ ftp://ftp.interlog.com/pub/windows95/web_browsers

The Interlog FTP site requires you to use FTP software to download archived browsers. This address has Internet Explorer and Netscape browsers only for the Windows operating system.

> **TIP** What is FTP? FTP stands for File Transfer Protocol, which, as the name implies, is a method for transferring files across the Internet. Computers set up to maintain files that can be accessed via FTP are called FTP servers.
>
> If you want to install FTP software on your machine, a number of good freeware and shareware FTP programs exist that you can download from places like http://www.tucows.com or http://www.downloads.com. Simply go to these sites, choose the operating system you want to get software for, and then use the search tools to locate FTP programs.

TEXT EDITORS

A number of different text editors are available for every platform. They range in price from free into the hundreds of dollars. The following sections describe the more popular text editors for each platform.

NOTEPAD (http://www.notepad.org)

If you're using a Windows operating system, there's no need to venture too far to find a text editor. Notepad certainly suffices, and it won't cost you anything. It is, however, extremely bare bones, and it does not support even the standard Windows keyboard shortcuts, but you can't beat the price tag.

TEXTPAD (http://www.textpad.com)

TextPad is a full-featured Windows application, providing multiple levels of undo and redo, find-and-replace tools, spell checking in ten languages, keyboard macros, drag-and-drop support, customizable syntax checking and coloring for different programming languages, as well as clip libraries that store reusable pieces of code to save on typing.

TextPad is *shareware*, which means you can download a free evaluation copy that will function indefinitely, but it is suggested that you register and pay for the program after 30 days if you intend to continue using it.

SimpleText (http://www.simpletext.com)

The Macintosh has SimpleText, which is on a par with Microsoft's WordPad. It ships with every Apple computer, so it too has a nice price tag. To quote the Apple Computer web site, "SimpleText is the utility knife of software." As the name implies, it is a simple tool for performing simple tasks. It is a basic word processor but is not intended for large files. (Anything over 32KB is out of the question.)

BBEdit (http://www.barebones.com)

Any software manufacturer whose slogan is "It Doesn't Suck" can't be all bad. This tool is to the Mac what TextPad is to Windows, and possibly more—also providing multiple levels of undo and redo, find-and-replace tools, an integrated spell checker, keyboard macros, drag-and-drop support, as well as extensive support for writing HTML and other programing language code.

Emacs (http://www.gnu.org/software/emacs) and vi (http://www.vim.org)

If you run a UNIX system, there are a number of popular editors—perhaps the most infamous being Emacs and the vi editor. Which one is the best is a highly contested subject, and programmers have been known to come to blows when this debate gets started. They also fight over the order in which the original Star Trek episodes were aired, so go figure.

Each of these editors is a full-featured, hard-core programming environment, but if you're savvy enough to be working with a UNIX computer, you're more than capable of using either of these tools. Both are free and are included in a number of UNIX distributions.

A Word about WYSIWYG Editors

The acronym WYSIWYG (pronounced *wizzy-wig*) stands for What You See Is What You Get. WYSIWYG tools allow you to build your web pages graphically, shielding you as little or as much from the HTML as you want. The three most popular web design packages available are Macromedia Dreamweaver, Adobe GoLive, and Microsoft FrontPage. Each of these has a price tag in the hundreds, although Macromedia does provide 30-day free demos of all its software on their web site. These tools essentially write HTML for you based on commands you enter from toolbars, menus, and dialog boxes. Each tool also provides access to the HTML source code of the documents you create, allowing you to use the program as a text editor if you choose. However, I suggest leaving these programs alone until you have a firm understanding of HTML.

You certainly won't need anything as complex as these tools to master HTML or to get something out of this book. If you have access to any of these programs, feel free to use them. The conventions in this book simply show HTML code, without implying or suggesting any preference for software, browser, or operating system.

Final Thoughts

You now have a little understanding about the origins of the Internet, how the World Wide Web came into existence, and the place of HTML within the bigger picture, including HTML's back-and-forth relationship with the web browser.

You know that the only tools you need to create a web page are a text editor and a browser to view it in, although having an Internet connection certainly helps. After all, the Web is obviously the best place to find examples of this thing you've set out to learn, and is loaded with resources to help you in your quest. Simply go to your favorite search engine and enter **HTML**. Are you ready? Let's get started.

The HTML Document

HTML is fairly simple to understand. However, when looking at all the code for a typical web page, it can all seem very intimidating. Try looking at the source code of your favorite web page. If you're using Internet Explorer, select View | Source, which opens a copy of the page's HTML code in Notepad. If you're using Netscape Navigator, select View | Page Source to open a separate window with the HTML displayed. There's probably a ton of code there, and you may need to scroll a full screen or two to view it all.

As you're looking at this code, it may seem like gibberish to you now, but by the time you've finished this chapter, you'll understand the basic structure of an HTML document. You'll recognize where the individual tags begin and end, see how the tags relate to the web page elements they define, and be able to recognize each tag's attributes that fine-tune an element's properties.

A SIMPLE HTML DOCUMENT

All HTML documents share the same basic structure: opening and closing `<html>` tags, inside of which sit the document header and document body, each defined by their own set of opening and closing tags, like so:

```
<html>
<head>
<title>A Simple HTML Document</title>
</head>
<body>
<h1>Welcome to my little Web Page!</h1>
They don't come much simpler than this.
</body>
</html>
```

The preceding code produces a page that looks like this:

Every web page you look at, regardless of its size, always contains these component parts. As you may recall from the last chapter, most tags act as containers. The `<html>` tags contain the document's head and body elements, each delimited by their respective tags. The `<head>` tags contain the document title as well as other information about the document. The `<body>` tags contain all the text and other HTML tags that make up the visible part of the web page you see in the browser window.

THE `<html>` TAGS

The `<html>` tags are used to define the type of document the browser is looking at. In most cases, the browser will be able to figure this out, whether these tags are present or not, by virtue of the file's .htm or .html extension. Consequently, it isn't strictly necessary to include them at all. This is true of a number of tags, where some browsers can determine which tag is required either by the type of content or by the presence of other tags. Some of this browser behavior harkens back to the early days of HTML when actions taken by the browser manufacturers were driving the HTML standard.

Never omit any tag when you write code. There are two primary reasons for this. First, not every browser will fill in the blanks left by missing tags and will simply fail to display the contents of your page if the correct tags are not present. Second, the new eXtensible Hypertext Markup Language (XHTML) standard, which is discussed in Chapter 12, requires that all tags use their closing form.

THE HEAD ELEMENT

The document header, or *head element,* holds information about the document that is not displayed in the browser window. However, the contents of the `<title>` tag do appear on the title bar of the browser window when displayed in Windows, or across the menu bar of a Mac when the browser window is active, as shown here:

The head element always follows immediately after the opening `<html>` tag, and it contains other elements used to pass information about the document to the web browser. Examples of such information include keywords and page descriptions for search engines, JavaScript declarations that need to be in place before the page is displayed, as well as cascading style sheet (CSS) information.

THE DOCUMENT TITLE

The `<title>` tags are the only required element within the document header, and they do pretty much what their name implies: define the title of the document. Not only do the contents of your `<title>` tags appear on the title bar of the browser, but they are also used as the descriptive text when users add your page to their favorites or bookmark list.

> **NOTE** Keywords and descriptions are defined by using the `<meta>` tag. In the early days, this tag was widely used because it could strongly affect your ranking in a search engine's database. When search engine companies realized they could make a killing selling keywords and ranking positions, `<meta>` tag use began to lessen, although in some cases, it can still be quite effective. See the HTML code reference in Appendix A to see notes on proper syntax and usage.

Be sure to give a little thought to the titles you assign your documents. A page should describe not only the document's contents, but also the document's relationship to the site of which it is a part. In other words, just titling your documents "Page One," "Contact Info," or "My Home Page" doesn't really do the job. Say, for example, you were converting this chapter to an HTML document. You'd want to give it a title like "HTML Virtual Classroom—Chapter 2" or "Chapter 2—The HTML Document." This way, there's a bit of description about what this document is, as well as a context for what it is a part of. Be aware that you have no formatting control over the text you place between the `<title>` tags, nor can you place any other HTML tags between them.

THE BODY ELEMENT

This is the big one. The document body, or *body element,* is essentially your web page. Everything that falls between the opening and closing `<body>` tags defines the portion of your document that is visible in the browser window. This leads to the next topic quite nicely.

HTML SYNTAX

You've just seen that the main HTML document consists of two primary elements, the head and body, which are defined by their respective opening and closing tags.

The keyword here is *element*. Everything you define with HTML tags is called an element—an image, a paragraph, a table—everything.

So elements are defined by HTML tags. HTML tags take two forms. Tags that require opening and closing sets are called *container tags*. Other tags have just a single tag, and they are referred to as *empty*. You can easily guess the difference between the two types of tags. Container tags have content in between them that they act on to define the specific element. They're used to create items with a physical beginning and end, like paragraphs, tables, lists, and forms. Empty tags don't need to surround anything to define an element. An example of an element defined by an empty tag would be a line break, which uses the `<br>` tag to place a line break in a block of text or to force an element onto the next line.

TAGS AND THEIR ATTRIBUTES

If tags define the elements within a document, how do you control the individual characteristics of these elements? What makes one table wider than another, or aligns one paragraph to the left and another to the right? *Attributes*. Nearly every tag supports a unique set of attributes whose values, when defined, allow you to control the specific properties of an individual element. The syntax for tags and attributes looks like this:

```
<tag attribute="value" attribute="value" attribute="value">content</tag>
```

For example, to answer the rhetorical question about tables and paragraphs, the width of a table is controlled (as luck would have it) by the `width` attribute, like this:

```
<table width="100">
```

100 is the number of pixels.

A paragraph's alignment is controlled by the `align` attribute, like so:

```
<p align="right">
```

As you can see, sometimes an attribute's value is numeric, whereas other times it might be a word (called a *token*), or a series of words or characters (called a *string*). At this point, you're probably wondering how you're supposed to know what the valid values are for the various attributes each tag has. Don't worry: each chapter to come answers that question case by case.

Quotation marks can be omitted depending on the type of value the attribute requires; for example, numeric values can usually stand on their own. In general, however, you should always include them. They will never prevent something from working, whereas forgetting them where they're needed can have catastrophic effects. Also, as your coding skills increase and you move on to other markup languages that require quotation marks, you'll be ready. (Two such languages include eXtensible Markup Language (XML) and the hybrid XHTML mentioned earlier, which joins XML and HTML together.)

CLOSING TAGS

The closing tags in a container tag set should always be used when writing HTML. Even though some browsers, particularly Internet Explorer, may be very lenient with dropped tags and make educated guesses about what you intended, don't use this as an excuse not to follow strict form. Another browser may not be as forgiving. Netscape Navigator, which prides itself on adhering more closely to the HTML standard than its competitors, although it can forgive the omission of some of the major tags, will simply not display certain parts of your page if the closing tag is missing.

The most important reason to follow proper HTML form and syntax is that HTML code is meant to be more than something a machine can understand—people are meant to understand it as well. By following proper form, you indicate what your intentions are to those who need to look at your code. The other point to keep in mind is that the future of web-based content lies in markup languages like XML and XHTML. And for these, you will need to adhere to strict form to get your pages to work.

CASE SENSITIVITY

HTML is not *case sensitive*. This means that `<head>`, `<Head>`, and `<HEAD>` are perfectly valid within HTML. However, XML and XHTML are case sensitive, and to make HTML more uniform with its brethren, the common practice now is to write all HTML in lowercase. Prior to XML and XHTML, uppercase was the norm when writing HTML, which proves one fact about the Web: it is always changing.

COMMENT TAGS

There is one form of HTML tag I want to discuss here in the early part of the book, and that's *comment tags.* Remember how I said an HTML document was meant to be read as much by people as by machines? This is exactly the purpose behind the comment tag. These are tags that you can use inside the body of an HTML document to enclose notes and instructions, concealing them from the browser so they are not displayed in the browser window when the document is displayed.

The syntax for a comment looks like this:

```
<!-- comment goes here -->
```

You can use comments to leave notes for yourself while you're working on a file or to demark the beginning and end of elements that run on for many screens. They're also good when you aren't the only person who's working on a particular file. You might build some part of a web page to which another person is then going to add other content. This is a perfect time to use comments to let someone else know what you've done or what you expect that person to expand on. Here's an example of comments in action:

```
<html>
<head>
<title>A Comment Example</title>
<!-- JOHN: please check with the client
and see if they have a description and list
of keywords they want included in the meta tags. -->

</head>

<body>
<!-- This is a heading tag. They're covered in Chapter 3. -->
<h1>This Page has Comment Tags</h1>

<!-- This is a paragraph. Notice the closing tag at the end. -->
<p>Try copying this page's code into your text editor. Save the file with
an .html or .htm extension and then open it in a browser. You notice right
away that the comments aren't visible except in the source code.</p>

</body>
</html>
```

MOVING FORWARD

Now you have a pretty good idea what a tag is and how to recognize one in an HTML document. You also understand that tags are required to create the visible content in your browser window. Every element you see is defined by its appropriate tags, and those elements are further refined by the attributes of those tags.

What's next? In the chapters to come, you'll learn about specific tags and their attributes, and how to use them to create content in your web pages. You'll also learn about some other related subjects, like cascading style sheets, to see what they offer you in terms of content control. And you'll look at what lies ahead for HTML and web-based content in terms of XHTML and XML.

 ON THE VIRTUAL CLASSROOM CD Don't let all that source code fool you! The basic structure of an HTML document isn't all that difficult to figure out. In Lesson 1, the instructor will break the HTML document into its component pieces, making it easy for the first-time coder to decipher any web page.

Formatting Text

There are scores of beautifully crafted graphic designs spread across the Web that give it life and vitality, but at its heart, the Web is a place for the free exchange of ideas and information. This means words, and if you think about it, most of the graphic design work you'll find out there is still intended to get you to read what the designers have to say. You may recall from Chapter 1 that markup has its origins in the world of typesetting. It's no coincidence, then, that the majority of HTML code is geared toward formatting the written word, and each successive version of the HTML standard has also attempted to improve the amount of control the web designer has over it.

HTML Text Formatting and Cascading Style Sheets

HTML may have a vast amount of markup devoted to formatting text, but this markup doesn't come close to what you find in the average word processor. As HTML has grown, however, so has its level of text formatting control, but HTML is capable of only so much. In 1996, a new method of text control was introduced, known as the cascading style sheet (CSS) specification, which is a separate standard in its own right. CSS offers nearly the same level of control as word processors do.

With the advancement of cascading style sheets, the recommendation of the World Wide Web Consortium (W3C), which develops and maintains both the CSS and HTML standards, is that text formatting on the HTML level is inherently inferior to CSS and should eventually be phased out altogether. Thus, HTML text formatting is now classified as *deprecated,* or disapproved of.

To date, HTML text formatting is still supported and widely used. Why? Well, browser manufacturers certainly weren't going to stop supporting the older HTML specifications. The dominant web browsers would have died slow and painful deaths if the millions of web sites out there had to retool the day CSS-compliant browsers were released. Not all users in the world were likely to run out and upgrade their browsers right away. In fact, many web designers are only now beginning to develop sites that are completely beyond the display capabilities of 3.0-generation browsers, and even then, many of us still include some level of backward compatibility for them.

To make matters more difficult, as has always been the case, no two browsers support the CSS specifications equally, which means you have to be judicious about how you employ CSS formatting. It is safe to say that regardless of what the W3C has recommended, HTML text formatting will be with us for some time to come.

Paragraphs, Line Breaks, and Headings

Sometimes, the best way to get a handle on something is to see it in action, so here's a little code example:

```
<html>
<head>
<title>Text Formatting</title>
</head>
<body>

'Twas brillig, and the slithy toves
Did gyre and gimble in the wabe;
All mimsy were the borogoves,
And the mome raths outgrabe.

"Beware the Jabberwock, my son!
The jaws that bite, the claws that catch!
Beware the Jubjub bird, and shun
The frumious Bandersnatch!"

-excerpt from Lewis Carroll's
"Jabberwocky"

</body>
</html>
```

This example is the first two stanzas of Lewis Carroll's famous poem
"Jabberwocky," laid out with minimal HTML code. It looks quite nice in this
printed form, but when you look at it in a browser, this is what you get:

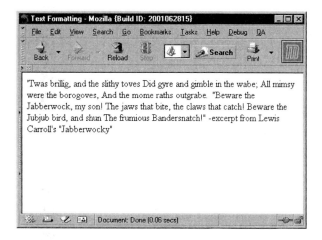

Not exactly pretty, is it? I did this to demonstrate a point. You can keep pressing
the ENTER key 'til the cows come home, putting in all the returns you like, but that

doesn't mean a thing in HTML or to your web browser. The tag determines appearances, not the keystroke.

PARAGRAPHS

Paragraphs in HTML have very little to do with what you learned in school. All that stuff about the optimal number of sentences a paragraph should have, how it should develop a concept, and proper indentation are lost on HTML. It doesn't understand English rules and usage—it's a markup language. It's up to you to be grammatically correct.

The tags that define the beginning and end of a paragraph are <p> and </p>. Anything placed between them begins on its own line, and any content that follows also begins on its own line, effectively forcing a blank line above and below the paragraph, except where to do so would cause two blank lines. For example, two concurrent paragraphs would not have two blank lines separating them.

By placing paragraph tags in the appropriate positions, the example document begins to take shape:

```
<html>
<head>
<title>Text Formatting</title>
</head>
<body>

<p>'Twas brillig, and the slithy toves
Did gyre and gimble in the wabe;
All mimsy were the borogoves,
And the mome raths outgrabe.</p>

<p>"Beware the Jabberwock, my son!
The jaws that bite, the claws that catch!
Beware the Jubjub bird, and shun
The frumious Bandersnatch!"</p>

<p>-excerpt from Lewis Carroll's
"Jabberwocky"</p>

</body>
</html>
```

This code creates a page that looks like this:

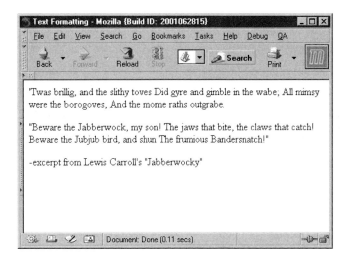

As you can see, you now have three distinct blocks of text, but you still have no control over line breaks, which at this point are governed by the width of the browser window. If you expanded the window far enough, you'd have three very long lines of text. Collapse it as far as you can, and you'd get about two words per line.

ALIGNMENT

You can control the alignment of a paragraph by using the `align` attribute. There are three value tokens for this attribute: `left`, `right`, and `center`. For example, you could take the first paragraph from the Carroll poem and align it to the right by rendering the opening tag `<p align="right">`, with the end result looking as you might expect—a right-justified paragraph.

By default, web browsers align page content left to right and top to bottom: in other words, the same order and direction in which western languages are read. This means you don't have to specifically set the alignment of an element to the left, except in instances where specifically defining a left alignment is necessary to achieve some effect: for example, when aligning graphics (Chapter 4) or tables (Chapter 7) within a block of text.

LINE BREAKS

At the moment, the example page's line breaks are governed by the width of the
browser window, which in this instance doesn't really provide the formatting you
might expect. This is where line breaks come into play. The line break tag is an
empty tag, or one without a closing form. Rendered <br>, it forces all page content
that follows it onto the next line. By placing these tags in the proper locations,
you can get these stanzas to appear as they were intended:

```
<html>
<head>
<title>Text Formatting</title>
</head>
<body>

<p>'Twas brillig, and the slithy toves<br>
Did gyre and gimble in the wabe;<br>
All mimsy were the borogoves,<br>
And the mome raths outgrabe.</p>

<p>"Beware the Jabberwock, my son!<br>
The jaws that bite, the claws that catch!<br>
Beware the Jubjub bird, and shun<br>
The frumious Bandersnatch!"</p>

<p>-excerpt from Lewis Carroll's<br>
"Jabberwocky"</p>

</body>
</html>
```

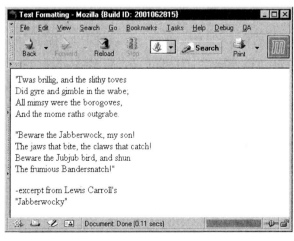

Now that looks a little better. You can use line breaks anywhere in a document to push content onto the next line, not just within paragraphs; and with the possible exception of poetry, you may never need to use them there, either. I'm just using them within paragraphs to demonstrate how they function.

HEADINGS

HTML heading tags are very similar to paragraphs in the way they force blank lines above and below. The difference is in how they treat the text you place between them. Look at the headings you see in this book. The chapter title has a very large font, the headings for major sections within the chapter have a smaller font, and the headings within a major section have an even smaller font. HTML headings work much the same way. There are six heading levels ranging from one down to six, in order of the significance they are intended to convey. The heading tags themselves look like this:

```
<h1>This is Heading One</h1>

<h2>This is Heading Two</h2>

<h3>This is Heading Three</h3>

<h4>This is Heading Four</h4>

<h5>This is Heading Five</h5>

<h6>This is Heading Six</h6>
```

And when displayed in a browser, this is how they appear:

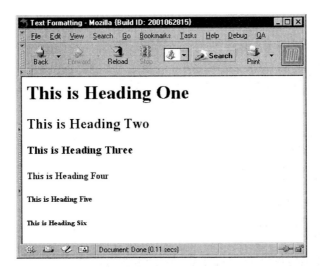

If you were to add an appropriate heading to the poetry example, it would look something like this:

```
<html>
<head>
<title>Text Formatting</title>
</head>
<body>
<h1>Text Formatting</h1>
<p>'Twas brillig, and the slithy toves<br>
Did gyre and gimble in the wabe;<br>
All mimsy were the borogoves,<br>
And the mome raths outgrabe.</p>

<p>"Beware the Jabberwock, my son!<br>
The jaws that bite, the claws that catch!<br>
Beware the Jubjub bird, and shun<br>
The frumious Bandersnatch!"</p>

<p>-excerpt from Lewis Carroll's<br>
"Jabberwocky"</p>

</body>
</html>
```

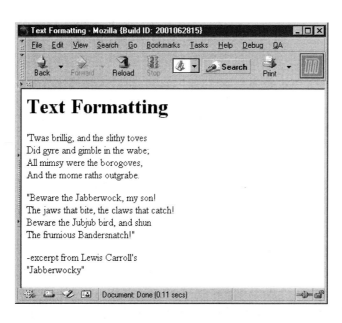

The recommended use for your main heading, as in the example, is to repeat the document's title. Like paragraphs, you can also use the `align` attribute to set the heading's alignment to the left, right, or center.

FONTS, SIZES, AND COLOR

I'm sure you're already familiar with selecting fonts and point sizes when you're working with a word processor. HTML also gives you a certain amount of control over font, size, and color of text. However, the web browser also plays a part in how text is displayed.

In the examples so far, there's no sight of the `<font>` tag, but you'll notice that there is a font being used: Times New Roman. This is because Times New Roman is the default font my browser is set to use. It's probably the one yours is using as well. After all, the browser has to make some choice if nothing is defined in the web page, right? Of course, users can change their default font at any time.

The fact that the users are in control of the viewing medium raises some important issues for us designers. In the world of print—for example, this book—the designer has the final say in just how the finished version will look: the book is a finite object, and each copy will look virtually alike to each person who buys one. Web designers, by comparison, have no control over visitors' browser settings or the fonts that may be on their computers. This impacts how you define the attributes for the tag that makes character-level formatting possible: the `<font>` tag.

THE `<font>` TAG

The `<font>` tag is another container tag, ending in the expected manner: `</font>`. By itself, it has no effect on text. The attributes you define for it do the magic.

THE `face` ATTRIBUTE

The `face` attribute is where you define the actual font you want your browser to use when displaying the marked text. For example:

```
<font face="Arial, Helvetica, sans-serif">
```

Wait a minute—why three font names? This is what I mean about not having control over the fonts that visitors may have on their computers. These three fonts listed together operate as a kind of wish list. The attribute is telling the browser,

"We want you to use Arial to display this text, but if the computer you're installed on doesn't have it, we'll settle for Helvetica. If you don't have either of these two sans-serif fonts, you, the browser, must have a default sans-serif font defined, so go ahead and use that."

The `face` attribute generally lists three or four fonts that possess similar characteristics. The object is to group a number of related fonts together in an attempt to guarantee the highest level of fidelity to your original design. If visitors don't have your first choice, perhaps they have one of the others. At the very worst, they won't have any of the fonts you prefer, in which case, make the last font option in the list either serif or sans-serif depending on the type of fonts you led off with.

> **NOTE** What's a serif? *Serif* comes from the Latin word *seraphim,* which is a type of angel. So serif can be loosely defined as "angel's wings." How does that relate to text? Serifs are the little flourishes on the ends of letters. For example, the body text of this book is laid out using a serif font. If you look at the headings in this book, by comparison, you'll see that the ends of each letter have no flourishes, so the font they're using would be called sans-serif, meaning "no serif."

In the "Jabberwocky" example, if you were to define a font for the first stanza, the code and resulting page would look like this:

```
<p><font face="Verdana, Arial, Helvetica, sans-serif">
'Twas brillig, and the slithy toves<br>
Did gyre and gimble in the wabe;<br>
All mimsy were the borogoves,<br>
And the mome raths outgrabe.</font></p>
```

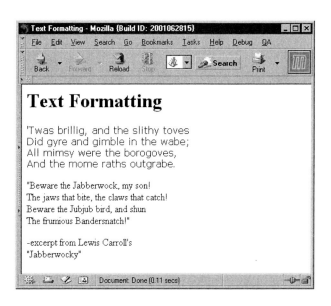

This is fine for one paragraph, but what about the rest of the document? What if you want this tag to format the whole thing? Remember, this is a container tag. Anything that lies in between will be formatted. Simply shifting the opening tag so that it immediately follows the opening `<body>` tag and moving the closing `</font>` tag so that it sits just before the closing `</body>` tag wraps the entire example in this formatting, affecting both the heading and the two paragraphs:

```
<html>
<head>
<title>Text Formatting</title>
</head>
<body>

<font face="Verdana, Arial, Helvetica, sans-serif">
<h1>Text Formatting</h1>
<p>'Twas brillig, and the slithy toves<br>
Did gyre and gimble in the wabe;<br>
All mimsy were the borogoves,<br>
And the mome raths outgrabe.</p>

<p>"Beware the Jabberwock, my son!<br>
The jaws that bite, the claws that catch!<br>
Beware the Jubjub bird, and shun<br>
The frumious Bandersnatch!"</p>

<p>-excerpt from Lewis Carroll's<br>
"Jabberwocky"</p>
</font>
</body>
</html>
```

THE size ATTRIBUTE

The `size` attribute is pretty self-explanatory—defining the font size controls how big or small the font appears in the browser. The syntax for the `size` attribute looks like this:

```
<font size="value">Text goes here</font>
```

The *value* is a number from one of two possible scales. Let me explain just what these scales are.

Unlike word processors, which use point sizes, HTML uses two numbered scales: absolute and relative.

▶ The *absolute* scale is numbered 1 through 7, 1 being the smallest and 7 the largest, with a size of 3 being equal to the default, or base font size set in a user's browser. Consequently, this scale isn't exactly "absolute" because any font size you set with this scale will still be relative to whatever base font size the visitor's browser is set to.

▶ The *relative* scale is numbered –7 through +7, and it sets the font size in relation to the base font of the visitor's browser. So if the visitor's browser is set to a base font of 12 points, setting the font size to +1 would make the text appear one size larger, or 13 points.

> **NOTE** The `<basefont>` tag lets you manually set the base font for your pages. By using the `size` attribute, like this, `<basefont size ="value">`, and placing the tag either in the head or the body, you could conceivably set a base font of -1 and then use a relative font size of +7 somewhere within the text. It's better to avoid the `<basefont>` tag, however, because its behavior is not consistent across multiple browsers.

The relative scale won't allow you to display a font size that falls outside of the absolute scale of 1 through 7, however. In the following illustration, you can see that the base font, regardless of what its point value might be, is always equal to a font size of 3. Consequently, you couldn't apply a relative size value below –2 or above +4. If you did, the font would simply stop at its maximum or minimum size.

Relative Scale: -7 -6 -5 -4 -3 -2   -1 | None | +1   +2   +3   +4   +5   +6   +7

Absolute Scale: 1   2 | 3 | 4   5   6   7

base font size

In my experience, few users even know they can change the base font setting, and I have found it safe to assume that the average user's browser is still set at the same size it started with when it was first installed on the computer. This setting is usually 12 points.

Now you will put this attribute into action. In the example, if you wanted to change the size of the font in that first paragraph, you'd simply squeeze the `size` attribute into the tag immediately following the `face` attribute defined previously, like so:

```
<p><font face="Verdana, Arial, Helvetica, sans-serif" size="5">
'Twas brillig, and the slithy toves<br>
Did gyre and gimble in the wabe;<br>
All mimsy were the borogoves,<br>
And the mome raths outgrabe.</font></p>
```

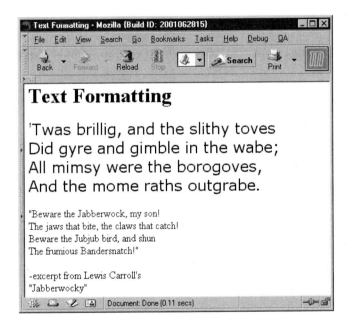

FONT COLOR

The `<font>` tag controls text color with—you guessed it—the `color` attribute. The syntax is no different than what you've used with the previous attributes discussed:

```
<font color="value">Text goes here</font>
```

The *value* is either one of a number of predefined color names, for example, `color="red"`, or a color value written in hexadecimal notation, for example, `color="#FF0000"`, which produces the same red value. Memorizing the entire spectrum of hexadecimal color values would be overly ambitious at this stage, so I've included a reference of the predefined color names and hexadecimal color values on the CD.

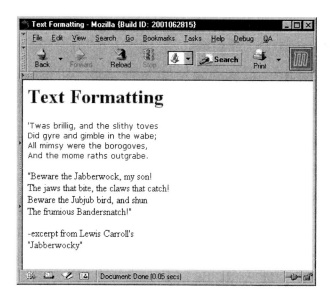

DEFAULT TEXT COLOR

The example you've been working with is pretty tame: basic black text (with one exception) on a white background. This is typically the default text/background color combo for a web browser if no specific color formatting has been defined. As you are no doubt aware from a quick perusal of the Internet, an infinite (or almost infinite) number of variations exist to this scheme. So what do you do if you don't *want* simple black on white as your default color scheme? You go and define a new scheme via the `<body>` tag discussed in Chapter 2.

You can control the default text color for an HTML document by using the `<body>` tag's `text` attribute. You'd use the same color options, either color name or hexadecimal value, that you use with the `color` attribute. If you wanted the default text to be blue, your `<body>` tag would be written `<body text="blue">`. This would make all the text in your document blue without using `<font>` tags. You control the background color of the document by using the `bgcolor` attribute of the `<body>` tag. Just as you did previously and will continue to do wherever you define a color, you use the color names or hex values.

PHYSICAL AND LOGICAL STYLES

You're already familiar with *physical styles* if you've ever made text bold or italic when using a word processor. In HTML, they tell the browser how text should literally look when displayed. *Logical styles*, in contrast, are descriptive terms applied to text that leave their interpretation and display up to the browser. To date, logical styles are displayed identically to the various physical styles. With the advent of text-to-speech technology, however, browsers may begin to read logical styles and alter the way words are pronounced that are formatted with them.

The following table represents the recognized physical styles and their corresponding tags:

PHYSICAL STYLES	TAGS
Bold	`<b></b>`
Italic	`<i></i>`
Underline	`<u></u>`
Strikethrough	`<strike></strike>`
Big	`<big></big>`
Small	`<small></small>`
Subscript	`<sub></sub>`
Superscript	`<sup></sup>`
Teletype	`<tt></tt>`

This table represents the recognized logical styles and their corresponding tags:

LOGICAL STYLES	TAGS
Citation	`<cite></cite>`
Code	`<code></code>`
Definition	`<dfn></dfn>`
Emphasis	`<em></em>`
Keyboard	`<kbd></kbd>`
Sample	`<samp></samp>`
Strong	`<strong></strong>`
Programming Variable	`<var></var>`

Figure 3-1 shows how each tag is displayed by a browser, indicating the corresponding similarities between the different style types.

NESTING TAGS

Sometimes, you will want to apply more than one set of tags to a single selection of text, particularly where physical styles are concerned. For example, you may want to make a word or sentence bold *and* italic. This is referred to as *nesting tags*, which you have basically already done. After all, you saw in Chapter 2 how the head and body elements are both nested inside the opening and closing `<html>` tags, how the `<title>` tags are nested inside the `<head>` tags, and how everything that makes up your visible design is nested inside the `<body>` tags. The important point to remember is how tags must be nested.

When nesting tags, think of each set of opening and closing tags like the layers of an onion, each surrounded by the layer outside it and surrounding the layer inside it. For example, if you were going to make a word both bold and italic, your tags would look like this:

```
<b><i>Lewis Carroll</i></b>
```

FIGURE 3-1

Logical styles mimic a number of the physical styles, and often, two logical styles have the same effect.

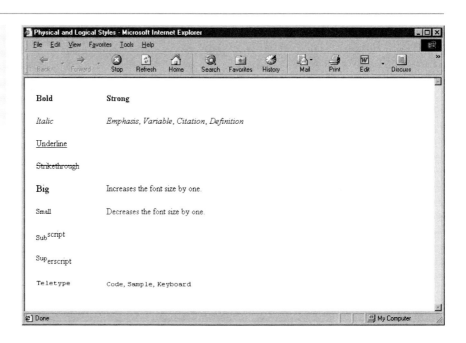

Notice how the closing tags reverse the order of the starting tags. You must follow this ordering of nested tags, or the browser may simply refuse to follow your instructions. This principle is particularly true when you're nesting tags that are used to create certain HTML structures like tables, lists, and forms. Fortunately, you don't need to worry about any rule governing the order in which style tags must be used when nesting; for instance, this example would have the same effect if the tags read as follows:

```
<i><b>Lewis Carroll</b></i>
```

PREFORMATTED TEXT

Remember when I said it's the tag that determines appearances, not the keystroke? There's a tag you can use that kind of reverses this principle, known as the `<pre>` tag. Any text that falls between the opening and closing `<pre>` tags is rendered exactly as it appears in the HTML file. That means that all line breaks and spaces are preserved just as you typed them into your text editor. So, for example, you could wrap `<pre>` tags around the entire "Jabberwocky" example as it was originally typed in the opening example:

```
<html>
<head>
<title>Text Formatting</title>
</head>
<body>

<pre>
'Twas brillig, and the slithy toves
Did gyre and gimble in the wabe;
All mimsy were the borogoves,
And the mome raths outgrabe.

"Beware the Jabberwock, my son!
The jaws that bite, the claws that catch!
Beware the Jubjub bird, and shun
The frumious Bandersnatch!"

-excerpt from Lewis Carroll's
"Jabberwocky"
</pre>

</body>
</html>
```

In this situation, your page would look like this:

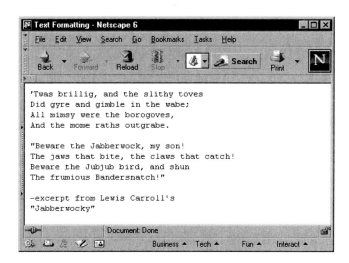

As the illustration shows, the drawback is that text formatted in this way is displayed with a monospace font, usually Courier, meaning the individual characters are all an equal distance apart, regardless of the width of each character. This prevents any sophisticated font treatment.

If you really wanted to, you could nest `<font>` tags within the preformatted text to control the font face and size, but this is considered bad HTML form, and it may not have the desired effect in all browsers. You'd lose the logical structure, as well as formatting options, created by using paragraphs. The most common uses for the `<pre>` tags are to render programming code examples or to construct columns of data where placing the information inside an HTML table is not a viable option.

> **TIP** Avoid using tab spaces inside `<pre>` tags to position text because different browsers each tend to interpret tabs differently, which can ruin whatever spacing effect you're trying to achieve.

BLOCK QUOTES

If you've ever had to write a term paper and quote a sizable selection from an outside source, you're probably familiar with block quotes. The traditional method for formatting block quotes is to apply additional indentation, and possibly change the text style.

HTML offers a tag that does the trick, and as luck would have it, it is properly named `<blockquote>`. Text placed within the `<blockquote>` tags is typically given wider margins, and like paragraphs and headings, additional white space above and below the enclosed text.

If you added a biographical paragraph about Mr. Carroll to the example, you might then consider setting off the poem with block quotes, like this:

```html
<html>
<head>
<title>Text Formatting</title>
</head>
<body>

<h1>Jabberwocky</h1>
<!-- Here's the new bio paragraph -->
<p>Lewis Carroll was born Charles Lutwidge Dodgson in Daresbury, Cheshire,
on January 27, 1832, and was educated at Rugby and at Christ Church
College, University of Oxford. From 1855 to 1881 he was a member of
the faculty of mathematics at Oxford. He was the author of several mathe-
matical treatises, including Euclid and His Modern Rivals (1879). In 1865
he published under his pseudonym Alice's Adventures in Wonderland. Its
sequel, Through the Looking-Glass and What Alice Found There, appeared
in 1871. These were followed by Phantasmagoria and Other Poems (1869),
The Hunting of the Snark (1876), and a novel, Sylvie and Bruno (2 vol.,
1889-93). He died at Guildford, Surrey, on January 14, 1898.</p>

<blockquote>
<i><p>'Twas brillig, and the slithy toves<br> <!--Notice the new italics -->
Did gyre and gimble in the wabe;<br>
All mimsy were the borogoves,<br>
And the mome raths outgrabe.</p>

<p>"Beware the Jabberwock, my son!<br>
The jaws that bite, the claws that catch!<br>
Beware the Jubjub bird, and shun<br>
The frumious Bandersnatch!"<br></p>

<p>-excerpt from Lewis Carroll's<br>
"Jabberwocky"</p></i>
</blockquote>

</body>
</html>
```

The result is the following:

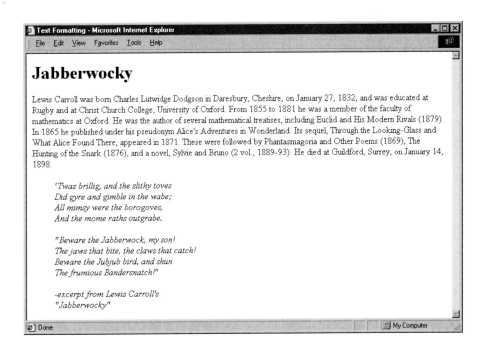

SPECIAL CHARACTERS

Sometimes the 100+ keys on your keyboard just aren't enough. You may need a copyright (©) insignia, trademark (™) symbol, or other nonstandard character. Fortunately, HTML recognizes this eventuality and makes some provisions for it.

These special characters, or *character entities*, as they're commonly referred to, can be placed inside an HTML document by using a unique code called ISO-Latin-1, courtesy of the International Organization for Standardization. The code for these characters is written as names or numbers bracketed between an ampersand (&) and a semicolon (;). For example, the character entity used to display the copyright symbol is written `&#169;` or `&copy;`, so if you wanted to place a small copyright mark at the bottom of a document, you'd insert a line of HTML that looked like this:

```
<font size="2"><sup>&copy;</sup> Robert Fuller, 2001</font>
```

Notice that I wrapped the copyright entity inside superscript tags to push it above the normal text line and decrease its size a little. The end result would be displayed like this:

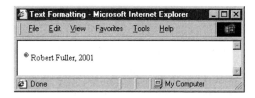

The HTML tag reference in Appendix A provides a complete listing of character entities.

 ON THE VIRTUAL CLASSROOM CD What a web page says may be its most important feature. Lesson 2 examines every aspect of formatting text in HTML, from block-level elements to individual characters—including special character entities.

4

Working with Images and Rules

I introduced the last chapter by saying that there are scores of beautifully crafted graphic designs spread across the Web that give it life and vitality. Then I quickly went on to imply that it doesn't matter how great the graphics are if the site has nothing to say, and that half the point of good graphics is to get you to read what the site says anyway. Well, I'll counter that here by asking a rhetorical question. Would the Web be the place it is today if it still supported only text? I don't think so.

IMAGE FORMATS

The two primary file formats for delivering images to the Web are the Graphics Interchange Format (GIF) and the format created by the Joint Photographic Experts Group (JPEG). These formats compress the image information they contain, decreasing the overall file size, which allows them to be quickly transmitted across the Web and then decompressed by your browser.

The GIF format was created by CompuServe in 1987. Because it was one of the first formats on the scene and is very good at what it does, it quickly became the standard for web-based images and helped speed the growth of the Web. Its compression methods are *lossless*, which means that you can compress an image without losing any information.

The JPEG format was created with photographs in mind, and it is particularly suited to compressing them while retaining a high level of fidelity. JPEG compression, however, is *lossy*; in other words, through the process of compressing the image, some information is lost. You can limit the degree of loss by controlling the level of compression through the software you use to create JPEGs. Basically, that's your trade-off with JPEG compression—loss of fidelity to the original image quality for small file size and download time.

GIF AND JPEG USAGE

The simplest rule of thumb concerning usage of these two formats is as follows: use JPEGs for photographs and GIFs for simple graphics like line art and icons. Without going into too much techno-babble, here are the reasons why:

GIFs support a maximum of 256 individual colors, which makes them great for images that don't have a lot of detail or that don't contain much color variation. For example, in an image with large areas of one color, GIF compresses it without losing any information or creating any distortion in these areas. In contrast, JPEG can't compress these large areas of color without introducing distortions. Also, JPEGs don't do well trying to render extremely sharp edges, which often occurs when two large areas of solid color are butted up against each other.

JPEGs, by comparison, are capable of displaying 16 million colors, so they do a much better job of rendering the subtle details found in photographs and photo-realistic images. They can also compress images much more than other formats, sometimes by as much as ten times. Of course, the drawback is that you lose some of the image information. However, because JPEG takes advantage of the fact that the human eye registers minute changes in brightness much better than minute changes in color (while still reproducing millions of colors), it can throw out a great deal of color information and still render an image that you and I perceive as being just fine.

INSERTING IMAGES

You insert images by using the `<img>` tag. This is an *empty* tag, which means it doesn't have a closing tag associated with it. This is because it isn't used to format something already in the document or define an area that will house other HTML content. An image stands alone as an independent object.

Like the `<font>` tag, the `<img>` tag does nothing all by itself. It's the attributes you define for the tag that allow you to select the image you want to insert and modify that image's properties. The following code illustrates an `<img>` tag in action:

```
<html>
<head>
<title>The Image Tag</title>
</head>
<body bgcolor="#FFFFFF" text="#000000">
<h3>The Image Tag </h3>
<img src="images/triangle.gif" width="84" height="83">

<!-- Below is the source code for the image formatted
in Courier font, and written with character entities
to mimic HTML tags so the browser isn't confused -->

<p><font size="2" face="Courier New, Courier, mono"><b>
&lt;img src=&quot;images/triangle.gif&quot; width=&quot;84&quot;
height=&quot;83&quot;&gt;</b></font></p>

</body>
</html>
```

When viewed in my browser, the page looks like this:

DEFINING THE SOURCE OF AN IMAGE

The first attribute you see in the example defines the source of the image, and it is written with the abbreviation src:

```
<img src="images/triangle.gif" width="84" height="83">
```

This code tells the web browser where to locate the image file to be used, using the file's uniform resource locator (URL). The *URL* is simply the path to the image on the web server. The written path to a file is called a *pathname*.

UNDERSTANDING PATHNAMES

You see pathnames all the time when you use tools like Windows Explorer or Macintosh Finder. Chances are, you've seen something like this before: C:\My Documents\My Pictures\. To understand a pathname, it's easier to read it backwards. This pathname tells you that you're in a folder called My Pictures. This folder is in the folder called My Documents, which, in turn, is on a hard disk labeled C.

This structure is all well and good for your PC, but what about a web server? Well, a web server isn't radically different from your own PC—they're both computers, and all computers have something called a *file structure*. The pathname is just the address of a file within that file structure.

Pathnames come in two different flavors: absolute and relative:

> **NOTE** All this information about pathnames will come in handy again in Chapter 5, during the discussion of hyperlinks.

▶ **Absolute** Declares the full address to a file, for example, http://www.your_site.com/images/ triangle.gif. This kind of pathname is best used when pointing to a file location on another web server.

▶ **Relative** Shortened addresses, best used for referencing files on your web server. This kind of pathname falls into two separate categories:

- **Document relative** Uses the document that the link or file reference is in as a starting point for looking to other files. For example, the pathname images/ triangle.gif tells the browser to start in the same folder the present document is in, locate the images folder, and look in that folder to find the triangle.gif file.

- **Site-root relative** Uses the web server's file structure as a base, using the root folder of the site as the starting point. For example, /html_virtual-classroom/ images/triangle.gif tells the browser to start at the very top of the file structure (/) and locate the html_ virtual-classroom folder, find the images folder within it, and then find the triangle.gif file in that folder.

SETTING IMAGE DIMENSIONS

The next two attributes are pretty self-explanatory—width and height control the physical dimensions of the image, expressed in pixels:

```
<img src="images/triangle.gif" width="84" height="83">
```

Make sure you always include these two attributes. If the browser can tell from the source code how much space is devoted to each image, it can render all the text-based stuff right away while the images are downloading. Otherwise, it has to wait for a picture to completely load and display before it can move on to the next element in the HTML document.

You aren't required to use the actual dimension of your image; for example, you could resize the image by using larger or smaller dimension values. However, you should avoid this. Drastic changes to an image's height and width values can cause it to distort. If you need to alter the scale of an image, use your favorite image editing software to reduce or enlarge an image before inserting it into your document.

SPECIFYING A BORDER WIDTH

I didn't use one in the example, but you do have the ability to place a border around an image by using the `border` attribute. By defining this attribute, you specify the border thickness in pixels, like so:

```
<img src="images/triangle.gif" width="84" height="83" border="2">
```

This would place a border two pixels thick around this image, as shown here:

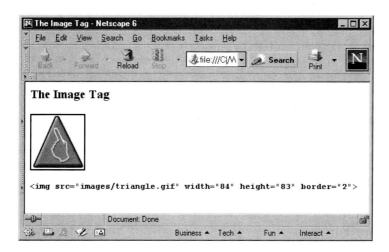

The `border` attribute will come in handy in Chapter 5, when you starting working with hyperlinks. When you format an image as a hyperlink, the web browser places a border around it by default, whether you specify one or not. If you don't want a border around your image link, you simply define a `border` attribute of 0, which removes the border created by the browser.

ALIGNING AN IMAGE

The `align` attribute has the greatest impact when an image is placed within a block of text. Although no longer a part of the HTML standard, deprecated in favor of style sheets, it is still supported by all modern browsers and will probably continue to be for the foreseeable future. The following list includes the possible values that the `align` attribute can accept, with examples of their effects:

▶ `align="left"` Anchors the image to the left of the document, table cell, or layer, and wraps text to the right of the image.

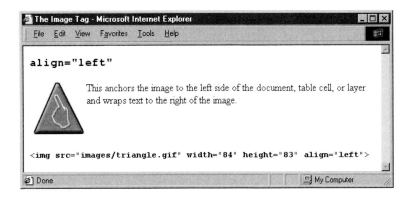

▶ `align="right"` Sets the image to the right of the document, table cell, or layer, and wraps text to the left of the image.

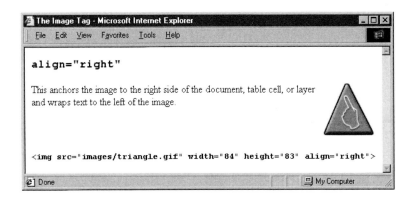

▶ `align="top"` Aligns the top of the image with the top of the tallest element on the same line. If that line of text wraps onto the next line, the second line begins below the image.

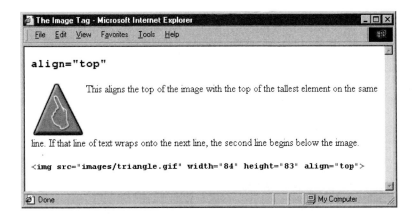

▶ `align="baseline"` Aligns the bottom of the image with the bottom of any content on the same line.

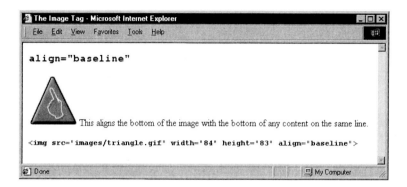

▶ `align="bottom"` Equivalent to `align="baseline"`.

▶ `align="middle"` Aligns the middle of the selected image with the baseline (bottom) of elements on the same line.

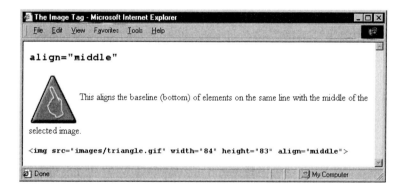

▶ `align="absbottom"` Aligns the bottom of the selected image with the absolute bottom of the other elements in the line.

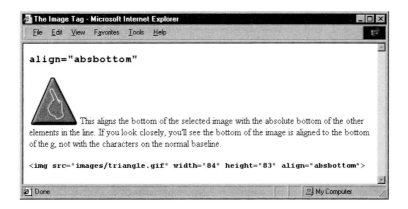

▶ `align="absmiddle"` Aligns the middle of the image to the absolute middle height of the line of text instead of to the baseline.

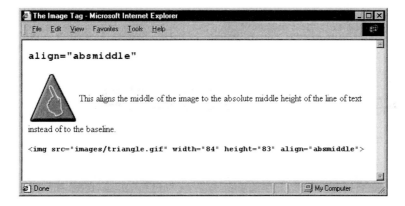

▶ `align="texttop"` Aligns the image with the top of the tallest text character in the line. Just like `align="top"`, if that line of text wraps onto the next line, the second line begins below the image.

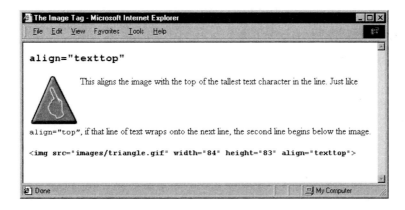

Having trouble with all this talk of baselines? Not to worry. Remember penmanship and writing out your letters on all those lines? The *baseline* is the line the text sits on. Some lowercase letters—*g, j, p, q,* and *y*—have *descenders,* or parts that drop below the baseline. This is where absolute bottom comes in. *Absolute bottom* aligns an image with the bottom of the descenders on a line instead of the text's baseline.

CENTERING AN IMAGE

You'll notice that there's no `"center"` value for the `align` attribute. That's because centering objects on a page has an interesting history. The original standard tags that were used to center anything were `<center></center>`. As the HTML standard evolved and the thinking about what constituted "proper markup" changed, these tags were pushed aside in favor of using the `align` attribute in either the `<p>` tag, where text was concerned, or within the `<div>` tag, both of which do accept a value of `"center"`.

The `<div>` tag is short for *division,* which is meant to be used wherever you intend a logical division of page content that doesn't lend itself easily to text markup like the `<p>` tag. So, in contemporary HTML 4.01, the proper way to center an image is to wrap the `<img>` tag inside a `<div>` tag, like so:

```
<div align="center">
<img src="images/triangle.gif" width="84" height="83">
</div>
```

Of course, just putting opening and closing `<center>` tags in place of the `<div>` tags would work just as well, and in some cases, it just seems to be easier. Again, this is another example of a deprecated tag that won't be going away any time soon.

You'll examine the `<div>` tag more closely when you learn about layers in Chapter 11; it is the primary tag that makes layers possible.

VERTICAL AND HORIZONTAL SPACING

Whenever you have an image alongside text, there's a slight gap between it and the text. If there weren't, the text would be pressed right up against the side of the image, making it rather difficult to read. That little gap, and in fact, any area that has nothing in it, is called *white space.* You can control the amount of white space that surrounds an image by using two attributes: `vspace` (vertical space) and `hspace` (horizontal space). Vertical space and horizontal space are measured in pixels. For example, if you defined a `vspace` value of 5, that would create five pixels of white space at both the top and bottom edges of the image, while the same value defined for `hspace` would place five pixels of white space on both the left and right.

Figures 4-1 and 4-2 show the example image located within a paragraph of text, with the horizontal and vertical spacing set to 0 and 10, respectively.

USING ALTERNATIVE TEXT

Chances are, if you're using a modem to connect to the Internet, you're connecting at 56 kilobytes per second, and this connection speed is nothing in comparison to the dedicated T1 lines many people have at the office, or DSL and cable modems. To give you an idea of how much technology has advanced, my first modem was 9600 *bytes* per second, and I was really excited when I made the big move to 14.4 Kbps.

In the early days, it was common practice to turn your browser's image-displaying capabilities off so you could load web pages without having to go out for coffee while you waited. This practice gave birth to an attribute that enabled the web developer to define an alternative piece of descriptive text to occupy the location assigned to the image, so site visitors could read it and decide whether they wanted to view the image. This attribute is appropriately labeled `alt` for *alternate text*. Figure 4-3 shows how alternate text appears in a browser whose images have been turned off.

Figure 4-4 provides an example of how the `alt` attribute is handled while the images are turned on.

FIGURE 4-1

Leaving the `hspace` attribute undefined results in a default horizontal spacing of 3.

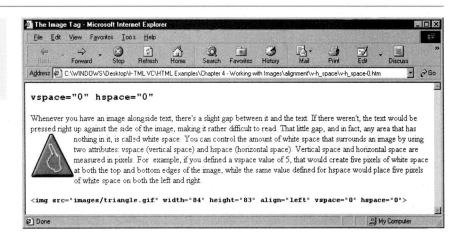

FIGURE 4-2

By comparison, an undefined `vspace` attribute is equal to setting it to 0.

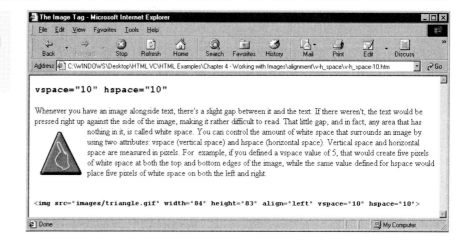

FIGURE 4-3

When images are disabled, a small icon representing an image file is displayed in the image's place, accompanied by the alternate text defined by the `alt` attribute.

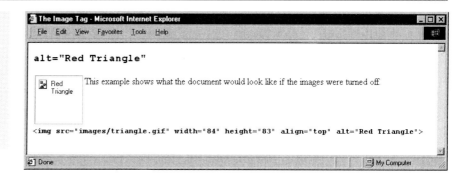

FIGURE 4-4

Since the release of Internet Explorer and Netscape Navigator versions 4.0, small tool tips are displayed when you hover the mouse over images with defined `alt` attributes.

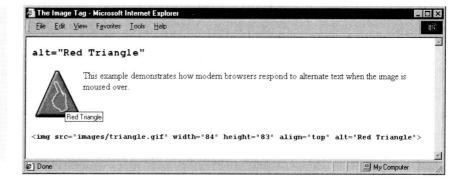

It has always been considered "good form" to define your image's `alt` attribute. You provide a text reference not only for users who may choose to turn off the images or who are in the process of waiting for them to load, but you also assist visually impaired visitors to your site who use text-to-speech software to browse the Web.

HORIZONTAL RULES

Horizontal rules are visible lines that you place in your document to section off regions of content; they are *not* laws that govern the horizontal placement of graphic elements on your page. They're generally used to add emphasis to a block of text's start and end points: for example, right under a heading or at the beginning and end of a specific topic.

THE `<hr>` TAG

Just like the `<img>` tag, the horizontal rule tag `<hr>` has no closing form. When placed in a document, it occupies its own line, without any additional space above or below. Its appearance, rather than coming from an image file you specify, is left up to the browser manufacturer—all you need to do is place the tag within your document and define a number of attributes to control its appearance. I'm sure you're getting tired of this old saw, but again, these attributes are all deprecated by the W3C, which would prefer that you use style sheets to control all this stuff.

THE width ATTRIBUTE

When left undefined, the width of a horizontal rule defaults to 100 percent of the browser window. You can easily modify the width of a horizontal rule by specifying a pixel value or a percentage of the browser window. For example, if you wrote the horizontal rule tag `<hr width="100">`, it would be only 100 pixels wide, but if you wrote it `<hr width="75%">`, the horizontal rule would run 75 percent of the browser window, no matter how you resized it.

Take a look at this code and the following illustration:

```
<p>These three horizontal rules are defined in pixel widths.</p>

50 pixels:
<hr width="50">
```

```
75 pixels:
<hr width="75">
100 pixels:
<hr width="100">

<p>And these three are using percentages:</p>

50 percent:
<hr width="50%">
75 percent:
<hr width="75%">
100 percent:
<hr>
<!-- notice that I need no width attribute to achieve 100 percent. -->
```

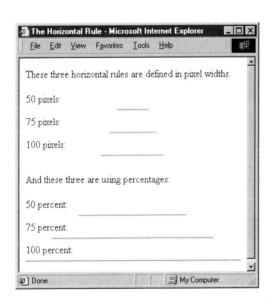

You probably noticed that each of these horizontal rules is centered.

THE align ATTRIBUTE

Three possible values exist for the align attribute of a horizontal rule—left, right, and center—although center is the usual browser default. The following code takes the first three <hr> tags from the previous example and applies the align attribute.

```
<p>Let's see how these look when we use the align attribute</p>

50 pixels, aligned left:
<hr width="50" align="left">
75 pixels, aligned center:
<hr width="75" align="center">
100 pixels, aligned right:
<hr width="100" align="right">
```

The following effect results:

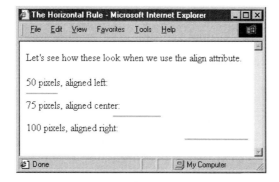

THE size ATTRIBUTE

You'd probably expect a horizontal rule's height, or thickness, to be controlled by a height attribute. After all, the examples in this chapter have used width and height to set dimensions thus far. Well, just to keep it interesting, instead of using height, the thickness of a horizontal rule is governed by the size attribute. Unlike width, you can use only pixel values to define this attribute.

Following the same theme as before, this code takes three horizontal rules and modifies them slightly by using the size attribute:

```
<p>Here are three more using the size attribute.</p>

size="10":
<hr size="10">
size="20":
<hr size="20">
size="30":
<hr size="30">
```

Generally, browsers display horizontal rules with a shaded, mock 3-D effect approximately two pixels thick. When you begin to modify the size attribute, the overall effect is that of an engraved impression in the document's surface.

THE noshade ATTRIBUTE

You can turn off the shading effect that browsers use to display horizontal rules by using the noshade attribute. Unlike all the attributes discussed so far, this one doesn't need to be set equal to a number or token value. You simply type it in as part of the tag, like so, <hr noshade>, and the browser won't shade the horizontal rule.

By adding the noshade attribute to the previous example, you get the following effect:

> **NOTE** Internet Explorer also provides a color attribute that you can define in the same manner as described in the previous chapter: by using either the predefined color names or hexadecimal values. If you choose to use that attribute, just be aware that only site visitors using Internet Explorer will be able to see the effect.

```
<p>Here they are again with the noshade attribute added.</p>

Just a plain horizontal rule with noshade added:
<hr noshade>
size="10":
<hr size="10" noshade>
size="20":
<hr size="20" noshade>
size="30":
<hr size="30" noshade>
```

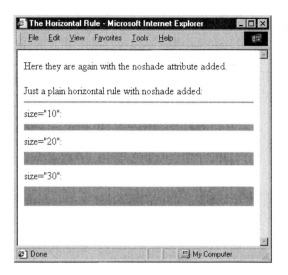

When the `noshade` attribute is applied, horizontal rules are generally displayed as dark gray lines in most browsers. Netscape Navigator goes one step further and rounds the ends of the horizontal rules.

ON THE VIRTUAL CLASSROOM CD **In Lesson 3, the instructor will demonstrate how to insert images into the HTML document and format image attributes.**

5

Hyperlinks

I have no doubt that if you've sat in front of a
computer connected to the Internet and opened a web
browser, you are intimately acquainted with the most
important component of hypertext that makes the whole
concept of a "web" possible—the hyperlink.

You've seen text underlined and highlighted in a different color, or you've seen some graphic image designed to look like a button or some other interface element that let you know that clicking it would cause your browser to display a different screen of information. What's more, I have no doubt that you've clicked one—and another, and another, and another...

WHAT'S IN A LINK?

Feeling confident that you've surfed the Web, I'll also assume you're familiar with the terms *web address*. I'm sure you have a favorite web site and know its address by heart—say, something like www.your_favorite_site.com. No doubt, you've typed this address into the address bar of your web browser on more than one occasion. You may have just started typing from the www. bit, or perhaps you included the full Hypertext Transfer Protocol (http://) at the beginning. It wouldn't really matter these days because most browsers will make the necessary adjustment and throw the protocol in there for you, so when the page loads, the address bar has the full http://www.your_favorite_site.com web address in place. The technical term for that web address, you might remember, is uniform resource locator (URL).

So how does this relate to links? A *hyperlink* is simply a section in your HTML code that has been marked up with a particular tag and has a URL associated with it via an attribute. When a web browser reads the HTML code, it knows that whatever is marked up by the tag needs to be displayed in a certain fashion, for example, underlined and highlighted in a different color. When the user clicks this section of the document, the browser looks to the referenced URL and attempts to load it into the browser window. The next section takes a look at the tag in question.

THE <a> TAG

Hyperlinks are also called *anchors,* and you create them by nesting either a section of text or an image tag between opening and closing anchor tags, written <a> and </a>. As you're probably getting used to by now, this tag is another one that doesn't do a whole lot without an attribute.

The attribute you define to create a hyperlink is called a *hypertext reference,* written href, and the value you assign to it is the URL to which you want the user to be sent when the hyperlink is clicked. So if you created a link that takes the visitor to your favorite web site, it would look something like this:

```
<a href="http://www.your_favorite_site.com">My Favorite Site</a>
```

The URL is always placed between quotes, and when displayed, it is typically underlined and highlighted in a different color than the surrounding text.

THE URL

It will probably help to dissect a typical URL before launching into how to use them properly in different linking situations. You see, the location of the file you're linking to relative to the document you're placing the link within impacts how you define the `href` attribute. Here's an example:

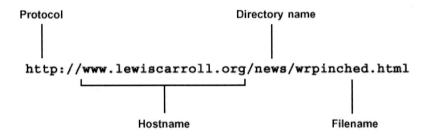

This URL is fairly typical. It includes the protocol—in this case, the Hypertext Transfer Protocol (http://), because that is the one you're most likely to be using when linking to other files on the Web—the hostname, a directory name, and the specific filename of the document.

HOSTNAME

The *hostname* is the base of the URL, and it represents the root, or primary directory, in which all of a web site's files and subdirectories are kept. *Directory* here means the same thing as folder: the two words are interchangeable.

DIRECTORY NAME

Some files on a web site might be within subdirectories off the main root, so to reference one of these files, the URL needs to include the directory name. Think of retrieving a document from a file cabinet. The cabinet is the Internet, the file drawer is the root directory represented by the hostname, a folder in that file drawer represents a directory, and inside it is a document that represents the web page.

FILENAME

This one is probably the most obvious. The *filename* is the name of the document, including its file extension. You might be thinking, "Wait a minute. When I go to my favorite web site, I'm usually only entering the hostname. What gives?"

Although I've made a lot of noise about different types of computers having many similarities, they obviously have some differences as well. Web servers recognize particular filenames as being the document they should display when a request comes in that references only the hostname or one of its other directories. Usually that magic filename is *index,* with either the .htm or .html file extension. For example, if you typed www.your_favorite_site.com into your web browser's address bar, the web server would look in the root directory for index.html and return its contents.

PATHNAMES REVISITED

The values you define for the `href` attribute are URLs, and URLs are *pathnames.* In other words, they describe the path you take through a computer's hierarchy of directories (the file structure) to get to a specific file. You learned about pathnames in Chapter 4, in the discussion about the `src` attribute of the `<img>` tag, but it certainly bears repeating. You'll recall that pathnames come in two forms: absolute and relative.

ABSOLUTE PATHNAMES

An *absolute pathname* contains the complete path to the file in question: protocol, hostname, and any required directory and filename. Going back to the file cabinet metaphor, think of an absolute pathname as giving explicit instructions to the new file clerk about where to get a specific file: go into the file room (protocol), open the file drawer marked "vendors" (hostname), find the folder marked "copiers" (directory name), and pull out the document titled "Xerox Information" (filename). If you wrote this out as a hyperlink, it might look something like this:

```
<a href="http://www.vendors.com/copiers/xerox.html">Xerox Information</a>
```

LINKING TO FILES ON OTHER SERVERS

When you need to link to a file on another web site, you need to use absolute pathnames. For example, the following illustration shows a file sitting on your web server and a file sitting on another web server somewhere out on the Web:

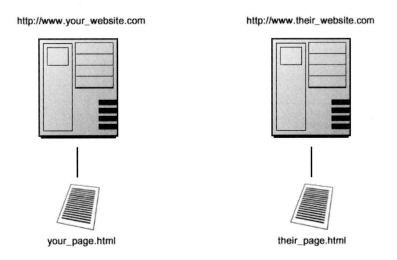

To create a link to that other file out there on the Web, you need to reference its complete address so a browser knows the route to take to find that document. So, the anchor tag required to link to that document on the other web server might look something like this:

```
<a href="http://www.their_website.com/their_page.html">Their Page</a>
```

RELATIVE PATHNAMES

Relative pathnames are *truncated,* or shortened versions, of their absolute counterparts. *Relative* is the keyword here, but relative to what? That depends on which type of relative pathname you use. You have two choices.

DOCUMENT-RELATIVE PATHNAMES

A *document-relative pathname* tells the browser to start from the current document that contains the link and look out to the rest of the present web server's file structure to locate the file to which the link points. For example, the following illustration shows a simple web site.

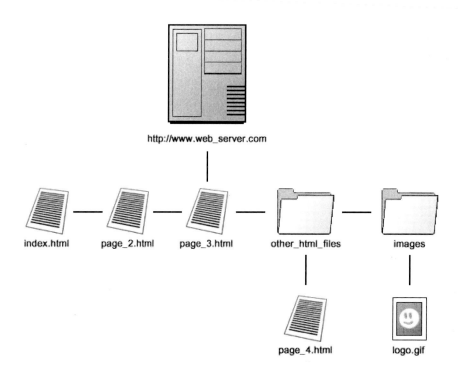

To make a link in index.html that takes the user to page_4.html, the anchor tag you create looks like this:

```
<a href="other_html_files/page_4.html">Page 4</a>
```

This syntax says, "Start from where you are in the server's file structure and locate the folder called other_html_files. Look inside this folder and find page_4.html and take users there when they click this link." Similarly, if you wanted to link to page_2.html or page_3.html, you would need to mention only the filename, for example, `<a href="page_2.html">`, because they're both in the same directory on the server as index.html.

You can use two dots at the beginning of a document-relative pathname to move up a directory in the file structure hierarchy. For example, if you wanted to create a link in page_4.html that opened the image file logo.gif, you'd write an anchor that looked like this:

```
<a href="../images/logo.gif">Our Logo</a>
```

This syntax says, "Step up one level out of the folder you're in and locate the folder called images. Then look in there and get the file called logo.gif." For each level you needed to move up to find a folder or file, you'd use another two dots and a forward slash. For example, ../../ would move you up two levels, and ../../../ would move you up three, etc.

SITE ROOT—RELATIVE PATHNAMES

A *site root–relative pathname* is less stringent than the absolute pathname, but not quite as relaxed as its document-relative sibling. This type of pathname uses the web server's file structure as the base reference for a link, using the root folder of the site as the starting point. In the diagram used in the previous example, the server root contains all the files and folders you can see. When writing a site root–relative pathname, the root directory is signified with an initial forward slash (/) and then followed by the full path down to the file to which you want to link. So, if you wanted to link to page_4.html as you did before, but using a site root–relative pathname, you'd write your link tag like this:

> TIP You should always use relative pathnames when creating hyperlinks to files inside your own web site. By using document-relative pathnames, you can move your site files from computer to computer or from web server to web server and not risk having the majority of your links break.
>
> For instance, imagine you have a folder on your current hard disk acting as the site root folder for the web server to which you plan to upload your documents. If you keep all of your links document-relative, it doesn't matter where those files ultimately wind up, provided that they maintain their position to one another and are moved as a unit.

```
<a href="/other_html_files/page_4.html">Page 4</a>
```

This syntax says, "OK, start at the root directory (/) and navigate down until you find the folder other_html_files. Then look inside that folder and find page_4.html, and take the user there when the link is clicked." With this type of link, because you're always referencing the site root, the URL you use to a particular file will always be the same regardless of which document you place the link in.

FORMATTING HYPERLINKS

A section of text or an image can be made into a link. It just depends on what you place between the opening and closing anchor tags. Figure 5-1 shows some typical

FIGURE 5-1

Generally, a text link appears
underlined, while an image
link has a colored border
around it.

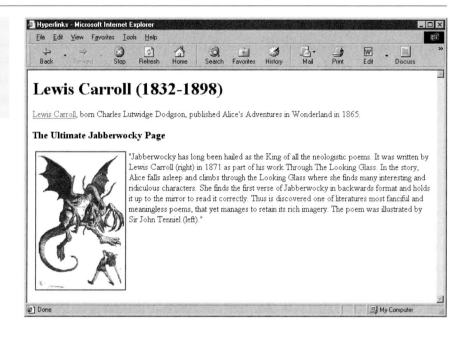

text and image links. Text-link colors and image-link border widths are controlled
by defining various tag attributes.

SETTING LINK COLORS

Links have three possible states—unvisited, activated (being clicked), and visited—
each of which can be assigned a color to let visitors know which links they've
been to and those they have yet to click. You define colors for these link states
via three attributes in the `<body>` tag: `link` (unvisited), `alink` (activated), and `vlink`
(visited). Just like any color you define in HTML, the value can be either one of
the predefined color names or a hexadecimal value. Simply place these attributes
in the `<body>` tag with appropriate values, as shown in the following example:

```
<body link="#0000FF" vlink="#660066" alink="#FF0000">
```

If left undefined, the browser will use whatever colors have been set in its defaults.

CONTROLLING IMAGE-LINK BORDERS

As discussed in Chapter 4, the border of an image is controlled by the `border`
attribute defined in the `<img>` tag; however, when an image tag is nested between

opening and closing anchors and becomes a link, a border is automatically placed around the image whether you've defined a border width value or not. This border typically shares whatever link colors you've assigned or uses the browser defaults if you haven't. The only way to remove the border from an image link is to intentionally define a border width of zero. For example:

```
<a href="index.html"><img src="home.gif" width="50" height="10" border="0"></a>
```

Named Anchors

The links we've made so far simply open the documents to which they point within a browser window. By using a different attribute for the anchor tag—the name attribute—you can use the anchor tag to create a specific location within a document, and then link to that location using a standard hyperlink. The named anchor effectively becomes a subaddress of the document in which it's located. When a visitor clicks a link that points to a named anchor, the document loads with that location at the top of the browser window.

The syntax for a named anchor looks like this:

```
<a name="location">content</a>
```

where *location-name* is a unique name you assign. Unlike a hyperlink, the content that falls between the named anchor tags isn't reformatted in any way. It simply becomes a point in the document that you can now reference.

Creating Named Anchors

Creating named anchors is really a two-part process: creating the named anchor, and then assigning a link to it. Imagine you have a heading and paragraph somewhere within a web page devoted to the game of darts. Your source code might look something like this:

```
<h3>Setting up the Board</h3>
<p>When setting up your dartboard,
the center of the bull's-eye must be
5' 8" from the floor, and the toe line
must be 7' 9.25" from the face of the board.</p>
```

To create a named anchor that would make "Setting up the Board" a location within the document to which a hyperlink could send a visitor, you'd place your anchor like so:

```
<h3><a name="board_setup">Setting up the Board</a></h3>
```

Be sure to use a name that makes sense to you so you don't have to think too hard later when you're creating the hyperlink. If you use two words, as I've done in this example, you don't want to leave spaces, so always use a hyphen (-) or an underscore (_).

LINKING TO NAMED ANCHORS

This imaginary anchor is now a subaddress of the HTML file that it's inside of. To link to a named anchor, you use the pound (#) sign. For example, say the link you create is within the same document as the named anchor. You simply need to reference the anchor name preceded by the pound sign, like so:

```
<a href="#board_setup">content</a>
```

Imagine that the document this anchor is within is called dartrules.html. As the hyperlink you create to this location gets farther and farther away, the URL pathname would grow as you might expect, and all the rules about pathnames would apply. For example, the pathname would grow in the following situations:

▶ If the link was in a different document but the same folder:
```
<a href="dartrules.html#board_setup">content</a>
```
▶ If the link was in a different document and a different folder:
```
<a href="darts/dartrules.html#board_setup">content</a>
```
▶ If the link was on an entirely different web server:
```
<a href="http://www.website.com/darts/dartrules.html#board_setup">
content</a>
```

USING THE id ATTRIBUTE

Another method exists for defining locations within a document, which involves attributing a unique ID to a specific HTML element. As luck would have it, the attribute you use is the id attribute, and it can be defined for any HTML tag. For instance, in the previous example, instead of setting up a named anchor within the <h3> tags, you could define an ID for the <h3> tag instead:

```
<h3 id="board_setup">Setting up the Board</h3>
```

As for linking to tag IDs, you use the same pound-sign methods as you do when linking to named anchors.

CREATING E-MAIL LINKS

There's one last linking method you need to know about before moving on, and one you've probably encountered: the e-mail link. This type of link allows you to define an e-mail address for the link instead of a file location so that when the link is clicked, the visitor's default e-mail application opens a blank message window with that address already filled in.

This type of link introduces you to yet another protocol, mailto:. The syntax for an e-mail link uses the href attribute, with a value that contains the mailto: protocol followed immediately by the e-mail address to which you want the visitor to send a message:

```
<a href="mailto:person@address.com">content</a>
```

 ON THE VIRTUAL CLASSROOM CD In Lesson 4, the instructor will demonstrate the steps involved in turning text and graphics into hyperlinks.

6

Creating Lists

Have you ever used a word processor and needed to make a list of bullet points or a numbered list of items? It's no great shakes with your word processor; just click the little button on the toolbar that corresponds to the style of list you want to make, and off you go. Don't worry, creating lists in HTML isn't much more complicated. Although you can't just click a button, the tags involved are very simple. What's more, they make sense when you look at them, but that's the whole point of HTML.

HTML offers three basic list types, shown here:

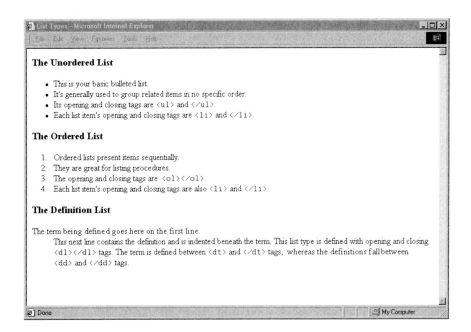

As you can see, I wasn't fooling when I said the tags make sense when you look at them. They're the initials for the type of list they define: `<ul>` is used for an unordered list, `<ol>` is used for an ordered list, and `<dl>` is used for a definition list. The first two list styles contain list items, `<li>`, while the definition list has terms, `<dt>`, and definitions, `<dd>`.

UNORDERED LISTS

Unordered lists allow you to emphasize major points without implying a sequence or priority to them. As you just saw, the tags used to create lists have a certain logic in their naming conventions. There is also a logic to how they are written in the HTML document, as seen here:

```
<html>
<head>
<title></title>
</head>
```

```
<body>

<h2>My Favorite Authors</h2>
<ul>
    <li>Robert A. Heinlein</li>
    <li>Robert Anton Wilson</li>
    <li>Roger Zelazney</li>
</ul>

</body>
</html>
```

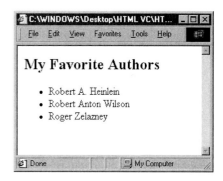

You can see that the HTML is written in basically the same manner as the list will be displayed in the browser window. Notice that the individual list item tags are indented from the opening and closing `<ul>` tags. This is done to make the source code easier to read and to demonstrate the relationship between the parent `<ul>` tags and their children, the `<li>` tags. Although the list items in both the unordered and ordered lists are indented slightly when displayed in the browser window, this has nothing to do with any indenting done in the source code. In fact, if you wanted to, you could write an entire HTML document out on one line—not that I'd ever recommend it, however.

MODIFYING THE BULLET STYLE

By default, most browsers display unordered list items by using a solid disc for a bullet. You can modify the bullet style by using the `type` attribute, which accepts a value of `square`, `circle`, or `disc`, as shown here:

`<ul type="square">`

■ Square

`<ul type="circle">`

○ Circle

`<ul type="disc">`

● Disc

The `type` attribute is usually applied to the `<ul>` tag to affect the entire list; however, you can also apply it to the individual `<li>` tags. The results vary from browser to browser. For example, in Internet Explorer, defining the type for a particular <li> tag affects only that lone list item, while Netscape Navigator makes each of the following bullets in the list adhere to that type attribute until you define a new one.

ORDERED LISTS

Ordered lists allow you to enumerate points and make procedural lists. Their basic structure is no different than an unordered list, other than the use of the <ol> tags:

```
<html>
<head>
<title></title>
</head>

<body>

<h2>The Steps to Dispatching a Jabberwock:</h2>

<ol>
    <li>Locate/Purchase one Vorpal Sword</li>
    <li>Track down Jabberwock</li>
    <li>Swing that blade - snicker-snack!</li>
</ol>

</body>
</html>
```

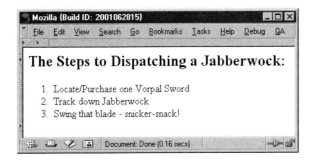

MODIFYING THE NUMBERING STYLE

Ordered lists also use the type attribute, which in this instance accepts the values shown next.

▶ `<ol type="1">` Setting the `type` attribute equal to 1 produces the traditional numbered list, as shown in the following illustration. This is also the usual browser default if the `type` attribute is left undefined.

▶ `<ol type="I">` Setting the `type` attribute equal to capital *I* creates an uppercase Roman numeral list, shown in this example:

▶ `<ol type="i">` Using a lowercase *i* to define the `type` attribute results in a lowercase Roman numeral list, like this:

▶ `<ol type="A">` Using a capital *A* to define the `type` attribute creates an upper-case alphabetical list:

▶ `<ol type="a">` Of course, using a lowercase *a* gives you a lowercase alphabetical list, as shown here:

As in unordered lists, you can apply the `type` attribute to list items in an ordered list with similar results varying from browser to browser. You are better off leaving the `type` attribute to be handled by the `<ol>` tag, and using the `value` attribute discussed in "The `value` Attribute" section of this chapter to manually set the number of the `<li>` tag in an ordered list.

THE start ATTRIBUTE

The `start` attribute allows you to define the point at which an ordered list begins counting. For example, you can start a numbered list with *4* or an alphabetical list with the letter *D* (the fourth letter in the alphabet) by giving the `start` attribute a value of 4. The following code demonstrates how each list type responds when the `start` attribute is set to 4.

```
<html>
<head>
<title>The Start Attribute</title>
</head>

<body>

<h2>The start Attribute set to 4</h2>
<ol type="1" start="4">
    <li>Number Four</li>
    <li>Number Five</li>
    <li>Number Six</li>
</ol>


<ol type="I" start="4">
    <li>Roman Numeral Four</li>
    <li>Roman Numeral Five</li>
    <li>Roman Numeral Six</li>
</ol>


<ol type="i" start="4">
    <li>Lowercase Roman Numeral Four</li>
    <li>Lowercase Roman Numeral Five</li>
    <li>Lowercase Roman Numeral Six</li>
</ol>


<ol type="A" start="4">
    <li>Uppercase Fourth Letter</li>
    <li>Uppercase Fifth Letter</li>
    <li>Uppercase Sixth Letter</li>
</ol>


<ol type="a" start="4">
    <li>Lowercase Fourth Letter</li>
    <li>Lowercase Fifth Letter</li>
    <li>Lowercase Sixth Letter</li>
</ol>

</body>
</html>
```

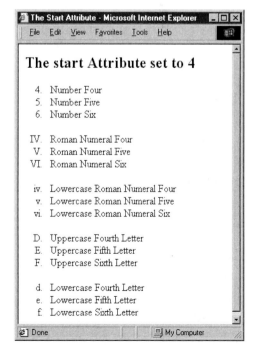

THE value ATTRIBUTE

First off, it's important to note that the value attribute can be defined for the <li> tag only when used in an ordered list. This attribute allows you to define the number or character of a list item. Each subsequent item's number will then follow in sequence, as the following code shows:

```
<html>
<head>
<title>The value Attribute</title>
</head>

<body>
<h3>The value Attribute</h3>
<ol>
    <li>By default this is Number One</li>
    <li value="3">This one has been changed to a value of 3</li>
    <li>This list item will automatically follow in sequence</li>
</ol>
</body>
</html>
```

The value attribute is equally supported by the major browsers, unlike defining the type attribute for an <li> tag in an ordered list, where display results will vary.

Just like with the start attribute, even though you're assigning a number to this attribute, the value attribute doesn't affect the list type. With list types that use characters, the number defined in the value attribute corresponds to the character's order in the sequence: 1 equals A, a, I, i, and 1; 2 equals B, b, II, ii, and 2, etc.

NESTING LISTS

To *nest* lists is to literally place the code for one list in among the code for another. For each successive *nesting*—list inside list inside list—the list items indent that much further from the left margin.

NESTING UNORDERED LISTS

In the following unordered list example, the main outer list has one list placed immediately after its first list item, another list inserted after the second list item, and within that second nested list, a third list has been inserted:

```
<html>
<head>
<title>A Nested Unordered List</title>
</head>

<body>

<h2>A Nested Unordered List</h2>

<ul>
    <li>First item in the outer list</li>

<!-- Nested list #1 -->
      <ul>
        <li>First nested list within the outer list</li>
      </ul>
      <-- end Nested List #1 -->

    <li>Second item in outer list</li>

      <!-- Nested List #2 -->
      <ul>
        <li>Second nested list within the outer list</li>

        <!-- Nested List #3 -->
        <ul>
          <li>A third list nested in the second nested list</li>
        </ul>
        <!-- end Nested List #3 -->
```

```
        </ul>
        <!-- end Nested List #2 -->
    </ul>

    </body>
    </html>
```

Notice that with each successive nesting, the default bullets change from disc to circle to square without the use of a `type` attribute. You can, of course, apply `type` attributes as you see fit to render the bullets you prefer.

Also notice that in the source code, each nested list is indented another level, mimicking the browser display. Again, this is done to make the code easier to read and has no bearing on how the browser displays the code.

NESTING ORDERED LISTS

By using this nesting method with ordered lists and taking advantage of the `type`, `start`, and `value` attributes to affect the list item's preceding characters, you can create complex list structures like formal outlines. For example, here's a formal outline that mimics the structure of this chapter:

```
<html>
<head>
<title>The Nested List</title>
</head>

<body>

<h2>Creating Lists</h2>

<ol type="I">
    <li>Unordered Lists</li>
        <ol type="A">
            <li>Changing the Bullet Style</li>
                <ol type="1">
                    <li>The type Attribute</li>
                        <ol type="a">
```

```
                    <li>disc</li>
                    <li>circle</li>
                    <li>square</li>
                </ol>
            </ol>
        </ol>
    <li>Ordered Lists</li>
        <ol type="A">
            <li>Changing the Numbering Style</li>
                <ol type="1">
                    <li> The type Attribute</li>
                        <ol type="a">
                            <li>1</li>
                            <li>I</li>
                            <li>i</li>
                            <li>A</li>
                            <li>a</li>
                        </ol>
                </ol>
            <li>The start Attribute</li>
            <li>The value Attribute</li>
        </ol>
    <li>Nesting Lists</li>
        <ol type="A">
            <li>Nesting Unordered Lists</li>
            <li>Nesting Ordered Lists</li>
        </ol>
    <li>Definition lists</li>
</ul>

</body>
</html>
```

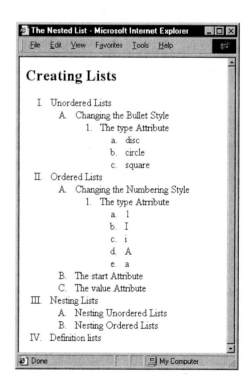

DEFINITION LISTS

Whereas the ordered list and the unordered list can be seen as siblings, the definition list is more like a distant cousin. These first two list styles have some kind of preceding symbol or character, and their contents are defined with a single common list item tag. Definition lists, in contrast, require two elements, a term and its definition, and have no preceding symbol or character.

A definition list is marked up with the opening and closing tags `<dl>` and `</dl>`. Instead of the common `<li>` tag to define an individual list item, you define two elements that are held between their own set of tags—`<dt></dt>` for the term, and `<dd></dd>` for the definition. The following code shows an example:

```
<html>
<head>
<title>The Definition List</title>
</head>

<body>
<h2>The Zoology of Lewis Carroll</h2>
<dl>
    <dt>Jabberwock</dt>
        <dd>A large, burbling, flame-eyed creature known to inhabit
        tulgey wooded areas.</dd>

    <dt>Bandersnatch</dt>
        <dd>A frumious creature, best avoided.</dd>

    <dt>Jubjub Bird</dt>
        <dd>A creature whose details are less clearly understood.
        In the same class as the Bandersnatch
and Jabberwock.</dd>
</dl>

</body>
</html>
```

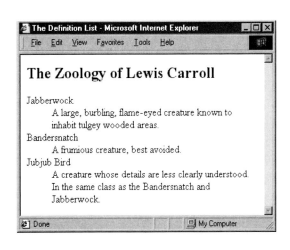

> **TIP** Each type of list has some generally accepted uses. For example, the definition list is specifically designed to provide what its name implies: a list of definitions. Any type of "this equals that" construction is right up its alley. Ordered lists are, again, great for outlines. This includes tables of contents, procedural lists, or any other type of sequential layout. The unordered list is perfect for setting off a list of hyperlinks, emphasizing points in a body of text, and listing anything where the order of the list items isn't particularly important.

Generally, browsers place the contents of the `<dt></dt>` tags on the left margin and indent the contents of the `<dd></dd>` tags underneath them. The contents of the `<dt></dt>` tags should be limited to a word or two. What is placed between the `<dd></dd>` tags is intended to be verbose, however, and can include other HTML markup-like paragraphs and images.

 ON THE VIRTUAL CLASSROOM CD Lists are a great way to display certain kinds of information. What's more, they're very easy to implement. In Lesson 5, the instructor will demonstrate how to create and format HTML's three list types.

7

Tables

When HTML was first developed, tables were intended to do what tables have traditionally done: display data. This means columns and rows of numbers and words, with headings and borders very much like traditional spreadsheets. This, in all likelihood, goes back to HTML's scholarly beginnings at CERN, an international high-energy physics research center in Switzerland where HTML was created.

The founders of the HTML specification were thinking more about research papers and thesis dissertations, where particularly in the hard sciences, there's a large quantity of data to be displayed. Initially, no one was considering the public and commercial expansion of this new medium, and with that expansion, the birth of web design.

Once that expansion began, it didn't take long before people realized tables could be used as more than just "tables." Tables also worked wonders as layout tools in a medium that possessed no inherent positioning attributes of its own. As time went by and the HTML specification grew, the number of attributes for the tags that create tables also expanded, making its layout capabilities even greater. Although the current recommendations for HTML/XHTML are toward the logical rendering of information, giving design and placement considerations over to cascading style sheets (described in Chapter 10), tables are still one of the most common layout elements used in web pages.

THE TABLE TAGS

Just like lists, tables are made up of a series of nested container tags, each opening and closing set defining a specific table element. In the HTML table model, tables contain rows and rows contain cells. For example, the opening and closing tags delineating the table are written `<table>` and `</table>`. Inside the `<table>` tags, each table row is defined by using `<tr>` and `</tr>`, the *tr* signifying *table row*. The individual table cells within each row are then defined with `<td>` and `</td>` tags, which stands for *table data*. The following code lays out a table in an HTML document, making this internal logic easier to see:

```
<table border="1">
    <tr>
        <td> One </td>
        <td> Two </td>
    </tr>
    <tr>
        <td> Three </td>
        <td> Four </td>
    </tr>
</table>
```

This source code creates a table two rows high by two columns wide, with the words "One" through "Four" as cell content, shown here. You can see that the column is not specifically defined. Columns lose out because HTML defines tables as a collection of rows that hold a number of cells, effectively creating columns by stacking rows on top of each other. What you might normally consider a column is just the inevitable result of that stacking. This idea can be a bit of a conceptual hurdle for people familiar with spreadsheets, where columns are a distinct entity.

FORMATTING TABLE PROPERTIES

That example table is as "vanilla" as they come. You can modify many different table properties by defining a number of attributes for each table element's opening tags. Because the `<table>`, `<tr>`, and `<td>` tags have many of the same attributes, it is possible to define properties that may effectively apply to the same spot in the table. For example, you can set the background color of a `<td>` tag to red by using the `bgcolor` attribute, and then use the same attribute to define the background color for the `<tr>` tag of the row that cell is in to make the row white. You could then define the `bgcolor` attribute for the `<table>` tag, making the entire table's background color blue. Which color is that cell going to wind up? Which tag's attribute takes precedence?

The general rule for HTML is that the specific element tops the general one. The hierarchy of table elements then is cell-row-table, meaning that cell formatting supersedes row formatting, and row formatting supersedes that of the table. Therefore, the hypothetical cell here would be red, the rest of the row it was in—provided no other cells had `bgcolor` defined—would be white, and the rest of the table would then be blue. With that said, it's time to look at the different ways to control table properties.

TABLE BORDERS

As you may have noticed in the opening example, the border around a table is controlled by the `border` attribute. This attribute accepts a numeric value that specifies the thickness of the border in pixels around the

perimeter of the table itself, as seen in the illustration. When using tables as layout elements where borders would detract from the design, you can set the border to a value of 0 and guarantee that they disappear.

Generally, a border is displayed using a 3-D effect with a highlight and a shadowed tone. Different browsers have slightly different display features; for example, the World Wide Web Consortium's browser/editor Amaya displays borders like this:

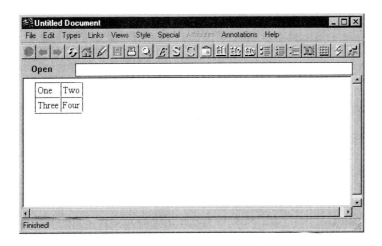

BORDER COLORS

Internet Explorer and Netscape Navigator allow you to specify border colors by using the `bordercolor` attribute. Internet Explorer even allows you to specify the highlight and shadow colors by using `bordercolorlight` and `bordercolordark`. In general, you should try to avoid using any tag or attribute that will put one group of viewers at a disadvantage. Unless you're working on an *intranet* (a self-contained network web server limited to specific users) and you know specifically which browser your audience is viewing your site with, stay away from browser-specific markup.

TABLE ALIGNMENT

Left to its own devices, a table will sit on the left margin and any page content that follows it will be placed on the next line, as shown here:

```
<table border="1">
  <tr>
    <td> One </td>
```

```
      <td> Two </td>
    </tr>
    <tr>
      <td> Three </td>
      <td> Four </td>
    </tr>
  </table>
  <p><i>'Twas brillig, and the slithy toves<br>
  Did gyre and gimble in the wabe;<br>
  All mimsy were the borogoves,<br>
  And the mome raths outgrabe.</i></p>
```

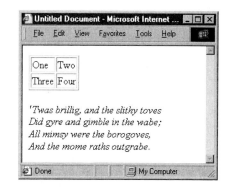

Similar to aligning an image, the `<table>` tag makes use of the `align` attribute, but with only three possible values: `left`, `right`, and `center`. Using the source code from the previous example and adding an `align` attribute to the opening `<table>` tag, these are the results:

▶ `align ="left"` Keeps the table to the left, wrapping other page content around the table's right side.

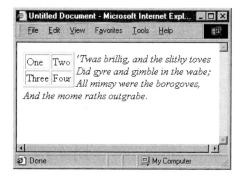

▶ `align="center"` Places the table in the center of the page, forcing page content onto the line beneath.

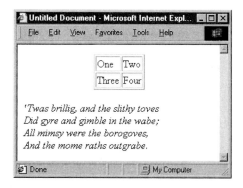

▶ `align="right"`   Sets the table to the right, wrapping other page content around the table's left side.

TABLE DIMENSIONS

By default, a table's dimensions are just sufficient to house whatever content is placed within their cells. In effect, the table shrink-wraps itself to its contents. You can apply dimension values to the `<table>` tag by using the `width` and `height` attributes. The values for these attributes can be either specific pixel values or a percentage of the browser's current window size. For example, `<table width="100" border="1">` results in a table that is 100 pixels wide, whereas `<table width="100%" border="1">` creates a table that will try to expand or contract to span 100 percent of the browser window, as shown here. If the content within a table can be scrunched only so much, the table simply stops shrinking.

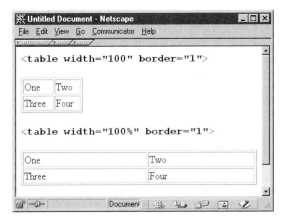

The `height` attribute for the `<table>` tag is not part of the HTML standard; rather, it was created by the browser manufacturers. In most cases, the height you specify will be adhered to unless the table content requires more space than the dimension permits, in which case, the value is ignored.

CELL PADDING AND CELL SPACING

Cell padding is used to control the amount of space between the cell walls and the content that rests inside them. *Cell spacing,* in contrast, controls the amount of space between the individual table cells. Both properties are controlled, fittingly, by the attributes `cellpadding` and `cellspacing`.

To demonstrate what I mean, the following code creates a table that consists of a single row with two cells. Two GIF images are placed inside the cells, a square and a triangle, so the source code and its corresponding appearance would be something like this:

```
<table border="1">
  <tr>
    <td><img src="square.gif" width="76" height="76"></td>
    <td><img src="triangle.gif" width="80" height="80"></td>
  </tr>
</table>
```

If you add the `cellpadding` attribute to the `<table>` tag and give it a value of 10, the interior of the table cells inflates by ten pixels around each side of the images within them, as seen here: `<table cellpadding="10" border="1">`.

Adding the `cellspacing` attribute and giving it the same value of 10 plumps up the interior cell "borders" to ten pixels in width. So `<table cellspacing="10" border="1">` results in the following:

It's important to realize that the `cellspacing` attribute is different from the `border` attribute. As you can see, there is no 3-D effect here. The `border` attribute affects only the perimeter border of the table. So, if you increase the `border` attribute to 10 and reapply the `cellpadding` attribute so the opening `<table>` tag reads `<table cellpadding="10" ccllspacing="10" border="10">`, you get a clearer picture of what each attribute affects, as shown in Figure 7-1.

CELL SPACING AND BORDERS

When left undefined, most browsers actually give tables a cell spacing of two pixels. This means that setting the `cellspacing` attribute equal to 2 has no noticeable effect. When I implied that the `border` and `cellspacing` attributes had nothing to do with each other, I was speaking only in the strictest possible sense. The two attributes do work hand in hand to create different effects.

For example, any `border` value of 1 or more when defined in conjunction with a `cellspacing` value of 0 creates 3-D, two-pixel wide interior borders around the table cells in most browsers. So, if you set the `border` attribute to 1 and the

FIGURE 7-1

Cell padding, cell spacing, and table borders each control specific regions of a table.

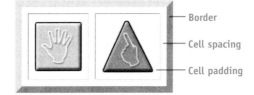

Border

Cell spacing

Cell padding

`cellspacing` attribute to 0, you get tight borders throughout the entire table, as seen here:

BACKGROUND COLORS AND IMAGES

The `<table>` tag supports two attributes that allow you to define either a background color or a background image for your table. To define a background color, use the `bgcolor` attribute much like you did for the `<body>` tag when specifying the background color for a document. This attribute, like all attributes pertaining to color, accepts either a hexadecimal value or a predefined HTML color name, for example, `<table bgcolor="#FF0000">` or `<table bgcolor="red">`.

Applying this attribute to the `<table>` tag gives all the table cells one underlying color, but as I mentioned at the start of the chapter, this attribute can also be applied to both the `<tr>` and `<td>` tags as well, allowing you to define specific colors to each region. Obviously, if you were to define a table background color and then define background colors for each cell, the `<table>` tag's `bgcolor` attribute would become superfluous.

The attribute for assigning a background image is simply written `background`. This attribute is not part of the HTML specification, but it is supported by both Netscape Navigator and Internet Explorer with slight differences. The value you define for this attribute is the URL of the image you want to use, for example, `<table background="images/bg.gif">`.

In Internet Explorer, this attribute tiles the image across the background, meaning that the image is repeated left to right and top to bottom across the expanse of the table. This has no effect on the table's dimensions, and the image is simply clipped off at the table edges. The cells of the table have no impact on the tiling of the image, as shown in Figure 7-2.

FIGURE 7-2
Internet Explorer tiles the image across the entire table background, as if the table were a window out onto the tiled image.

In Netscape Navigator, however, using this attribute with the `<table>` tag has the same effect as if it were assigned to each of the `<td>` tags, beginning the image tiling anew in each table cell, as shown in Figure 7-3.

FORMATTING ROW AND CELL PROPERTIES

As previously mentioned, each of the opening tags used to construct tables accept many of the same attributes, occasionally with minor differences in interpretation.

TABLE HEADERS

Creating column and row headings isn't the work of a particular attribute setting, but a fourth type of table element tag. Used in place of the cell's `<td>` and `</td>` tags, the `<th>` and `</th>` tags render all text inside them bold and centered. For example, the following table replaces some of the traditional cell tags with the results shown in the following code.

FIGURE 7-3
Netscape Navigator begins the tiling effect over again within each cell.

```
<h3>Relative Ferocity of Creatures Beyond the Looking Glass:</h3>
<table border="1" cellspacing="0" cellpadding="10">
  <tr>
    <th>Jabberwock</th>
    <th>Bandersnatch</th>
    <th>Jubjub bird</th>
    <th>Snark</th>
  </tr>
  <tr align="center">
    <td>OFF THE SCALE!</td>
    <td>10</td>
    <td>9.5</td>
    <td>Much too elusive</td>
  </tr>
</table>
```

The `<th>` tag accepts all the same attributes as the `<td>` tag.

ROW AND CELL ALIGNMENT

The same `align` attribute used for aligning the `<table>` tag is also accepted by the `<tr>` and `<td>` tags, but with a slightly different interpretation. Whereas the `align` attribute for the `<table>` tag affects how the table is aligned in the HTML document, when used with the `<tr>` and `<td>` tags, it affects the alignment of content *inside* the rows and cells.

The possible values for the `align` attribute are the same as well: `left`, `right`, and `center`, and again by default, browsers align cell content to the left. When applied to the `<tr>` tag, this attribute affects the alignment of content in each cell in the row, whereas if applied to the `<td>` tag, it simply affects that individual cell, as seen in the following illustration.

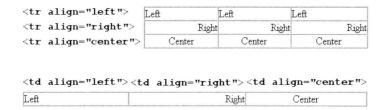

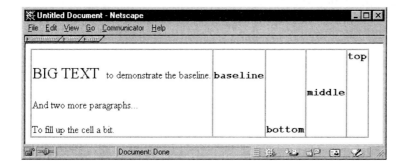

VERTICAL ALIGNMENT

So far, I've discussed alignment only on the horizontal plane, but you can also control the vertical. To do this, you use the `valign` attribute. This attribute accepts four possible values: `baseline`, `bottom`, `middle`, and `top`. By default, most browsers render cell content with a vertical alignment equal to a value of `middle`. Again, this attribute can be used in either the `<tr>` or `<td>` tag to equal effect.

In the following example, I've placed three one-sentence paragraphs in one cell to help illustrate how the different values of the `valign` attribute work. In each of the following cells, I've placed a word corresponding to an attribute value and then applied the attribute accordingly:

There is a difference between setting the `align` attribute of cells and rows and formatting the alignment of the specific content within them. Imagine you set a row's alignment to the right. This is equivalent to hanging a sign on that row that says, "Anything falling into these cells lines up on the right side." However, you could also place a paragraph or other element that accepts the `align` attribute in one of those cells and align it to the left. Here's another dilemma about formatting precedence. In HTML, the specific element always beats the more general one, so although cells beat rows, and rows beat tables, formatting applied to specific content inside the table cells trumps them all.

WIDTH AND HEIGHT

You can use both `width` and `height` attributes to specify the dimensions of individual `<td>` tags just like you would the `<table>` tag. Watch out that the values you define don't conflict with each other, however. For example, two cells in the same row can't have different heights, nor can two cells that would be considered part of a "column" have different widths.

Where the `<table>` tag is concerned, if you've defined a table width of 100 percent, you can't set pixel width values for each cell in a row without causing problems. One of your columns must be free to expand and contract with the browser window. Likewise, if you set a table's width equal to 500 pixels and then set cell widths across all the cells in a row that add up to only 300 pixels, web browsers won't be able to tell how the table should be rendered. They'll attempt to compensate the best they can, but the overall effect will not be what you were originally intending.

If you set cell heights and widths to specific values, those settings will be adhered to unless you place content inside them that is bigger than the allotted space. In most cases, a cell's height will always expand to fit content regardless of any height value specified. Width values will force text in a cell to wrap unless the text is a continuous string without any spaces. In this case, the cell and table will expand to fit the text line.

THE `nowrap` ATTRIBUTE

You can turn the automatic wrapping of cells off by using the `nowrap` attribute. This attribute does not accept any value but is instead a toggle, turning wrapping on or off with its inclusion in a `<td>` tag, like so:

```
<td width="200">
```

```
Yada Yada Yada Yada
Yada Yada Yada Yada
Yada Yada Yada
```

```
<td width="200" nowrap>
```

```
Yada Yada Yada Yada Yada Yada Yada Yada Yada Yada Yada
```

SPANNING ROWS AND COLUMNS

When building a table, you may want a particular cell to span across a number of rows or columns, in effect, merging the cell with the ones beside it. The two attributes used to accomplish this feat are `colspan` and `rowspan`. Each attribute accepts a numeric value corresponding to the number of columns or rows you want the cell to span across. For example, if you want a cell to span across two columns, you'd write the opening table cell tag like this:

```
<td colspan="2">
```

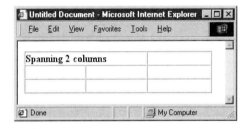

Conversely, if you want to span across two rows, the tag is written like this:

```
<td rowspan="2">
```

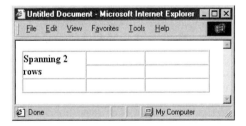

You can define both attributes for a `<td>` tag simultaneously. For example, if you wanted to merge all cells across three columns and three rows, you'd apply attributes like this:

```
<td colspan="3" rowspan="2">
```

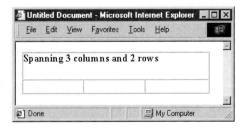

The order in which you define them is not important.

Be sure you don't have a greater value set for your span than the number of rows or columns in your table. If you do, some browsers will attempt to compensate for your mathematical error by extending the row or column to cover cells that aren't there. This problem can have some very peculiar effects.

NESTING TABLES

Just like nesting HTML lists, you can also nest complete tables within other table cells. This technique is extremely useful for displaying complex data and positioning content when tables are used as layout elements. Here's a very simple example:

```
<table cellpadding="3" cellspacing="0" border="1">
  <tr>
    <td>
    <!-Here's the first nested table -->
    <table cellpadding="3" cellspacing="0" bgcolor="yellow" border="1">
      <tr>
        <td> content </td>
        <td> content </td>
      </tr>
      <tr>
        <td> content </td>
        <td> content </td>
      </tr>
    </table>
    </td>
    <td> content </td>
    <td> content </td>
  </tr>
  <tr>
    <td> content </td>
    <td> content </td>
    <td> content </td>
  </tr>
</table>
```

Something interesting happens to a table width when it's defined as a percentage while nested inside another table. It becomes a percentage of the cell width in which the table is nested. For example, you might have a cell with a width of 80 pixels. If you nest a table inside it whose table width is 50 percent, that table stretches across only half the cell, for a total of 40 pixels.

Nested tables are a panacea for positioning elements while retaining backward compatibility with older browsers that don't support cascading style sheets. By using tables to constrain other page elements, and nesting tables to gain greater control over a region of a page and then hiding the table borders, you escape from the traditional left-to-right, top-to-bottom word processor-esque feel. Figure 7-4 shows an example of the type of effect I mean.

Figure 7-5 shows the same document with the borders revealed and cell padding increased to better indicate where tables begin and end.

Here's the source code for the document shown in Figure 7-4:

```
<html>
<head>
<title>HTML VIRTUAL CLASSROOM</title>
</head>
<body bgcolor=#ffffff text=#000000>


<table border="0" cellpadding="5" cellspacing="0" width="760" align="center">  <tr>
```

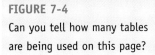

FIGURE 7-4

Can you tell how many tables are being used on this page?

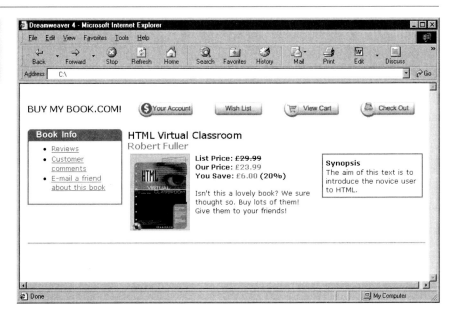

FIGURE 7-5

There are eight tables in all.

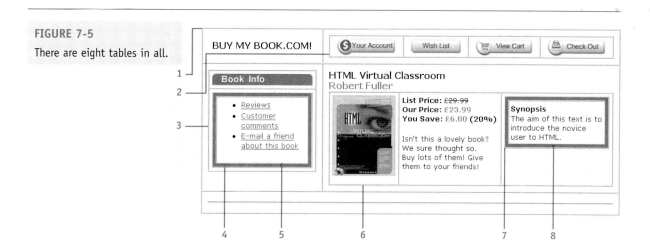

```
<td align="center">
<font face="verdana, arial, helvctica, sans-serif">
<b>BUY MYBOOK.COM!</b>
</font>
</td>


<td>
<table border="0" cellspacing="0" cellpadding="10" width="100%">
<tr align="center">

  <td>
  <a href="acounts.html">
  <img src="images/button1.gif" width="105" height="33" border="0">
  </a>
  </td>

  <td>
  <a href="wishes.html">
  <img src="images/button2.swf"width="93" height="33" border="0">
  </a>
  </td>

  <td>
  <a href="cart.html">
  <img src="images/button3.swf" width="105" height="33" border="0">
  </a>
  </td>
```

```
    <td>
    <a href="checkout.html">
    <img src="images/button4.swf" width="105" height="33">
    </a>
    </td>

  </tr>
  </table>
  </td>
</tr>

<tr>

  <td valign="top" align="center">
  <table border="0" cellpadding="0" cellspacing="0" width="180">
    <tr>

      <td><img src="images/book-info.gif" width="180" height="20"></td>
    </tr>
    <tr>

      <td>
      <table width="100%" border="0" cellpadding="0" bgcolor="#336699">
      <tr>
        <td>
        <table border="0" width="100%" cellpadding="3" cellspacing="0"
        bgcolor="#ffffcc">
        <tr>

          <td>

            <ul>
              <li>
              <font face="verdana, arial, helvetica, sans-serif" size="2">
              <a href="../reviews.html">reviews</a></font>
              <br>
              </li>

              <li>
```

```
            <font face="verdana, arial, helvetica, sans-serif" size="2">
            <a href="../comments.html">customer comments</a></font>
            <br>
            </li>

            <li>
            <font face="verdana, arial, helvetica, sans-serif" size="2">
            <a href="../email.html">e-mail a friend about this book</a>
            </font>
            </li>
         </ul>

      </td>

   </tr>
   </table>
   </td>

 </tr>
 </table>
 </td>
</tr>
</table>
</td>

<td valign="top" align="left">
<font face="verdana, arial, helvetica, sans-serif" size="4">
HTML Virtual Classroom</font>
<br>
<font face="verdana, arial, helvetica, sans-serif" color="#336699">
<b>robert fuller </b></font>
<br>

<table border="0" cellpadding="5" cellspacing="0">
<tr valign="top">

  <td width="112">
  <img src="images/html-vc.jpg" width="112" height="140">
  </td>
```

```
<td align="left">
<font face="verdana, arial, helvetica, sans-serif" size="2">
<b>List Price: <s>&pound;29.99</s></b>
<br>
<b>Our Price: <font color="#336699">&pound;23.99</font></b>
<br>
<b>You Save: <font color="#336699">&pound;6.00</font> (20%)</b>
<br>
<br>
Isn't this a lovely book? We sure thought so. Buy lots of them!
Give them to your friends!</font>
<br>
</td>

<td align="left" width="166">
<table width="190" border="0" cellpadding="2" bgcolor="#336699"
cellspacing="0">
<tr>

 <td width="386">
 <table border="0" cellpadding="3" bgcolor="#ffffcc">
 <tr>

   <td align="left" valign="top">
   <font face="verdana, arial, helvetica, sans-serif" size="2">
   <b>Synopsis</b>
   <br>
   The aim of this text is to introduce the novice user to HTML.
   </font>
   </td>

 </tr>
 </table>
 </td>

</tr>
</table>
</td>
```

```
      </tr>
      </table>
      </td>

</tr>
<tr>
    <td valign="top" align="center" colspan="2">
    <hr>
    </td>

</tr>
</table>

</body>
</html>
```

ON THE VIRTUAL CLASSROOM CD In Lesson 6, the instructor will demonstrate how to construct tables, focusing on how they can be used to house and constrain information within a page, providing structure to the entire page.

8

Forms

HTML *forms* allow information to be passed between
the visitor (also referred to as the user) and the web server.
Some examples include the following: a guestbook, where visitors enter their names and comments, which are posted to
the site for other visitors to read; your favorite search engine,
which takes a word or phrase that you enter and returns
matching entries from its database; or an e-commerce site
like Amazon.com, where visitors fill out forms providing book,
credit card, and shipping information.

If you've filled out web forms, then you know that you not only enter information, but something also becomes of that information once you submit it, sending it on its way. This makes web forms a two-part proposition: the HTML-based interface that your visitors enter information into, and an application on the web server that processes that information. What is this "application" stuff all about? Enter the Common Gateway Interface (CGI).

CGI is a standard used for external programs and scripts to communicate with web servers. The application is usually a script or program written in any of a number of programming languages, for example, Perl, C++, or VBScript. The form page on the web site packages the information up and sends it to the web server where the external application resides. The application processes the information and either has the web server pass some response back to the visitor, or holds and maintains the data for a future purpose. CGI scripting is a whole book unto itself, whereas this chapter concentrates on only the HTML part of the form equation.

DISSECTING A FORM

The following illustration shows a simple form followed by its source code. Without reading ahead, see if you can interpret which code creates the various form elements:

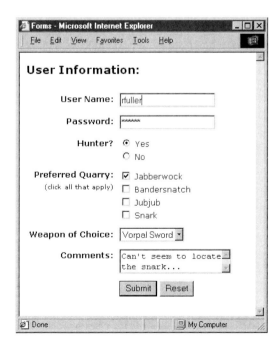

```
<html>
<head>
<title>Forms</title>
</head>

<body>

<font face="Verdana, Arial, Helvetica, sans-serif" size="4">
<b>User Information:</b></font>

<form name="myForm" method="post" action="http://www.highstrungproduc-
tions.com/cgi-bin/process.pl">

<!- I've thrown in some added spacing between rows and cells
    to make this easier to read -->

<table border="0" cellspacing="0" cellpadding="5">
    <tr>

      <td align="right" valign="top">
      <font face="Verdana, Arial, Helvetica, sans-serif" size="2">
      <b>User Name:</b></font>
      </td>

      <td align="left" valign="top"><input type="text" name="user"></td>

    </tr>
    <tr>

      <td align="right" valign="top">
      <font face="Verdana, Arial, Helvetica, sans-serif" size="2">
      <b>Password:</b></font>
      </td>

      <td align="left" valign="top">
      <input type="password" name="password">
      </td>
```

```
</tr>
<tr>

    <td align="right" valign="top">
    <font face="Verdana, Arial, Helvetica, sans-serif" size="2">
    <b>Hunter?</b></font>
    </td>

    <td align="left" valign="top">
    <input type="radio" name="hunter" value="yes">
    <font face="Verdana, Arial, Helvetica, sans-serif" size="2">Yes</font>
    <br>
    <input type="radio" name="hunter" value="no">
    <font face="Verdana, Arial, Helvetica, sans-serif" size="2">No</font>
    </td>

</tr>
<tr>

    <td align="right" valign="top">
    <font face="Verdana, Arial, Helvetica, sans-serif" size="2">
    <b>Preferred Quarry:</b><br>
    <font size="1">(click all that apply)</font></font>
    </td>

    <td align="left" valign="top">
    <input type="checkbox" name="quarry" value="jabberwock">
    <font face="Verdana, Arial, Helvetica, sans-serif" size="2">
    Jabberwock</font>
    <br>
    <input type="checkbox" name="quarry" value="bandersnatch">
    <font face="Verdana, Arial, Helvetica, sans-serif" size="2">
    Bandersnatch</font>
    <br>
```

```html
<input type="checkbox" name="quarry" value="jubjub">
<font face="Verdana, Arial, Helvetica, sans-serif" size="2">
Jubjub</font>
<br>
<input type="checkbox" name="quarry" value="snark">
<font face="Verdana, Arial, Helvetica, sans-serif" size="2">
Snark</font>
</td>

</tr>
<tr>

  <td align="right" valign="top">
  <font face="Verdana, Arial, Helvetica, sans-serif" size="2">
  <b>Weapon of Choice:</b></font>
  </td>

  <td align="left" valign="top">
  <select name="weapon">
     <option value="smart" selected>Vorpal Sword</option>
     <option value="stupid">Pointed Stick</option>
     <option value="insane">Bare Hands</option>
  </select>
  </td>

</tr>
<tr>

  <td align="right" valign="top">
  <font face="Verdana, Arial, Helvetica, sans-serif" size="2">
  <b>Comments:</b></font>
  </td>

  <td align="left" valign="top">
  <textarea name="comments"></textarea>
  </td>
```

```
    </tr>
    <tr>

        <td align="right" valign="top"> </td>

        <td align="left" valign="top">
        <input type="submit" name="Submit" value="Submit">
        <input type="reset" name="Reset" value="Reset">
        </td>

    </tr>
    </table>
    </form>


    </body>
    </html>
```

That's an awful lot of code for such a little form, but as you look through it, you'll see that most of it is stuff you're already familiar with from previous chapters. This should tell you something about forms—form elements are simply part of the larger HTML document, they aren't the document itself. In other words, a check box means nothing to a visitor unless you include some kind of textual reference explaining its significance, and you need to think about page layout as well.

If you look at the example code, you'll see that there's a table present with its border set to 0, used to structure the form elements and accompanying text. The tags you haven't seen before are `<form>`, `<input>`, `<textarea>`, `<select>`, and `<option>`. These tags create the individual interface elements of the form: the text fields, radio buttons, check boxes, and Submit buttons. These elements are referred to as *form controls,* and it's by modifying these controls (entering text, clicking check boxes, etc.) that site visitors complete a form before using the Submit button to send the form data to a web server for processing.

THE `<form>` TAG

Although the opening and closing `<form>` tags don't define a form control, they are the most important tags in the example. Without them, there is no form. In fact, without the opening and closing `<form>` tags, some browsers fail to display the form controls at all. Two attributes are required for the `<form>` tag: `action` and `method`. The `action` attribute tells the browser where to submit the data, and the `method` attribute tells the browser how the data should be submitted.

THE `action` ATTRIBUTE

The `action` attribute, which in the previous example reads `action=http://www.highstrungproductions.com/cgi-bin/process.pl`, tells the browser where the information gathered in the form should be submitted; it supplies the URL of the script or application that will process the form data. The pathname you specify will depend on where the script or application is located in relation to the document containing the form. If the script or application were located on a different server than your form document, you'd want to use an absolute pathname, like the one referenced in the example. If the script or application were located on the same server the form document is on, then of course you'd use a relative pathname.

Notice that the URL points to a file called process.pl, which resides in a folder called cgi-bin. The .pl file extension, in this case, refers to a script written in the Perl programming language. The cgi-bin stands for *Common Gateway Interface binaries,* and it is a directory name common to web servers for the storage of CGI scripts.

THE `method` ATTRIBUTE

The `method` attribute defines the method by which the data is submitted to the web server. There are two possible choices:

▶ `method="post"` With this method, the browser first contacts the web server on which the application defined in the `action` attribute resides. When contact is established, the browser then sends the information on to be processed.

▶ `method="get"` This method, instead of contacting and then sending the data, transmits the data to the server in a single step.

Ultimately, your web server configuration and processing script determine the appropriate method for your form. Generally, if the data you are sending to the application will be added to a database or will in some other way modify some existing data on the server, use the post method. If you're just sending a small amount of data from a few fields that don't produce any side effects, like updating a database, use the get method.

FORM CONTROLS

The first thing you'll discover about form controls is that most of them are created with the <input> tag. What separates one form control from another is how its type attribute is defined. The following examples show the results depending on how you define the type attribute:

▶ <input type="text"> Creates a text field.

rfuller

▶ <input type="password"> Creates a password field.

****

▶ <input type="checkbox"> Creates a check box.

☑

▶ <input type="radio"> Creates a radio button.

⊙

▶ <input type="submit"> Creates a Submit button.

Submit

▶ <input type="reset"> Creates a Reset button.

Reset

▶ `<input type="file">` Creates a file field.

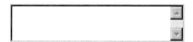

▶ `<input type="hidden">` Creates a field hidden from the user. Hidden fields are used to pass information to the server unbeknownst to the user.

▶ `<input type="image">` Inserts a graphic image within the form.

There are only two other form control elements:

▶ `<textarea></textarea>` Creates a multiline text area used for longer responses than a simple text field allows.

▶ Combination of `<select>` and `<option>` tags Creates a menu list.

```
<select name="weapon">
     <option value="smart" selected>Vorpal Sword</option>
     <option value="stupid">Pointed Stick</option>
     <option value="insane">Bare Hands</option>
</select>
```

This code is laid out in much the same way as ordered and unordered lists. The list appears as a drop-down menu from which a user can make a selection, as you can see in the preceding illustration: either Vorpal Sword, Pointed Stick, or Bare Hands.

THE name ATTRIBUTE

Every form control must have a `name` attribute defined for it so that the processing script can make sense of the data it receives. For example, if you created a text field into which you wanted users to enter their first name and didn't associate a `name` attribute with that field, the script would simply receive a text string without any reference about what the string was for. It wouldn't "know" what the string was supposed to represent. By defining a `name` attribute for each of your form controls, you create what is called a *name/value pair*. The syntax looks something like this:

```
<input type="text" name="first_name">
```

By defining a `name` attribute for this text field, a name/value pair gets created from the `name` attribute and the content a user enters into the field (its value): for example, `first_name=Robert`. This name associated with the value gives the script or program a handle it can take hold of to manipulate the incoming data. In other words, the script or program can be told to do something with the value of `first_name`.

When naming your form controls, avoid using spaces or uppercase characters. If you must have some type of separator, use underscores. For example, you could use `my_form` for a form name, or `first_name` for a text field.

Don't confuse defining a `name` attribute for a form control with providing some kind of textual clue for visitors reading the form. Visitors can't see the attribute, can they? You need to provide some kind of logical labels for your form controls so your visitors understand which specific information they're being asked for.

In the example at the beginning of this chapter, notice that the table holding the form controls is made up of two columns: the form controls in the right column and regular HTML text in the left column telling visitors which information you want entered into those controls. The check boxes and radio buttons also have individual words right beside them to tell visitors what their choices are. You could remove all this text content from the document, and the form would still function properly with the script it is sending data to, but what would be the point? Visitors would have no idea what they should do with the form controls.

FORMATTING TEXT BOXES

The most common type of data passed to forms is text: for example, names, addresses, passwords, and numeric strings like ZIP codes, phone numbers, and credit card numbers. The form controls used to enter this kind of data are generically referred to as *text boxes,* and there are three specific types.

▶ **Text fields** Fields most commonly used for single-line, short responses like names, addresses, phone numbers, etc.

```
<input type="text" name="content">
```

▶ **Password fields** Fields used to receive passwords. They are simply text fields formatted so that text entered into them is hidden, usually appearing as asterisks.

```
<input type="password" name="content">
```

▶ **Text areas** Larger, multiple-line text windows, typically used to receive some kind of extended written response like a user's comments.

```
<textarea></textarea>
```

TEXT FIELDS

By default, if you place a *text field* form control into a document with only the type and name attributes defined, most browsers display a text field approximately 20 characters long. At the same time, there is no limit on the number of characters a user can type into the field. The cursor just keeps moving ever rightward, accepting whatever content the user feels like entering.

THE size AND maxlength ATTRIBUTES

You can control both the size of the text field and the maximum number of characters it will accept by using the size and maxlength attributes. For example, you may have two fields for ZIP codes: one for the primary five numbers, and a second for the four-digit "ZIP Plus 4" number that specifies the building. You certainly wouldn't want two big 20-digit fields taking up all kinds of space in your form.

For the first five-digit field, your tag would look something like this:

```
<input type="text" name="zip" size="5" maxlength="5">
```

For the second ZIP Plus 4 field, you might write your tag this way:

```
<input type="text" name="plus_four" size="4" maxlength="4">
```

The size attribute controls how many characters the text field is, and the maxlength attribute defines how many characters the field can accept. There's no rule that says your size and maxlength attributes have to be the same. The information you're trying to gather and the aesthetics of the overall form might dictate slightly different values. Obviously, really lopsided numbers like a `size` attribute of 60 and a `maxlength` attribute of 2 wouldn't make sense.

THE `value` ATTRIBUTE

Sometimes, you may want an initial value to be already present in a text field when the browser loads the page. Remember that a form control creates a name/value pair when submitted, so to define a prefilled value for the text field, you use the `value` attribute, logically enough.

For example, here's a small form with three fields the visitor is required to fill in. To indicate that the user must enter values in these fields, I've chosen to place the text `"***REQUIRED***"` in each text field by using the `value` attribute:

```
<form name="form1" method="post" action="../cgi-bin/user_info.pl">
<table border="0" cellspacing="0" cellpadding="3">
  <tr>
    <td>First Name:</td>
    <td><input type="text" name="name" value="***REQUIRED***"></td>
  </tr>
  <tr>
    <td>E-mail Address:</td>
    <td><input type="text" name="email" value="***REQUIRED***"></td>
  </tr>
  <tr>
    <td>Phone Number:</td>
    <td><input type="text" name="phone" value="***REQUIRED***"></td>
  </tr>
</table>
</form>
```

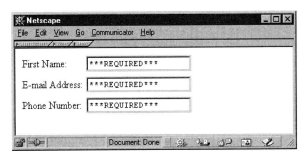

PASSWORD FIELDS

Password fields respond to the same `size`, `maxlength`, and `value` attributes as text fields. Of course, the difference between a text field and password field is how you define the `type` attribute, in this instance, `<input type="password">`. The resulting effect is that any text entered into a password field is displayed as asterisks in a browser.

Other than hiding sensitive information from prying eyes that might be peeking over a user's shoulder, the password field does not encrypt or scramble the information it submits to the processing application on the web server. To provide secure data transmission between form and web server requires that specific software be installed on that web server.

TEXT AREAS

Text areas provide large scrollable fields for entering multiline responses. They're most commonly used for sending messages and comments about a site, and they appear in message boards, guest books, and survey forms. Unlike the other two form controls for handling text, the text area is not created with the `<input>` tag. Instead, it has a set of opening and closing tags unto itself, written `<textarea>` and `</textarea>`. By default, most browsers display a text area field unfettered by any attributes as a box about 20 characters wide and two lines high, with visible scroll bars running along the bottom and right sides.

You control the dimension of a text area field with two somewhat deceiving attributes, `cols` and `rows`, representing columns and rows. I say *deceiving* because there really are no columns in a text area, and the value you define for `cols` is instead the number of characters wide you want the text area to be. The `rows` attribute, by comparison, is a bit more logical: there actually are obvious rows of text entered into a text area field. The number you define for the rows attribute then determines how many lines of text high the text area will be. For example, a text area defined as

```
<textarea cols="30" rows="5"></textarea>
```

produces a text area 30 characters wide by 5 rows high, plus any space the browser devotes to scroll bars.

Whereas you'd use a `value` attribute to include prefilled text in a text field or password field, the text area requires only that you place plain text between its opening and closing tags. You can't use any other HTML text formatting or include other form controls. In many respects, it is like the `<pre>` tag discussed in Chapter 3. The text you place within the `<textarea>` tags is displayed exactly like you type it in the HTML document, using a monospaced font and preserving line breaks and word spacing. For example, the following source code produces this text area in a browser window:

```
<textarea cols="30" rows="5">Monkey see        Monkey do
Monkey
     Monkey
          Monkey</textarea>
```

```
Monkey see        Monkey do
Monkey
     Monkey
          Monkey
```

By default, a text area field keeps placing text on a single line until the user presses the ENTER key. You can control how text wraps within a text area by using, as luck would have it, the `wrap` attribute. The `wrap` attribute allows you to control how a visitor's text is displayed when input goes beyond the original dimensions of the text area, as well as how that data gets submitted to the script. The `wrap` attribute accepts three possible values: `off`, `virtual`, and `physical`:

▶ `wrap="off"` Prevents Internet Explorer from wrapping text in the browser window. Data is still submitted as a single line of text.

▶ `wrap="virtual"` Wraps the displayed text in the browser window for both Netscape and Internet Explorer, but still submits the text in a single line.

▶ `wrap="physical"` Wraps the displayed text in the browser window for both Netscape and Internet Explorer. The data is then submitted with line break codes included, indicating the end of each displayed line in the text area.

FORMATTING CHECK BOXES

You create *check boxes* by defining the `<input>` tag's `type` attribute as `checkbox`. They function as a kind of switch that the user can toggle on or off to make a selection. In addition to the required `type` and `name` attributes, check boxes also need a `value` attribute. Whereas the `value` attribute prefills the content of a text field, when defined for a check box, it supplies the value that will be passed to the CGI application if the check box is selected. So in this case, you define both halves of the name/value pair. Whether or not the visitor checks the box determines if the data is sent to the server.

In the example at the beginning of this chapter, I included four check boxes and asked the visitor to click each box that applied to the implied question, "What's you're favorite quarry?" I then provided the appropriate text for the visitor and defined each check box like this:

```
<input type="checkbox" name="quarry" value="jabberwock">
<input type="checkbox" name="quarry" value="bandersnatch">
<input type="checkbox" name="quarry" value="jubjub">
<input type="checkbox" name="quarry" value="snark">
```

As you can see, multiple check boxes can share a `name` attribute, which in effect lets a visitor supply multiple answers to a single question.

If you want a check box to be preselected when the browser loads the page, you can include the `checked` attribute. It doesn't need to be set equal to something. Just including the word among the tag's attributes ensures that the box is initially checked, as shown in this example:

```
<input type="checkbox" name="quarry" value="jabberwock" checked>
```

FORMATTING RADIO BUTTONS

You create *radio buttons* by defining the `<input>` tag's `type` attribute as `radio`. They are similar to check boxes in that they require the same attributes: `type`, `name`, and `value`. However, when a number of radio buttons share the same `name` attribute, only one radio button is capable of being selected at a time. If one is already selected, clicking another radio button in the list turns the initial one off. Use them when you want a visitor to make only one selection from a number of choices. Obviously, you need to include at least two radio buttons with identical `name` attributes. You should also make sure that one of the radio buttons is initially selected by using the `checked` attribute. The following code shows an example:

```
<form name="reservation" method="post" action="../cgi-bin/ticket_purchase.pl">
<b>Type of Seat Preferred:</b>
<table cellpadding="0" cellspacing="0">
  <tr>
    <td>Window</td>
    <td><input type="radio" name="seat" value="window" checked></td>
  </tr>
  <tr>
    <td>Aisle</td>
    <td><input type="radio" name="seat" value="aisle"></td>
  </tr>
</table>
</form>
```

As you see here, I've added the `checked` attribute to the radio button for choosing a window seat, and both radio buttons share the same `name` attribute: `seat`. When testing your form, if you are able to select two radio buttons that are supposed to be in the same group, check to see that you've named them properly.

FORMATTING MENUS AND LISTS

You can create *drop-down menus* in your forms by using the opening and closing `<select>` tags. You lay these out in much the same way as you would an ordered or unordered list. Use opening and closing `<option>` tags to define each menu choice, as shown in this example:

```
<select name="weapon">
    <option value="smart" selected>Vorpal Sword</option>
    <option value="stupid">Pointed Stick</option>
    <option value="insane">Bare Hands</option>
</select>
```

The first option in the menu is displayed when the page loads, and no particular item is selected. You can use the `selected` attribute within an `<option>` tag if you want a specific option to be displayed other than the first one:

```
<option value="insane" selected>Bare Hands</option>.
```

As you can see in these examples, I'm using the `value` attribute with the `<option>` tag to define the value sent to the server when a menu option is selected. If no `value` attribute is defined, the content between the selected `<option>` tags is sent on to the server.

Menus make excellent use of screen real estate by letting you offer as many choices as you like while occupying only a single line in your document. If you want to conserve even more screen space, instead of devoting a portion of your document to traditional HTML text that informs the user what the menu is for, you can make the first `<option>` tag an instruction, leaving the `value` attribute undefined and applying the `selected` attribute. To make a visual break between this instructional prompt and the rest of the menu options, make the second set of `<option>` tags a line by typing hyphens between them, as shown in this example:

```
<select name="weapon">
    <option selected>Choose a Weapon</option>
    <option>------------</option>
    <option value="smart" selected>Vorpal Sword</option>
    <option value="stupid">Pointed Stick</option>
    <option value="insane">Bare hands</option>
</select>
```

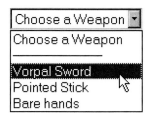

By default, the user can choose only one menu option. You can format a menu to allow multiple choices by adding the `multiple` attribute to the opening `<select>` tag. For users to make multiple selections on a menu, they need to hold down either the CTRL key if using a PC, or the COMMAND key on a Macintosh. You should provide these instructions with your form so users understand their available options.

To turn a menu into a *list*, you simply add the `size` attribute to the `<select>` tag. This attribute accepts a numeric value signifying the number of list options to display. As the following example shows, if there are more options in the list than the number of lines defined, the list sprouts scroll bars:

```
<select size="3" name="creatures">
    <option>Jabberwocky</option>
    <option>Bandersnatch</option>
    <option selected>Jubjub</option>
    <option>Snark</option>
</select>
```

FORMATTING FILE FIELDS

The *file field* form control, written `<input type="file">`, allows your visitors to locate files from their hard disk and upload them to the web server. Be sure your web server permits this activity before you implement this type of form control, however.

When included in a form, the file field appears as a text field accompanied by a Browse button, as shown here. Visitors have the option of entering the local pathname of the file they want to upload, or using the Browse button to locate the file via a dialog box.

Along with the required `name` attribute, you can use both the `size` and `maxlength` attributes to modify the text box just as you would with an ordinary text or password field. You can also limit the type of files a visitor can submit by using the `accept` attribute. The values you define for this attribute are called Multipurpose Internet Mail Extensions (MIME types). For example, if you want your visitors to submit only GIF images, you'd define the `accept` attribute this way:

```
<input type="file" name="new_files" accept="image/gif">
```

Now that value sort of looks like a pathname, but it's not. It's a value pair that says to accept image files that are only in the GIF format. By contrast, if you wanted to accept only HTML files, the value would be `text/html` because HTML documents are text-based files that use an .html extension.

FORMATTING HIDDEN FIELDS

You create a *hidden field* with the `<input>` tag, defining the `type` attribute as `hidden`. Hidden fields allow you to pass information to the web server that you don't want the visitor to see. Why would you ever need this type of form control? Many times when dealing with CGI scripts and web forms, the pages that the visitor sees are actually being generated dynamically by the CGI script in response to information the visitor has submitted. Sometimes, the CGI script needs to include information submitted previously, but you don't want the visitor to have to reenter that information a second time. The CGI script can dynamically supply that required information via hidden fields.

Obviously in this case, you wouldn't be the one writing the hidden field controls— the script would. But in some situations, you might want to generate them yourself; for example, if you used one script to process forms from a number of web sites, you could include a hidden field in each example of the form that specified which web site it was from.

The hidden information the field supplies when the form is submitted is defined in the `value` attribute, like in this example:

```
<input type="hidden" name="data_origin" value="highstrung_productions">
```

FORMATTING SUBMIT AND RESET BUTTONS

Your visitors use form buttons to send the completed form to the server or to clear the form if they make a mistake. These types of form controls are again created with the `<input>` tag. The button's function is determined by the value associated with the `type` attribute:

▶ `<input type="submit">` As this `type` value implies, it submits the form data to the server, or technically, it invokes the form's action by using the specified method.

▶ `<input type="reset">` This `type` value is also rather self-explanatory. It clears the form if the visitor makes a mistake and wants to start over.

Form buttons are generally gray and 3-D in appearance, with black text on their faces indicating their function. You don't have a great deal of formatting control over buttons, other than what the text on them says. Whatever text you set the `value` attribute equal to appears on the button's face, as shown in this example:

```
<input type="submit" name="submit" value="Finished">

<input type="reset" name="reset" value="Start Again">
```

The previous code produces a set of buttons like this:

USING GRAPHIC IMAGES FOR SUBMIT BUTTONS

If the default rectangular gray buttons insult your sense of style, you can substitute graphics for your buttons by using an image field. Be forewarned: you can use *graphic images* only for Submit buttons, and some older browsers don't support this form control well.

Instead of defining the `type` attribute as `submit`, give it a value of `image`. To tell the form control which image to use, define an `src` attribute equal to the pathname of the image file. You can use the same attributes covered in Chapter 4 for the `<img>` tag to control the graphic's appearance, as shown in the following example:

```
<input type="image" name="submit_button" src="images/my_button.gif" width="50"
height="10" alt="submit">
```

When the visitor clicks the image, the form data is submitted just as if you used a traditional Submit button.

ON THE VIRTUAL CLASSROOM CD Forms are an important part of many web sites. In Lesson 7, the instructor will demonstrate the process of creating form controls and formatting them for logical and intuitive use by site visitors.

9

Frames

Frames give you the ability to display a number of documents in a single browser window. The browser window gets divided into individual panes, each displaying the contents of a separate HTML document. Each frame can be independently scrollable, and you can also make hyperlinks that are displayed in one frame open new documents inside another frame. By keeping certain content permanently on the screen while other content is scrolled through or swapped out, you can maintain a level of consistency in your site design.

UNDERSTANDING FRAMES-BASED WEB PAGES

In a certain sense, a frames-based site turns the browser window into a giant table with rows and columns that contain entire web pages. The effect is controlled by a governing HTML file called the *frameset document,* which defines the layout of the frames, their properties, and the filenames of the other HTML documents displayed within them. This means that if you create a three-framed web page, actually a minimum of four HTML documents are involved: the frameset document, and one document for each frame that the frameset creates. Figure 9-1 shows a sample frames-based site.

Think of the frameset document, then, as a set of instructions for how the browser window should be divided, rather than as a web page with its own content. In fact, a frameset has no `<body>` tags, so it can't display any content of its own.

THE FRAMESET DOCUMENT

In a frameset document, the opening and closing `<frameset>` tags replace the `<body>` tags used in regular HTML files. The `<frame>` tags that fall between the

FIGURE 9-1

Frames give you more bang for the buck: in other words, more documents per browser window.

First document —

Second document —

Third document —

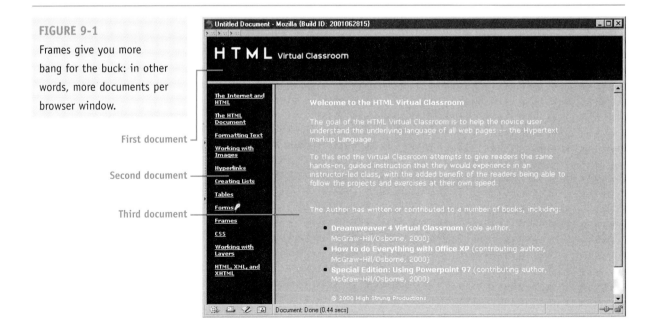

opening and closing <frameset> tags tell the browser which HTML files go in each frame, placing them in order from left to right across the columns and from top to bottom down the rows. Because it has no <body> tags, no regular HTML markup can be used in a frameset document. Here's an example:

```
<html>
<head>
<title>Frames</title>
</head>
<frameset cols="200, *">
    <frame src="left.html" name="left_frame"
    <frame src="right.html" name="right_frame">
</frameset>

</html>
```

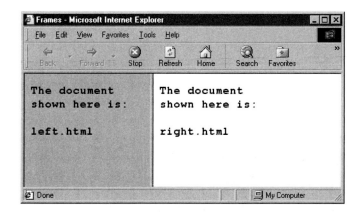

This simple two-column frameset still has the normal opening and closing <html> tags and document header you're familiar with. The new tags specific to framesets are the <frameset> and <frame> tags. The column widths, row heights, borders, and scroll bar properties are all defined by various attributes for the <frame> and <frameset> tags. Notice that the two <frame> tags both reference other HTML files. These are ordinary HTML files that define the content displayed within their respective frames.

DEFINING COLUMNS AND ROWS

The number of columns and rows in a frameset, as well as their dimensions, are defined with the `cols` and `rows` attributes of the `<frameset>` tag. You can define one or both attributes, depending on how you want to divide the browser window.

The values you assign to these attributes are slightly different than anything covered thus far. Instead of entering a value that corresponds to the number of rows or columns you want to create, you enter column width and row height values in the order each frame will appear in the browser window—columns being created from left to right, and rows from top to bottom. The more values you include for each attribute, the more columns or rows you create. Each value is separated by commas, creating syntax that looks like this:

```
cols="width of the first column, width of the second column, etc."
rows="height of the first row, height of the second row, etc."
```

The values you define for these attributes can take any of four possible forms: pixel values, percentage values, relative values, and mixed values.

PIXEL VALUES

Using an absolute *pixel value* ensures that a row or column is always an exact size. Be careful how you use pixel values, however. If you create a frameset defining all of your `cols` or `rows` attributes with pixel values, like so, `<frameset cols="100, 100, 100">`, the browser attempts to create a three-column frameset, with each column 100 pixels wide.

Now here's the tricky part. The previous values would mean that the browser window would have to be 300 pixels across in order to divide equally into three 100-pixel frames. You have no control over the size of a visitor's browser window, however. So what happens? The browser compensates and makes each frame one third of the screen, effectively giving you percentage widths. To ensure that a frame stays a specific pixel dimension, you need to mix absolute pixel values with percentages and relative values: for example, `<frameset cols="100, 200, *">`. (See the "Mixed Values" section coming up.)

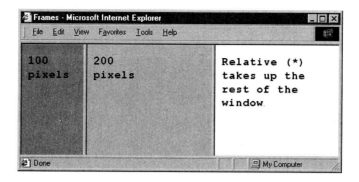

PERCENTAGE VALUES

As you might have guessed, *percentage values* create frames that take up the specified percentage of the browser window, like so, `<frameset cols="20%, 80%">`. The first column takes up 20 percent of the width of however wide the browser window is open, and the second columns takes up the remaining 80 percent. Of course, your percentages need to total 100 percent. If they don't, the first value (or values, depending on the number of columns and rows you define) will be adhered to, and the last frame will stretch to complete 100 percent of the screen.

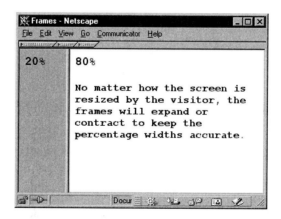

RELATIVE VALUES

Relative values allow you to set a frame's dimension relative to the other frames in the frameset. These types of values are written with an asterisk. For example, a value written `<frameset cols="3*, 2*, 1*">` creates three columns that are, in this case, relative sixths (3 + 2 + 1 = 6) of the browser window width. Just like percentage values, the frames expand and contract with the resizing of the browser window to maintain their relative dimensions.

MIXED VALUES

Mixed values are pretty much what you'd expect—a combination of pixel, percentage, and relative values. In fact, you're more likely to use a set of mixed values than any of the other three exclusively.

By combining an asterisk with a pixel or percentage value, the column or row afforded the asterisk will occupy the rest of the remaining browser window. For instance, `<frameset cols="200, *">`, from the first example in this chapter, creates an initial column that is 200 pixels wide and then gives the rest of the browser window to the second frame. The second frame is now free to expand and contract with the resizing of the browser window, leaving the first column fixed.

NESTING FRAMESETS

With tables, you can span columns and rows to create certain layouts. Unfortunately, that option is not available in framesets. You can, however, nest framesets inside each other to create a similar effect. For example, if you wanted to have a single row running across the top of the browser window with two frames dividing the row below it, you'd define your frameset something like this:

```
<frameset rows="100, *">
  <frame src="top.html" name="top_frame">
  <frameset cols="200, *">
   <frame src="left.html" name="left_frame">
   <frame src="right.html" name="right_frame">
  </frameset>
</frameset>
```

Notice that the opening `<frameset>` tag calls for two rows: the first one is 100 pixels high, and the second one below it takes up the remainder of the page by virtue of the relative value. Now take a look at the code in the middle. The first tag is the `<frame>` tag for the first row. That's all well and good, but where's the `<frame>` tag for the second row? That's where the nesting part comes into play: instead of a second `<frame>` tag, there's a complete frameset stuck in there occupying the spot

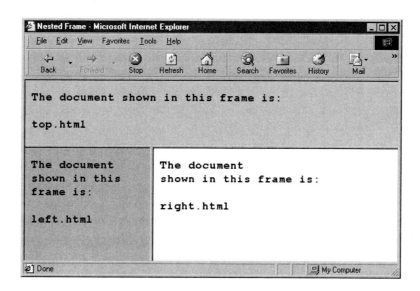

the second `<frame>` tag would normally sit in. That's really all there is to it. You simply nest a complete frameset in place of one of the `<frame>` tags.

FORMATTING BORDER PROPERTIES

Borders—and what you do with them—are the linchpins in a frame-based design. You can leave them to their own devices so they're free to be repositioned by the visitor, or you can lock them in place to enforce a specific boundary. You can modify their color, define their thickness, make them flat, or hide them completely.

THE `frameborder` ATTRIBUTE

By default, most browsers display frame borders as gray 3-D bars, approximately five pixels thick. The `frameborder` attribute, which can be defined for both the `<frameset>` and `<frame>` tags, accepts a `yes`/`no` value that produces the following effects:

▶ `frameborder="yes"` Displays borders in their default fashion: gray, 3-D, and about five pixels thick. Border thickness is controlled with the `border` attribute discussed in the following section.

▶ `frameborder="no"` Flattens the borders. Internet Explorer then displays them roughly two pixels thick if no value has been defined for the border attribute, as shown in the following illustration. Netscape Navigator simply flattens the borders, leaving their thickness at five pixels.

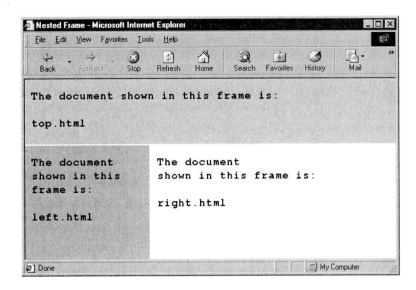

Use this attribute with the `<frameset>` tag to govern the border appearance across the entire page, and use it with the `<frame>` tag to affect specific frames. However, frames sharing a common border can't have conflicting `frameborder` attributes. In other words, when setting the `frameborder` attribute at the frame level, you can't set one frame's borders to `no` and set the adjacent frame to `yes`. If you try this, the `yes` value usually wins out.

THE `border` ATTRIBUTE

The `border` attribute is defined only for the `<frameset>` tag, and it is used to control the thickness of the borders in your frameset, as opposed to the `frameborder` attribute, which is more of a toggle controlling their 3-D qualities. The `border` attribute accepts a numeric value. Because the default border thickness is in the neighborhood of five pixels, you should set the value to something significantly different to achieve a noticeable result. Here's an example:

```
<frameset cols="200, *" border="10">
   <frame src="left.html" name="left_frame">
   <frame src="right.html" name="right_frame">
</frameset>
```

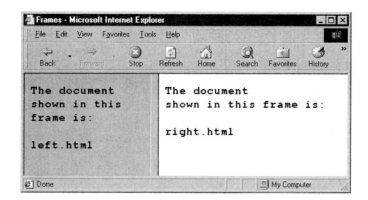

Setting it equal to 0 completely hides the borders in Netscape. However, Internet Explorer also requires you to set the `frameborder` attribute equal to `no` to achieve the same effect, as you can see in this example:

```
<frameset cols-"200, *" frameborder="no" border="0">
  <frame src="left.html" name="left_frame">
  <frame src="right.html" name="right_frame">
</frameset>
```

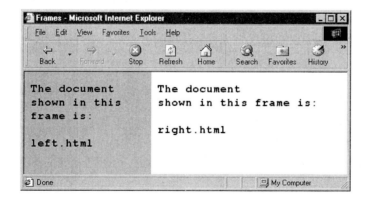

THE noresize ATTRIBUTE

Ordinarily, a site visitor can resize a frame by simply grabbing the frame border with the mouse and dragging it to a new location. As a designer, you might have other plans. You can fix a frame border in place by adding the `noresize` attribute to the `<frame>` tag, which represents the frame you want to lock down. This attribute doesn't accept any values; it's simply a toggle whose presence in the `<frame>` tag disables the ability to resize the frame.

THE bordercolor ATTRIBUTE

Just like in tables, you can also define the border colors of your frames. Using the bordercolor attribute, you can define either a hexadecimal value or a predefined color name. You can define the bordercolor attribute for both the <frame> and <frameset> tags, but remember, HTML always gives precedence to the most specific element. As a result, bordercolor attributes defined for a <frame> tag override those defined for the <frameset> tag.

SETTING SCROLL BAR PROPERTIES

Frames display scroll bars whenever the content inside them is too big to be seen within their defined dimensions. Consequently, scroll bars often pop up when the browser window is resized, or if the visitor's monitor resolution is set sufficiently low. Again, as a designer, you may not want scroll bars to appear under any circumstances.

You can control the appearance of scroll bars by using a simple attribute for the <frame> tag, appropriately called the scrolling attribute, which accepts the following values:

► scrolling="yes" Displays scroll bars regardless of the amount of content in the frame.

► scrolling="no" Disables scroll bars entirely.

► scrolling="auto" Displays scroll bars if the amount of content requires them. By not defining the attribute, most browsers' default is equal to "auto".

If you set the scrolling attribute to no, be sure to test your site across as many browsers and platforms as you can. Because text, borders, and the browser window all display differently across different browsers, operating systems, and monitor resolutions, your layout can vary from visitor to visitor. You want to avoid a situation where a visitor is unable to see all the content in one of your frames because you've disabled scrolling.

SETTING FRAME MARGINS

In the frameset document, you can control the margins of individual frames by applying the marginwidth and marginheight attributes to their <frame> tags. Each attribute accepts a numeric value, as follows.

▶ `marginwidth="pixel value"` Defines the pixel distance between a frame's contents and its left and right frame borders.

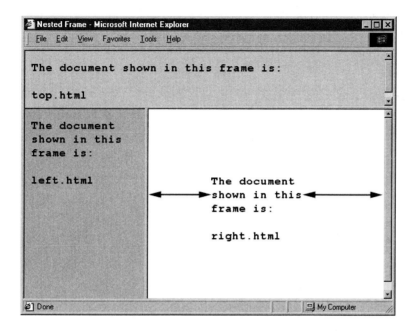

▶ `marginheight="pixel value"` Defines the pixel distance between a frame's contents and its top and bottom frame borders.

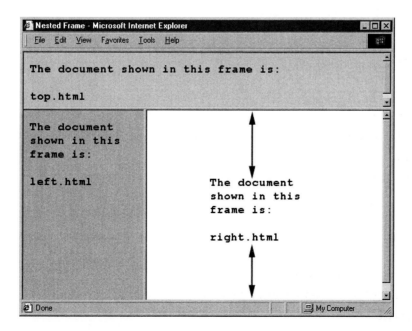

Don't set a value for just one margin attribute and leave the other alone. If you did, the undefined attribute would automatically be set to 0, which would slam your content flush to whichever margin you didn't define. Also be aware that some old browsers don't recognize margin attributes and will simply ignore your settings.

LINKING BETWEEN FRAMES

As mentioned at the start of this chapter, the hyperlinks displayed in one frame can be written in such a way that the documents they point to are opened within other frames in your frameset. The most common practice is to use one frame like a navigation bar, while another frame displays the documents that the links in that navigation bar open. The process of telling links where to open their referenced documents is called *targeting*. In other words, one frame aims its links at, or "targets," another frame.

As you see in each of the examples in this chapter, the `<frame>` tags all have a `name` attribute defined for them, just like the named anchors discussed in Chapter 5. By naming your frames, you can reference those names when you create your links. For example, the following frameset creates two columns whose names are `left_frame` and `right_frame`.

```
<frameset cols="200, *">
  <frame src="left.html" name="left_frame">
  <frame src="right.html" name="right_frame">
</frameset>
```

Basically, a frame is a little browser window unto itself. This means any hyperlinks appearing within the frame simply open the documents to which they point inside that same frame, just like links in a regular browser window. To make links in `left.html` open inside the frame named `right_frame`, you need to incorporate the `target` attribute into the code you write for the hyperlink, and use the frame name as the attribute's value. The following example illustrates:

```
<a href=" products.html" target="right_frame"> content </a>
```

SPECIAL TARGET NAMES

Besides the frame names you defined, HTML also has a number of predefined target names that produce various effects when used to target your links:

▶ `target="_blank"` This target name opens the document in a new browser window. You can use it in ordinary hyperlinks as well to force a new browser window.

▶ `target="_parent"` If the link is in a nested frameset, this target name opens the document in place of the parent frameset.

▶ `target="_self"` This target name opens the document in the current frame, which is equivalent to not defining a target at all.

▶ `target="_top"` This target name displays the new document in the entire browser window, replacing the frameset altogether.

SETTING A BASE TARGET

You can tell a document to target a specific frame by default, without assigning individual targets to each link, by using the `<base>` tag and the `target` attribute. Simply place the tag in the document header after the `<title>` tags, like this:

```
<head>
<title>Document Title</title>
<base target="frame name">
</head>
```

Any hyperlink within the document will now automatically open within the frame you've specified.

Using the `<base>` tag can create a situation where the _self target might come in handy. With the `target` attribute defined, the targeted frame is now the default frame for all links in that document. You'd now have to use the _self target if you wanted a link in that document to open inside its own frame.

ACCOMMODATING OLDER BROWSERS

A small portion of visitors may have browsers that do not support frames, in which case, you want to define some content they'll be capable of viewing. This concept is referred to as creating *no frames content,* because you are entering the equivalent of a regular web page between `<noframes></noframes>` tags at the bottom of the frameset's HTML code.

You can enter any HTML code you'd normally place between the opening and closing `<body>` tags. The usual practice is to simply inform visitors that they've reached a frames-based site, and redirect them to another version of your site that isn't frames-based. The following code provides an example:

```
<html>
<head>
<title>Frames</title>
</head>
<frameset cols="200, *">
    <frame src="left.html" name="left_frame">
    <frame src="right.html" name="right_frame">
</frameset>
<noframes>
We're sorry, your browser isn't able
to display frames. Don't worry, we have
a solution right <a href="no_frames.html">this way...</a>
</noframes>
</html>
```

You can't view the no frames content of your frameset unless you have a browser that doesn't support frames to test it in. You can copy and paste the content into an ordinary document, save it, and test it from there.

THE PROS AND CONS OF FRAMES

With all the technical aspects of frames out of the way, it's a good idea to discuss their pros and cons. Let's face it: there are just some things frames can do that nothing else can. Frames provide for the display of multiple documents within a single screen, which can be scrolled, frozen in place, and resized. Frames also let you maintain a consistent navigation area that never leaves the screen, while new content is swapped in and out, allowing for an overall consistency of design.

On the downside, frames can be slower to load because you're providing more than one document at a time. Visitors have a hard time bookmarking a specific document within a frames-based site, simply because the URL in the browser's cache is that of the main frameset: the URL never changes as new points within the site are navigated to.

Framesets cause a problem for some search engines as well. The only document the search engine sees is the frameset document, not all the content inside the individual documents that are displayed inside the frames. Because some search engines rank a page based on its content, a frameset's total lack of content really hurts it. It has no content of its own, only the frameset instructions. Because some search engines crawl through a site following the hyperlinks from one page to the next, the fact that a frameset has no links also prevents the search engine from finding all the associated documents.

Solutions? Don't have your entire site depend on a single frameset. If you have a site with a number of distinct sections to it that each contain a lot of information, make each section its own frameset. This way, visitors can at least bookmark the main section and then navigate to a specific part, instead of having to start at the home page and dig down to find what they're looking for. If you depend on search engines to drive your page hits, you might want to consider making the home page nonframed, with links to the frameset or framesets. This way, you have a home page that has actual content and links to be referenced and crawled.

 ON THE VIRTUAL CLASSROOM CD Frames can be tricky for both the designer and the site visitors. In Lesson 8, the instructor will demonstrate how to create and format a frames-based site.

Cascading Style Sheets

When you look at the pages of this book, you notice that all the chapter headings are formatted in a specific way, as are the all the tips, figure captions, and of course, the page text. Imagine recreating this book as a web site. Using the methods you've learned so far, you'd probably go through and format all those elements using heading tags and the `<font>` tag. Imagine the site was finished and sitting on a web server somewhere. If you wanted to change the formatting of those headings and body text, you'd have to go in and make the changes manually, one at a time. Style sheets change all that.

INTRODUCTION TO STYLE SHEETS

When HTML was born, it attempted to do a number of different tasks simultaneously. It defined specific elements of the web page, as well as formatted them. For example, the `<p>` tag defines a block-level text element, while the `<font>` tag allows you to format how the text within that element appears. One tag creates a logical construct, while the other tag deals with matters of design. As web design and development have advanced, there has been a move to separate design from content, and this is the whole purpose of style sheets—to let HTML worry about the content in a document, defining the elements in a logical fashion, while *cascading style sheets* (CSS) control design issues like text formatting and element positioning.

In Chapter 3, you learned how to format text and discovered all the different tasks you can do using the `<font>` tag. You can define the `face`, `size`, and `color` attributes to make text appear nearly any way you want. Styles allow you to bundle all those different attribute settings into single, stand-alone units. You can then apply those styles wherever you see fit. The great advantage is that you don't have to modify each instance where you use the style in your document. Instead, you have to change only the properties of the style itself. This idea will make a little more sense when you see how individual styles are defined and then applied to your HTML document.

Like so many other aspects of web design, the CSS specifications developed by the World Wide Web Consortium (W3C) have yet to be fully supported by the major browser manufacturers, and some have created their own proprietary style properties. Of course, older browsers (versions prior to 4.0) do not support the CSS specifications at all. To date, Netscape 6.0 is the most compliant browser on the market.

When attempting to include styles in your documents, you will need to experiment with a number of different browsers to find out which styles produce a uniform look across as many browsers as possible. Also keep in mind that, although it's fairly simple to pick up, CSS is a big subject worthy of a book all its own. This chapter doesn't aim to be all-inclusive, but rather, functions as an introduction. For a complete discussion of CSS, you can visit the W3C's site at http://www.w3c.org/Style/CSS.

CSS SYNTAX

Styles bundle a number of different formatting options and assign them to specific HTML tags or to custom style elements called *classes*. Whenever that tag or class is used to mark up a region in a web page, all those formatting attributes get applied simultaneously.

An individual style is known as a *style rule*. The syntax of a style rule is fairly simple to dissect. Where HTML uses angle brackets, equal signs, and quotation marks, CSS syntax uses curly braces, colons, and semicolons. For example, the following rule turns all paragraph text green and uses a Verdana font face:

```
p { color: green; font-family: Verdana, Arial, sans-serif }
```

So, a *style* is a rule you define for how a specific web page element should be displayed. A *style sheet* contains a collection of these rules that you can then apply to any number of HTML documents.

STYLE RULES

A style rule has two parts: a *selector*, which is a specific HTML tag (sans angle brackets) or a class name, followed by a *declaration*. The declaration appears between curly braces and defines the properties of the selector. The following example illustrates:

```
p { color: green }
```
Selector   Declaration

The selector identifies which HTML tag or class name is acted upon; the declaration defines the properties of the selector.

DECLARATIONS

Just like style rules, a declaration also has two parts: the *property*, and its *value*, each separated by a colon, as illustrated in the example on the following page.

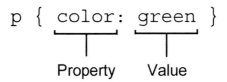

You can include as many declarations for a selector as necessary. You simply need to separate each declaration with a semicolon, as this example shows:

```
p   { color: green;
        font-family: Arial, Helvetica, sans-serif;
        font-size: 12px }
```

To make your CSS code easier to read, it's best to place each of your declarations on a new line, as shown in the previous example. Just like HTML code, your browser ignores any extra line breaks and white space.

If you want a number of selectors to share common properties, simply attach the selectors to your declaration, separating each with a comma:

```
h1, h2, h3 { color: blue;
                font-family: Arial, Helvetica, sans-serif }
```

CONTEXTUAL SELECTORS

You can set selectors so that they affect a tag only when it occurs in a specific circumstance. By separating a number of selectors with just a space, you are in effect saying, "Only assign this style to the last selector if it is nested within the preceding selector(s)." Here's an example:

```
h2 b { color: green }
```

This style tells a CSS-capable browser to make anything between <b> tags green *only* when those <b> tags are nested within <h2> tags.

STYLE CLASSES

Style classes allow you an even greater level of control over elements on your web pages than normal selectors do. A *style class* is simply a style rule that has a unique selector that you create. Instead of using one of the many HTML tags, you define your own name for the class and then attach your declarations to it.

SELECTOR CLASSES

Selector classes act as amendments to traditional tag-based selectors. Separating the selector and class name with a period, you can effectively create a number of style possibilities for one selector. For example, you may have a document that contains a series of questions and answers, each defined as paragraphs. You could create a specific style for the question paragraphs and another for the answer paragraphs, like so:

```
p.question { color: blue }

p.answer { color: red }
```

When you are applying the style classes to the specific paragraphs in the actual HTML code, as luck would have it, you use the `class` attribute, as shown here:

```
<p class="question"> content </p>
```

STANDARD CLASSES

Standard classes are similar to selector classes, except that instead of using a traditional HTML tag selector, they simply use a period followed by a unique class name, as in this example:

```
.bombastic { color: purple;
             font-family: comic sans, sans-serif;
             font-size: 18pt }
```

Because this kind of class isn't assigned to a specific HTML tag selector, you are free to use it on any element you want simply by defining the element's `class` attribute and setting it equal to the class name. Here's an example:

```
<h2 class="bombastic"> content </h2>
```

Notice that the period used to define the class name is dropped when it is used to define the `class` attribute.

ID CLASSES

The *ID class* provides yet another syntax method for applying styles. An ID class takes advantage of the `id` attribute instead of the `class` attribute for a given HTML tag. With the `id` attribute, technically, no two `id` values for a common element should be identical. In other words, you shouldn't have two `<p>` tags with the same `id` value. Therefore, you should use ID classes to specify only unique, one-time styles. Granted, most browsers allow you to get away with almost anything, but that flexibility is bound to change as they start adhering more closely to the XHTML standard.

When you define this type of style, instead of using a period, you precede the class name with a pound (#) sign. The following example demonstrates:

```
p#first { color: blue }

p#second { color: red }

#main { color: purple;
        font-family: comic sans, sans-serif;
        font-size: 18pt }
```

In this instance, you'd render your HTML as follows:

```
<p id="first"> content </p>

<p id="second"> content </p>

<h2 id="main"> content </h2>
```

STYLE SHEET TYPES

With that introduction to CSS syntax out of the way, how do you actually attach your styles to a specific HTML document? Four different methods exist for incorporating styles into your web pages:

▶ Inline styles
▶ Embedded style sheets
▶ Linked style sheets
▶ Imported style sheets

These style methods are listed in order of precedence. You may recall from the discussion of tables in Chapter 7 that HTML's precedence always works from the specific to the general. For example, the formatting of a specific cell overrides that of the row it is in; in turn, the formatting applied to a row generally takes precedence over the formatting applied to a table. Cascading style sheets are no different. In fact, that's where the "cascade" comes from. Styles *cascade* from the specific to the general. This means that inline styles supersede embedded styles, which supersede linked and imported style sheets.

INLINE STYLES

You use *inline styles* to apply style rules to specific portions of your document by actually inserting a style rule directly into an HTML tag. This requires the `style` attribute. For example, if you wanted to modify the color and font of a specific `<h1>` tag, you'd write the tag like this:

```
<h1 style="color: blue; font-family: Arial, Helvetica, sans-serif">
```

You can use the `style` attribute with nearly every HTML tag. However, even though this method of employing styles gives you the expanded range of properties that CSS provides, it obviously doesn't give you the ability to create a style and apply it across a number of locations. Therefore, you can't simply edit a single style sheet to impart changes on a sitewide scale.

EMBEDDED STYLE SHEETS

Embedded style sheets, as the name implies, are embedded inside the HTML document within the document header of a web page, and they define styles only for that document. This task is accomplished by using the `<style>` tag, like so:

```
<head>
<title>Jabberwocky</title>
<style type="text/css">
<!--
    p  { color: green;
         font-family: Arial, Helvetica, sans-serif;
         font-size: 12px }
    h1, h2, h3, { color: blue;
                  font-family: Arial, Helvetica, sans-serif }
-->
</style>
</head>
```

Notice that the `<style>` tag makes use of an attribute called `type`. The `type` attribute tells the browser which kind of style the following code refers to. For example, `"text/css"` indicates that the following information is written in regular text format and uses CSS syntax. Netscape has a JavaScript style sheet specification of its own that is referred to with `"text/jss"`; however, this style format has never really caught on. Although you can completely omit the `type` attribute and be relatively sure that your style sheet will be properly implemented by most browsers, you're better off including it to prevent any possible errors.

LINKED STYLE SHEETS

Using a *linked style sheet,* you can create an entirely separate document containing nothing but style rules and then link it to any number of HTML documents. In this manner, you can effectively control the formatting of an entire site (or sites), and have to implement changes only in a single document to change the look and feel of elements sitewide.

Style sheet documents are saved with a .css extension, and then they are referenced in the head section of the HTML document to which they're linked using the `<link>` tag, as shown here:

```
<html>
<head>
<title>Introduction to CSS</title>
<link rel="stylesheet" type="text/css" href="http://www.site.com/my_styles.css">
</head>
```

The `<link>` tag accepts the following attributes:

▶ `rel` This attribute lets the browser know what relationship the linked document has to the web page. In the case of style sheets, use the value `stylesheet`.

▶ `type` This attribute is no different than when it's used with the `<style>` tag discussed in the previous section.

▶ `href` This attribute informs the browser of the style sheet document's URL.

IMPORTED STYLE SHEETS

Using an *imported style sheet* is another way you can attach an external style
sheet to a document using the `<style>` tag, as shown in the following code:

```
<head>
<title>Introduction to CSS</title>
<style>
<!--
@import "http://www.site.com/my_styles.css";
-->
</style>
</head>
```

This method takes advantage of a command called `@import`. The `@import` command
is followed by the URL of the style sheet, either placed within quotes and followed
by a semicolon, or placed within parentheses after something called a `url` keyword,
like so:

```
@import url(http://www.site.com/my_styles.css);
```

Both syntaxes work equally well; just be sure to end the line with a semicolon.

STYLE PROPERTIES

Up to this point, I've been describing style declarations like `{ color: red }` or
`{ font-family: Arial, Helvetica, sans-serif }`. You may have wondered just
where and how you were supposed to learn the CSS declaration properties. This
section defines the units of measure that CSS uses to define property values, and
the individual declaration properties to which they are attributed.

UNITS OF MEASURE

The units of measure for defining property values are much more specific than tag
attributes, allowing for effects and levels of control that plain HTML can't dupli-
cate. Four different units of measure can be used to define property values: length
values, percentage values, color values, and URLs.

In some situations, property values don't accept a specific unit of measure and instead take keyword values, for example, bold. In cases where keywords are the accepted value (or another convention that is not a distinct unit of measure), they have been so noted.

LENGTH VALUES

"Length" can be a bit deceiving here, in that in some cases within CSS, you could easily substitute the word "size." Be that as it may, *length values* fall into two categories: absolute and relative. The absolute length values recognized by the CSS specification include the following: inches (in), millimeters (mm), centimeters (cm), points (pt), and picas (pc).

When using these values to define a length, they follow immediately after the numeric value you specify, without any spaces. Here's an example:

```
{ margin-left: 1in }

{ width: 115mm }

{ height: 2cm }

{ font-size: 12pt }

{ font-size: 3pc }
```

Relative length values indicate a length comparative to some other property. In CSS, you can define length relative to three different measures:

▶ The font height of the specific element's capital letters (em).

▶ The height of the letter *x* within a given element (ex). This doesn't mean an *x* must be written in the element; instead, it generally refers to the height of lowercase characters within the font being used.

▶ The resolution of the user's computer screen, using a pixel value (px).

Examples include these:

```
{ font-size: 12px }

{ margin: 1em }

{ margin: 2ex }
```

You can also use the optional plus (+) and minus (–) symbols to increase or decrease the length of a declaration property, as well as decimal values, as this example shows:

```
{ font-size: -3pt }

{ margin: +0.5in }

{ height: 3.5ex }
```

PERCENTAGE VALUES

Percentage values set a property value relative to another characteristic of the element being defined; for example, the size of the element's font. As you'd expect, percentage values are written using the percent (%) symbol, and they can be preceded by an optional plus (+) or minus (–). For example:

```
{ line-height: 110% }
```

This syntax sets the space between lines equal to 110 percent of the current font height of the element.

COLOR VALUES

Three possible methods exist for defining a *color property value,* two of which you're already familiar with: the predefined color name (also called a *keyword*) and the hexadecimal value. The syntax for these methods is much what you'd expect:

```
{ color: red }

{ color: #ff0000 }
```

The third method makes use of the RGB color model, where values are written in a comma-separated list, one value each for the red, green, and blue component of a color. Each component's value is defined using a scale from 0 to 255, 0 being the total absence of color, and 255 its total saturation point. For example, the RGB value for black, which is the absence of color, is written `rgb(0, 0, 0)`, meaning Red = 0, Green = 0, and Blue = 0; the value for white, which is the presence of all colors, is written `rgb(255, 255, 255)`, meaning Red = 255, Green = 255, and Blue = 255.

When written in CSS syntax, an RGB value uses what is called *functional notation,* where you cite RGB and follow it with the appropriate values in parentheses, as in this example:

```
{ color: rgb(255, 0, 0) }
```

You can also use percentages with the RGB method, where instead of using the RGB scale numbers, you use intensity percentages for each color, as shown here:

```
{ color: rgb(100%, 0%, 0%) }
```

URLs

When you need to reference a URL in CSS syntax, you also make use of functional notation. If, for example, you wanted to assign a background image to the body of your web page, you'd do so using the `<body>` tag as a selector and the `background-image` property in the declaration:

```
body { background-image: url(images/bg.gif) }
```

PARENTS AND CHILDREN

The definitions in the following section refer to parent elements, which require a short explanation. You've seen how HTML favors a specific element's formatting over the general element to which it is related; for example, the table cell takes precedence over the row it is in, which in turn takes precedence over the entire table of which it is a part.

When elements are connected in this way, it is referred to as a *parent/child relationship.* For example, if the table is the parent, then the rows are its children. In turn, the row's children are the individual cells. This begs the question: who is the table's parent? If that table were nested, then the cell it was nested in would be its parent. If, on the other hand, the table was just out in the document itself, then the document is its parent, which, in terms of tags, means that the `<body>` tag is the parent element. Of course ultimately, the `<body>` tag is just about every element's sire because it contains all the visible elements of a web page.

So, the term *parent element* simply means the next element higher up in the chain. This doesn't mean the previous element in the document, however. If you have two unnested tables on a page, the second table is not a child of the first. They're both siblings—the document is their parent. Get it?

So what does all this talk of family have to do with CSS? Inheritance. Child elements will often *inherit* certain style properties from their parents, as you can see in this example:

```
h1 { color: blue;
     font-family: Courier, Courier New, serif;
     font-size: 12px }

em { font-size: 13px }

<h1>The <em>Big/em> Kahuna</h1>
```

In this example code, the emphasis tag `<em>` has only a font size associated with it, whereas the `<h1>` tag has a color, font, and size. The word "Big" in the sample heading would not only have the `<em>` tag's size applied to it, but it would *inherit* the color and font from its parent element, the `<h1>` tag.

FONT PROPERTIES

Font properties cover many of the same aspects as the `<font>` tag attributes do, as well as a few of the physical style tags like `<b>` and `<i>`. The font properties include `font-family`, `font-size`, `font-style`, `font-weight`, and `font-variant`.

THE `font-family` PROPERTY

This property is the equivalent of defining the `face` attribute of the `<font>` tag. It accepts the same comma-separated list of font names you're used to, as you can see in this example:

```
{ font-family: Arial, Helvetica, sans-serif }
```

As you may recall from Chapter 3's discussion of text formatting, the reason you use three values is to group a number of related fonts together in an attempt to guarantee the highest level of fidelity to your original design. You're hoping that

if some of your visitors don't have the first choice, perhaps they have the second.
The last font option in the list is either serif or sans-serif, depending on the type of
fonts you led off with—this way, the visitor can at least get a general feel for what
you intended.

THE font-size PROPERTY

This property accepts a number of absolute and relative values consisting of
keywords and length values, as well as percentages. The absolute scale this property accepts is made up of the keywords xx-small, x-small, small, medium, large,
x-large, and xx-large. They correspond to the absolute scale of 1 through 7 used
by the size attribute of the <font> tag, as demonstrated in this example:

```
{ font-size: small }
```

The relative keyword values simply increase or decrease the font size in relation to
the absolute scale, using the keywords larger and smaller. For instance, if the current element's font size is medium and you attached a style of larger, it would be
bumped to large.

You can also use length values like points and picas, as well as the relative units of
pixels and percentages:

```
{ font-size: 12pt }
{ font-size: 2pc }
{ font-size: 12px }
{ font-size: 50% }
```

Although points and picas are traditional typesetting units, pixel measurements
tend to display with a higher level of fidelity across a range of browsers and operating systems. Percentages simply increase or decrease the font by a percentage of
the original font size.

THE font-style PROPERTY

This property accepts any of three keywords: normal, italic, or oblique, normal
being the default value. Here's an example:

```
{ font-style: italic }
```

The difference between a font's italic and oblique style is sometimes difficult to distinguish, depending on the font being used. In the serif font families, the italic and oblique styles differ in the shape of the serif and may look entirely different. Sans-serif families often display oblique and italic the same. If the font you're using wasn't created with a specific oblique state, italic will be used instead.

THE font-weight PROPERTY

This property affects the boldness of the font. You can use an absolute scale that runs in increments of 100 from 100 (lightest) to 900 (boldest), where normal is 400 and bold is 700. You can also use the relative keyword values lighter, normal, bold, or bolder.

THE font-variant PROPERTY

This property toggles between the normal font and the font displayed using small caps, which places all the text in capital letters of a decreased size. This property is equally supported in Netscape Navigator 6.0 and Internet Explorer 5.0 and later. Netscape Navigator version 4.76 and earlier do not support this feature, and Internet Explorer 4.0 simply capitalizes the text.

COLOR AND BACKGROUND PROPERTIES

In regular HTML, you have control over only a few backgrounds: the document's via attributes for the <body> tag and the table elements via attributes for the <table>, <tr>, and <td> tags. There's the page itself, tables and their cells, and the backgrounds of layers. (See Chapter 11). With CSS, almost everything supports its own background. Want the background color to be different behind a particular paragraph? Not a problem! Just define the background-color property for a class or selector, and away you go. The color of text is often referred to as the *foreground* color in CSS, so it's included here as well to cover the spectrum of foreground and background possibilities. The *color and background properties* include color, background-color, background-image, background-repeat, background-attachment, and background-position.

THE color PROPERTY

As you saw in the "Color Values" section, you define the color property by using a keyword, hexadecimal value, or RGB triple. For example, if you wanted to make the color of a specific text element red, you'd use any of the following values.

```
{ color: red }
{ color: #ff0000 }
{ color: rgb(255, 0, 0) }
{ color: rgb(100%, 0%, 0%) }
```

THE background-color PROPERTY

As I just stated, CSS allows most elements to have a background. The background-color property accepts the same values as the color property. The general effect is similar to that of a highlighter across text in a book. For example, if you defined the background-color property for the body of your document in one color and a paragraph class in another, you might write something like this:

```
body { background-color: #999999 }
p { background-color: #ffffcc }
```

If you placed a simple paragraph into an HTML document with this style information attached, the end result would look something like this:

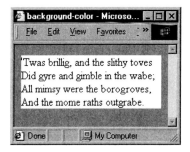

THE background-image PROPERTY

Just like the background attribute of the <body> tag, the background-image property lets you place an image behind web page elements. This property accepts a URL pathname, as shown here:

```
{ background-image: url(images/texture.gif) }
```

THE background-repeat PROPERTY

This property is used in conjunction with the background-image property and controls how a background image tiles behind an element. You have a choice of the following four keyword values.

▶ `repeat` Tiles the image both horizontally and vertically behind the element; the browser default

▶ `no-repeat` Fixes a single instance of the image beginning in the upper-left corner of the element

▶ `repeat-x` Tiles the image only horizontally behind the image

▶ `repeat-y` Tiles the image only vertically behind the image

THE `background-attachment` PROPERTY

This property also depends on the `background-image` property. The `background-attachment` property determines whether the background image is fixed, or whether it scrolls along with the rest of the page's content. Ordinarily, when you have to scroll down in a document, the background image scrolls along with the rest of the page. This property accepts the keywords `fixed` and `scroll`, `scroll` being the default browser behavior. When the `fixed` keyword is used, the background image appears to stay put while only the page content scrolls. Internet Explorer browsers 4.0 and later support this functionality, as does Netscape Navigator 6.0. Earlier versions of Netscape Navigator do not.

THE `background-position` PROPERTY

If a background image has been defined, the `background-position` property determines the image's initial position in the browser window. The value for this property is expressed as a comma-separated value pair, using length values, percentages, or keywords.

Length values, rendered, for example, `{ background-position: 50px, 50px }`, use these values to determine the image's position from the upper-left corner of the element being defined. So the first value is the distance over from the left, and the second value is the distance down from the top.

Percentage values behave similarly. A value of `50%, 50%` places the upper-left corner of the image directly in the center of the element being defined. A value of `0%, 0%` places it firmly in the upper-left corner of that element.

The accepted keywords are `left`, `right`, `top`, `bottom`, and `center`. These keywords allow you to place the image at all the compass points as well as the center of the element being defined. They are simply separated with a space instead of a comma, as this example shows:

```
{ background-position: top left }
{ background-position: top center }
{ background-position: top right }
{ background-position: center left }
{ background-position: center   }
{ background-position: center right }
{ background-position: bottom left }
{ background-position: bottom center }
{ background-position: bottom right }
```

TEXT PROPERTIES

Font properties deal with the style of the text—its color, font, size, etc. *Text properties* deal with the physical characteristics of the text itself—character, word, and line spacing, alignment and indentation, etc. The text properties include word-spacing, letter-spacing, text-decoration, vertical-align, text-transform, text-align, text-indent, and line-height.

THE word-spacing PROPERTY

As you may have guessed, this property adjusts the amount of space between words. Any absolute or relative length value that you specify adds that much to the normal word spacing used by the browser. For example:

```
{ word-spacing: 2em }
```

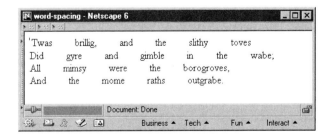

This property can become distorted if the text has been justified, which is a function of the `text-align` property covered later in this chapter. Negative values can be set, but different browsers may not honor them.

THE `letter-spacing` PROPERTY

You can increase the amount of space between individual characters by using the `letter-spacing` property. With the `word-spacing` property, any absolute or relative length value you specify adds that much to the normal letter spacing used by the browser. Again, text justification can influence how the browser displays letter spacing. You can set negative values, but different browsers may not honor them.

THE `text-decoration` PROPERTY

The `text-decoration` property allows you to place a line under, over, or through the text, accepting the following keyword values: `underline`, `overline`, and `line-through`. There is also a `blink` keyword; however, only Netscape Navigator supports this value.

THE `vertical-align` PROPERTY

The `vertical-align` property allows for exact control over the vertical positioning of elements. This property accepts the following keyword values:

▶ `baseline` Aligns the element's baseline with the baseline of the parent element

▶ `middle` Aligns the middle of the element with the baseline of the parent element

▶ `sub` Subscripts the element

▶ `super` Superscripts the element

▶ `text-top` Aligns the top of the element with the top of the parent element's tallest text character

▶ `text-bottom` Aligns the bottom of the element with the bottom of the parent element's lowest character: for example, the bottom of a *g, j, p, q,* or *y*

You can also use these relative keywords:

▶ `top` Aligns the top of the element with the tallest element on the line

▶ `bottom` Aligns the bottom of the element with the lowest element on the line

Percentage values are also acceptable, and they are relative to the line spacing of the parent element. Using a percentage value raises the element's baseline the defined percentage above the baseline of the parent element. For example, setting the vertical alignment to 110 percent increases the element's line spacing 10 percent over that of the parent element. You can control the actual line spacing by using the `line-height` property discussed later in this chapter.

THE `text-transform` PROPERTY

You can capitalize the first letter of each word or set the entire word to upper- or lowercase by using the `text-transform` property. This property accepts the following keyword values:

▶ `capitalize` Capitalizes the first letter of each word

▶ `uppercase` Capitalizes each letter in the element

▶ `lowercase` Lowercases each letter of the element

▶ `none` Turns off any `text-transform` value inherited from the parent element

THE `text-align` PROPERTY

This property defines the text alignment of the element, and it accepts these keyword values:

▶ `left` Aligns text to the left

▶ `right` Aligns text to the right

▶ `center` Aligns text in the center

▶ `justify` Aligns text to both left and right, properly spacing the interior text

THE `text-indent` PROPERTY

You can define how far the first line in a block of text is indented by using the `text-indent` property. You can use both length and percentage values. For example, { `text-indent: .5in` } increases the first line's indent by half an inch, and { `text-indent: 5%` } increases the first line's indent by 5 percent of the width of the parent element.

You can create a *hanging indent,* in which the first line hangs out to the left of the text beneath it, by using a negative value. But you should use this in conjunction with the `margin-left` property discussed in the "Box Properties" section. You'd want to increase the left margin of the element by the same amount you decreased the indent of the first line, as this example shows:

```
{ text-indent: -.5in;
  margin-left: .5in }
```

The overall effect would be to push the entire element in a half inch from the left margin, and then pull the first line back a half inch, creating the hanging indent.

THE `line-height` PROPERTY

This property controls the distance between baselines in a text element. For those of you who are familiar with publishing terminology, this is identical to *leading.* This idea is similar to single-spacing and double-spacing in a word processor. In fact, you can even use numeric values to define this property in just that fashion. For example, `{ line-height: 2 }` is equivalent to double-spacing. The `line-height` property also accepts length values to set specific line heights, as well as percentage values.

BOX PROPERTIES

The *box properties* supply styles with many of the same qualities you are familiar with from working with tables, for example, width, height, and padding. The CSS box model assumes a simple rectangular area surrounding all element content. Picture this box as a rectangular bulls-eye with four regions radiating out from the center. At its heart is the *content area,* which contains the text or image element. Outside of this region is the *padding area,* followed by the *border area,* and finally, the *margin area.*

Each of the three outer areas (padding, border, and margin) can be divided into four parts: left, right, top, and bottom. The perimeter of all four areas (content, padding, border, and margin) is called an *edge,* giving each box four distinct edges: the content edge, padding edge, border edge, and margin edge. These

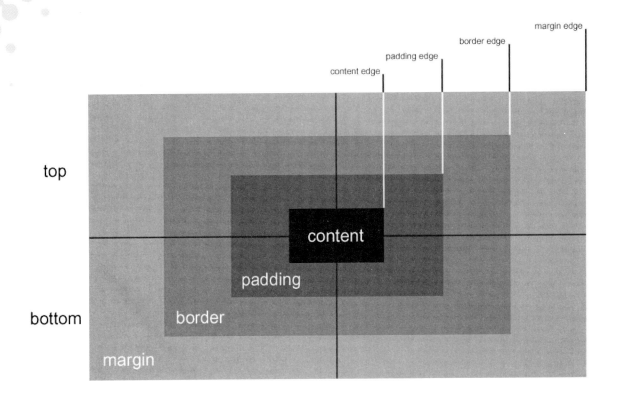

edges, in turn, can be divided in the same fashion as the areas, giving you left, right, top, and bottom edges.

PADDING PROPERTIES

The *padding properties* control the width of the padding area of an element box. These properties accept both length and percentage values. A value of 0 collapses the area completely. Negative values will not work. These properties include `padding-top`, `padding-right`, `padding-bottom`, and `padding-left`.

BORDER PROPERTIES

The *border properties* specify the width, color, and style of the border area of the element's box.

BORDER WIDTHS

Four properties govern the width of the border area: `border-top-width`, `border-right-width`, `border-bottom-width`, and `border-left-width`. They accept any positive length value. A value of 0 collapses the area entirely. You can also use the following keyword values: `thin`, `medium`, and `thick`.

BORDER COLORS

The four properties governing the border color are `border-top-color`, `border-right-color`, `border-bottom-color`, and `border-left-color`. They accept color values expressed in any of the three possible methods described in the "Color Values" section, as well as the keyword `transparent`, which renders the border invisible without collapsing any width value you set.

BORDER STYLES

The properties governing border style break down as you might expect: `border-top-style`, `border-right-style`, `border-bottom-style`, and `border-left-style`. Each property accepts the following keywords:

▶ `none` Hides the border, forcing border width values to 0

▶ `dotted` Makes the border a dotted line

▶ `dashed` Makes the border a dashed line

▶ `solid` Displays the border as a solid line

▶ `double` Creates a border of two solid lines

▶ `groove` Creates an engraved 3-D border effect

▶ `ridge` Creates an embossed 3-D border effect

▶ `inset` Makes the content area appear inset into the document surface

▶ `outset` Makes the entire content area appear embossed from the document surface

UNIQUE BOX PROPERTIES

There are four other box properties, which can be applied to any element but are most commonly used to affect images: `width`, `height`, `float`, and `clear`.

THE width PROPERTY

As the name implies, this property governs the width of an element. When applied to images, it is best to use a pixel length value, although it will accept any length or percentage value, as shown here:

```
img { width: 110px }
```

This property also accepts the keyword auto. This value is good to use in conjunction with the height property when you want to fix one dimension but have the other dimension scale appropriately, as in this example:

```
img { width: 110px;
      height: auto }
```

This syntax fixes the width of the image to 110 pixels, but maintains the image's proper aspect ratio so it doesn't distort.

THE height PROPERTY

As you may have guessed, this property is the opposite of the one just described and works in exactly the same way.

THE float PROPERTY

This property governs how text wraps around an element. It is similar to the align attribute in HTML for the <table> and <img> tags; however, in CSS, you can apply it to any element with equal success. The float property accepts the following keyword values:

▶ left Places the element on the left margin, wrapping content to the right

▶ right Places the element on the right margin, wrapping content to the left

▶ none Disables the float property

THE clear PROPERTY

This property governs whether an element permits floating elements to its sides. The clear property accepts the following keyword values that dictate which sides do not allow floating elements:

▶ left Clears floating elements from the left side of an element

▶ right Clears floating elements from the right side of an element

▶ `both` Clears floating elements from both sides of an element

▶ `none` Allows floating elements on either side of an element; the default browser behavior

MARGIN PROPERTIES

The *margin properties* govern the width of the margin area. They accept both length and percentage values. The margin properties include `margin-top`, `margin-right`, `margin-bottom`, and `margin-left`.

CLASSIFICATION PROPERTIES

By *classification,* CSS means that these properties set elements off into categories rather than control some obvious display property they may have. The *classification properties* include `white-space`, `display`, `list-style-type`, `list-style-image`, and `list-style-position`.

THE `white-space` PROPERTY

The `white-space` property affects how the browser displays spaces and tabs. The property accepts the following keyword values:

▶ `normal` Collapses any extra white space; the default browser behavior

▶ `pre` Behaves just like preformatted text tags (`<pre></pre>`), maintaining all white space

▶ `nowrap` Prevents text from wrapping, forcing you to use `<br>` tags to force line breaks; supported only by Netscape

THE `display` PROPERTY

The `display` property determines whether the element is treated like the following:

▶ **A block element** Like a paragraph, heading, or table

▶ **An inline element** Like an image

▶ **A list item** Like the `<li>` tag—without the element necessarily being part of a traditional HTML list

You use this property to fully define a unique class of your own, for example, when you aren't redefining the behavior of a preexisting tag. You could also use this property to do just that—change the native behavior of a tag, turning some element into a list element so you could ascribe bullets to it, for example. The property accepts these appropriate keyword values: `block`, `inline`, `list-item`, and `none`.

THE `list-style-type` PROPERTY

This property controls the style of the marker (bullet or character) that precedes the list item, making it similar to the `type` attribute of the `<ol>`, `<ul>`, and `<li>` tags. The property accepts these keyword values: `disc`, `circle`, `square`, `decimal`, `lower-roman`, `upper-roman`, `lower-alpha`, `upper-alpha`, and `none`.

THE `list-style-image` PROPERTY

This property allows you to insert an image for a list item marker, and it accepts a URL value. For example:

```
ul { list-style-image: url(images/bullet.gif) }
```

THE `list-style-position` PROPERTY

The `list-style-position` property lets you indent the bullet or character in one character space on the first line of a list item, should that list item's content wrap onto a second line. The property accepts the two keyword values `inside` and `outside`, the latter being the default browser behavior. For example, `ul { list-style-position: inside }` produces the following effect:

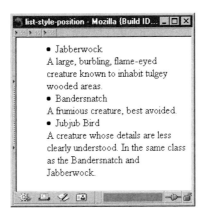

ON THE VIRTUAL CLASSROOM CD Cascading style sheets are the future of element formatting in HTML. In Lesson 9, the instructor will demonstrate how to define styles and implement them in your HTML documents.

Layers

The word "layer" almost speaks for itself. What does *layer* conjure in your mind? Something on top of, over, or around something else? Whether you're thinking winter clothes, coats of paint, layer cakes, or the skins of an onion, the idea is basically the same. In HTML, layers are a metaphor for the positioning capabilities of CSS.

By creating layers, you define separate levels of page content that can be manipulated in these ways:

▶ Given an exact position anywhere on the screen

▶ Stacked in front of each other

▶ Revealed independently, while other layers remain hidden

Because layered content is a function of the CSS specification discussed in Chapter 10, you may want to read that chapter first if you haven't done so already. CSS-capable browsers first appeared with version 4.0 of both Internet Explorer and Netscape Navigator, and even then, they were only partially compliant with the first CSS specification. Earlier browsers, not being CSS-compliant at all, obviously can't support any layering effects. What's more, both Netscape Navigator and Internet Explorer do not support CSS positioning exactly the same way.

Understanding CSS-Positioning

The first CSS standard created by the World Wide Web Consortium (W3C), called CSS1, focused predominantly on controlling how content *looked*. An extension to CSS1 was then created, called CSS-Positioning (CSS-P), which dealt—as you might expect—with *where* content was positioned. CSS1 was expanded on and melded with the CSS-P extension into a unified specification called, simply enough, CSS2, which is the standard we have today.

Prior to CSS, a page element's location had been strictly 2-D, limited to its order within the document and simple alignment. Using layers, elements can be given exact placement in 3-D: from left to right (the X axis), from top to bottom (the Y axis), and from front to back (the Z axis). You can even control a layer's visibility, effectively turning the layer "on" or "off." Think of layers, then, as physical, 3-D objects—like transparency sheets on an overhead projector—instead of the typical 2-D content you've read about thus far.

Because you need only a simple style rule declaration to position an element wherever you'd like, in theory, anything can be treated as a layer. In practice, however, you may want to curb any enthusiastic tendencies. There's little point in giving an exact position to something like an `<i>` tag without properly setting the position

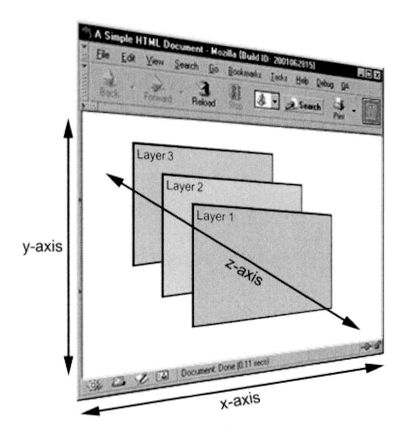

of the `<p></p>` tags that the italicized word might be sitting within. If you did, that italicized word could find itself floating off in left field somewhere completely out of context with the text to which it relates.

As I just mentioned, the easiest way to think of layered content is like transparency sheets on an overhead projector, each sheet holding various kinds of page content. The metaphorical transparency sheets, when written in HTML, should probably be made from some kind of generic container tag: in other words, one that doesn't already have some other logical purpose like the `<i>` or `<p>` tags do. You could then place any content you liked inside this tag and position the entire block as a whole. Here's an example:

```
<some tag with positioning magic>
   <img src="images/jabberwocky.gif" width="50" height="50" align="left">
   <p>The Jabberwocky is a beast with jaws that bite
```

```
    and claws that catch, even more nasty
    than the <i>frumious</i> Bandersnatch.</p>
</some tag with positioning magic>
```

THE <div> AND <span> TAGS

So, where to find "some tag with positioning magic"? As you might recall back in Chapter 4, I mentioned the <div> tag in the section "Aligning an Image." The <div> tag is a generic tag that has no predefined display characteristics of its own. "Div" is short for "division," which means the <div> tag is meant to be used wherever you intend a logical division of page content. Well, a layer is certainly a logical division, so the <div> tag sounds like the perfect tag for the job.

The <span> tag is another generic tag, which you generally use to apply an inline style to some piece of page content, instead of defining some larger block-level element the way the <div> tag does. In this respect, the <span> tag is to the <div> tag what the <i> tag is to the <p> tag—a paragraph is a block-level element, while italic is simply a way to modify a single word.

HOW CSS CREATES LAYERED CONTENT

Because layering is a function of CSS, it stands to reason—based on what you learned in Chapter 10—that certain CSS properties must exist that govern this layering behavior. Basically, a CSS-compliant browser needs to know two pieces of information to position an element:

▶ How it's to be positioned
▶ Where it's to be positioned

The "how" part of the equation is covered by the position property. The "where" is determined by coordinates specified through these four properties: top, left, bottom, and right.

Unfortunately, as of this writing, support for each of these properties is not universal, as shown in Table 11-1. Until the release of the most recent versions of Internet Explorer and Netscape Navigator, top and left were the only two properties you could count on. Until browsers supporting the complete CSS specification are commonplace, it's best to stick with the top and left properties.

TABLE 11-1 CSS SPECIFICATION

| | NETSCAPE NAVIGATOR | | INTERNET EXPLORER | | | | | | |
| | WINDOWS & MACINTOSH | | WINDOWS | | | | MACINTOSH | | |
	4X	6.0	4.0	5.0	5.5	6.0	4.0	4.5	5.0
top	*Partial	Yes	Partial	Yes	Yes	Yes	Partial	Partial	Yes
left	*Partial	Yes	Partial	Yes	Yes	Yes	Partial	Partial	Yes
bottom	No	Yes	No	No	Yes	Yes	No	No	Yes
right	No	Yes	No	No	Yes	Yes	No	No	Yes

*In the 4X versions of Netscape Navigator, the positioning coordinates are lost whenever the browser is resized. This problem requires the use of JavaScript to reload the document each time it is resized to refresh with the original coordinates.

UNDERSTANDING CSS-POSITIONING PROPERTIES

The most common method for positioning a <div> tag is to use the style attribute to create an inline style, like so:

```
<div id="jabberwocky" style="position: absolute; left: 150px; top: 75px;
width: 200px; height: 100px; visibility: visible; z-index: 1">
   <img src="images/jabberwocky.gif" width="50" height="50" align="left">
   <p>The Jabberwocky is a beast with jaws that bite
   and claws that catch, even more nasty
   than the <i>frumious</i> Bandersnatch.</p>
</div>
```

As you can see in this example, the style attribute has a number of new properties in evidence, which, when combined, determine how and where this element is positioned.

THE position PROPERTY

If you look at the previous code, you see that the first property defined inside the style attribute is the position property. This property defines the element as positionable, and it dictates which positioning method to use by way of these three keyword values: absolute, relative, and static.

position: absolute

Absolute positioning places the element in a specific location with respect to its parent element, using the coordinates supplied with the top, left, bottom, and `right` properties. If the parent element is the body of the document, the element is positioned in relation to the browser window. For example, `position: absolute; left: 50px; top: 50px` places the upper-left corner of the element 50 pixels over from the left and 50 pixels down from the upper-left corner of the browser window, affixing itself permanently to that location within the document.

position: relative

Predominantly used with the `<span>` tag, the `relative` property value uses the coordinates specified in the `top`, `left`, `bottom`, and `right` properties to place the element relative to its normal position within the flow of the document. For example, when the following code is applied to a word in a sentence, it shifts that word 50 pixels over from the left and 50 pixels down from its original position within the parent element, leaving a gap where it would normally be positioned:

```
<span id="example" style="position: relative; left: 50px; top: 50px">
```

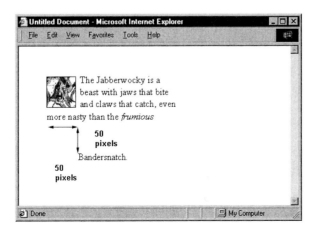

position: static

Static positioning is traditional HTML browser default positioning: in other words, no CSS capabilities at all. Defining the position property as static guarantees that the element will stay in its normal position within the flow of the document.

THE COORDINATE PROPERTIES

The left, top, bottom, and right properties are used in conjunction with the position property to specify the coordinates for the element's position. Each of these properties accepts both length and percentage values, which are discussed in Chapter 10. Traditionally, designers use pixel (px) length values because they retain the highest level of fidelity across different browsers, operating systems, and monitor resolutions.

In the code samples in this chapter, I've defined two of these properties (for the most part, left and top), and together, they effectively plot the x and y coordinates of the upper-left corner of my element. As the older versions of Internet Explorer and Netscape Navigator become used less frequently, using different combinations of left, top, bottom, and right will allow designers to be more free in their positioning habits.

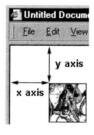

THE left PROPERTY

The value you define for the left property indicates where the left edge of an element gets positioned. Of course, how you define the position property makes all the difference.

When you define the position property as absolute, the value represents how far the left side of the element is offset from the left side of the parent element.

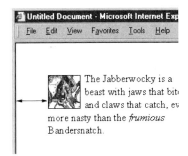

When you define the `position` property as `relative`, the value represents how far the left side of the element is offset to the right of its normal static location:

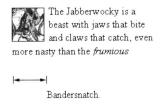

THE top PROPERTY

The `top` property defines how far the top edge of an element is offset from the top of the parent element, in the case of absolute positioning:

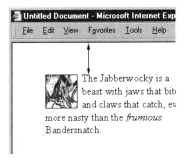

The `top` property also defines how far the top edge of the element is shifted from its normal static location, if it's relatively positioned:

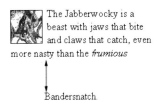

VIRTUAL CLASSROOM   179

THE bottom PROPERTY

The `bottom` property, as you may have already guessed, is used to determine the location of the bottom edge of a positioned element.

When the element is positioned absolutely, the offset distance is between the element's bottom edge and the bottom of the parent element:

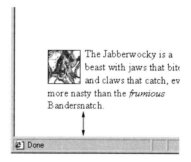

When the element is relatively positioned, the value represents how far the bottom edge of the element is offset above its normal static location:

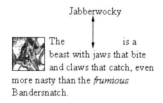

THE right PROPERTY

The `right` property determines how far the right side of the element is offset from the right side of the parent element, if the element is absolutely positioned:

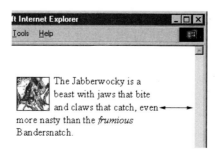

The `right` property also determines how far the right side of the element is offset from the right of the element's normal static position, if the element is relatively positioned.

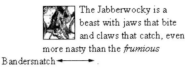

DEFINING LAYER DIMENSIONS

Now that you have a handle on positioning an element left to right and top to bottom, it's time to discuss its physical size. Logically enough, you control an element's dimensions with the `width` and `height` properties. Both accept length and percentage values, as discussed in Chapter 10.

```
<div id="jabberwocky" style="position: absolute; left: 150px; top: 75px;
width: 200px; height: 100px; visibility: visible; z-index: 1">
   <img src="images/jabberwocky.gif" width="50" height="50" align="left">
   <p>The Jabberwocky is a beast with jaws that bite
   and claws that catch, even more nasty
   than the <i>frumious</i> Bandersnatch.</p>
</div>
```

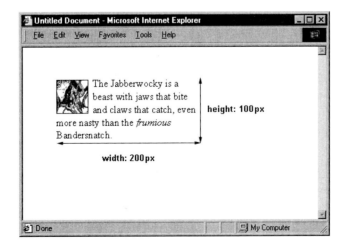

THE visibility PROPERTY

The visibility property lets you make an element either visible or invisible. You define this property by using one of the following keyword values: visible, hidden, or inherit, the visible keyword being the default, of course. The first two keywords should be fairly obvious. And you use the inherit value to make the element inherit the visibility of its parent element.

Why would you want to make a layer invisible? Well, in combination with a little JavaScript, layers can be made to appear and disappear based on the actions of the user. When you combine the three elements JavaScript, CSS, and HTML, the fusion is commonly called dynamic HTML (DHTML). Alas, the proper use of JavaScript is a whole other book. Some good sources for JavaScript are the following:

► http://www.javascript.com

► http://javascript.internet.com

► http://www.webmonkey.com

For sites devoted exclusively to DHTML, check these sites out:

► http://www.dynamicdrive.com

► http://www.dhtml-zone.com

► http://www.dhtmlshock.com

THE z-index PROPERTY

The left, top, bottom, and right properties help you position your content along the X and Y axes, but that leaves one more axis to be reckoned with: the Z axis. This is where the z-index property comes into play. Returning to the imaginary transparency sheets on the overhead projector for a moment, imagine having a number of sheets (layers) on the glass, one on top of the other. They'd create a stack, wouldn't they? When you have a number of overlapping layers in a document, their position front to back is called the *stacking order*. The z-index property defines a layer's place in that stacking order and accepts a numeric value. The lower a layer's z-index number, the deeper its position in the stack. For example, if you had three layers in a document, with z-indexes of 1, 2, and 3, z-index 3 would be on the top of the stack, 2 would be in the middle, and 1 would be at the bottom.

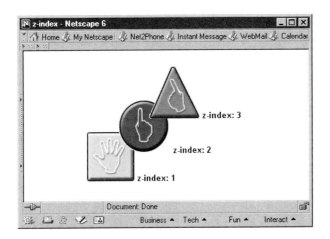

If, on the other hand, none of these layers had their z-index property defined, then the order in which the elements appear in the HTML code of the document determines their stacking order: first one on top, second in the middle, third on the bottom.

CONTROLLING LAYER OVERFLOW

What happens if the contents of a layer exceed the dimensions you set for it? You get *overflow*, which, reasonably enough, is controlled with the overflow property. You can set four possible keyword values for this property:

▶ visible Displays the full contents of the layer, regardless of actual layer dimensions. Using this keyword is equivalent to not defining a value at all.

▶ hidden Obscures any content that falls outside of the layer's dimensions.

▶ scroll Maintains the layer's dimensions, adding scroll bars to accommodate the expanded content. Scroll bars are added regardless of whether the content exceeds the layer's dimensions. This keyword is supported only in Internet Explorer 5.0 and later, and Netscape Navigator 6.0.

▶ auto Adds scroll bars only when a layer's contents exceed its dimensions. In Netscape Navigator 4X versions, auto is equivalent to hidden. Internet Explorer treats it as scroll.

DEFINING A CLIPPING AREA

By defining a *clipping area*, you mask the content around a layer's edges, marking off a rectangular region of the layer that remains visible to the visitor. The property used to define the clipping is called `clip`, and the syntax is written like this:

```
clip: rect(top right bottom left)
```

The words "top," "right," "bottom," and "left" represent pixel values which specify offsets from their respective sides of the layer.

Clipping does not delete content; it only hides it. Any images in a layer that you apply clipping to still retain their original file size and affect download time the same way. By default, any clipping area values are considered pixels, unless you specify otherwise using any of the length value abbreviations discussed in Chapter 10.

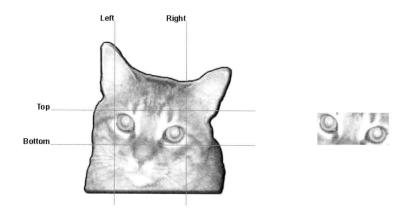

 ON THE VIRTUAL CLASSROOM CD CSS makes layered content, allowing for the exact placement of page elements. In Lesson 10, the instructor will demonstrate the process of creating layers and populating them with content.

The Future of HTML

As of this writing, HTML is a "dead" language.

"NOW YOU TELL US!" you're screaming. Don't get excited.
I'm sure all your HTML files work just fine when you open
them in a browser, don't they? Just because there will never
be an HTML 5.0 specification doesn't mean HTML is pushing
up the daisies. It's simply evolving.

THE DEATH OF HTML

The last HTML specification was version 4.01, delivered on Christmas Eve, 1999, by the World Wide Web Consortium (W3C) as the last word on a language that had seen the Web through its first decade. It wasn't perfect, and sometimes it was far from pretty, but it had done the job—and without it, there'd have been no Web. The Web had grown tremendously, brimming with new capabilities and technologies. HTML's creators had concluded that aesthetics and content were best addressed separately, and they developed the CSS specification to deal with HTML's shortcomings and expand the possibilities of web design.

There was still more to be done, however. You see, HTML is actually a subset of a vast *metalanguage* called the *Standard Generalized Markup Language* (SGML). This metalanguage is a set of rules governing how electronic markup languages should behave. HTML was meant to be fast and easy, so it's compliance to the SGML standard was always a bit lax. Combine that with the history of browser development, where everyone was out for themselves creating proprietary markup, and you can imagine how far afield HTML strayed. With each successive version of HTML, the W3C has tried to bring it back in line with the SGML standard. Unfortunately, only so much could be done. SGML is just too vast a standard to emulate. There is no way HTML could be perfectly compliant and still be easy enough for the average person to pick up. A middle ground was needed.

XML

The eXtensible Markup Language (XML) is that middle ground. Like its parent SGML, XML is also a metalanguage, but a fairly easy one to grasp. And unlike HTML, it is completely SGML-compliant. Instead of being a markup language with a defined set of tags, XML is a set of rules by which you can convert any type of logically ordered data into a tag-based text file. This means you use XML to create your own tags that logically represent the data you're working with.

Well, nothing works better than a demonstration, so here goes. In XML, you need to create an element that defines your *base data type*. What's a base data type? I might as well use the thing you're holding in your hands—this book—as an example. If you ran a book store and had a large inventory, all the information about those books, in itself, is a vast quantity of logically ordered data.

A bookseller needs to keep track of quite a bit of information about a book: the title, the author, the publisher, the ISBN number, the page count, the list price, etc. Imagine you have a whole database worth of books, and these six items comprise the component pieces of data you need to maintain. How do you express them in XML? Here's a possibility:

```
<book subject="computer">
  <book.title>HTML Virtual Classroom</book.title>
  <author>
    <firstname>Robert</firstname>
    <lastname>Fuller</lastname>
  </author>
  <pub>McGraw-Hill</pub>
  <isbn>0072192569</isbn>
  <pages>300</pages>
  <list.price>$29.99</list.price>
</book>
```

This code provides an example of the basic element in your XML document, the `<book>` element; that element, in turn, is composed of component elements. As you can see, the `<book>` element even has an attribute. Looks a lot like HTML doesn't it? Unlike HTML, however, XML's tags have no intrinsic display characteristics of their own. Their interpretation is left up to whatever application reads them. In fact, nothing in XML even assumes these elements will be "displayed." How the data is used is ultimately up to the people who need it.

There's a little more to XML than just thinking up some tags, however. You need to define these tag elements and their attributes someplace before you actually start using them. You accomplish this task by using something called an XML *document type definition* (DTD), using *element* and *entity declarations*. The DTD is typically a separate document, although it can be written at the beginning of the XML file as well. The DTD defines each element and its component parts. The syntax looks like this:

```
<!ELEMENT book ( book.title, author+, pub, isbn, pages, list.price ) >
<!ELEMENT book.title ( #PCDATA ) >
<!ELEMENT author ( firstname, lastname ) >
<!ELEMENT firstname ( #PCDATA ) >
<!ELEMENT lastname ( #PCDATA ) >
```

```
<!ELEMENT pub ( #PCDATA ) >
<!ELEMENT isbn ( #PCDATA ) >
<!ELEMENT pages ( #PCDATA ) >
<!ELEMENT list.price ( #PCDATA ) >
<!ATTLIST book subject (computer|fiction|nonfiction) #REQUIRED >
```

The element declarations in the previous code define the individual tag elements. The values in parentheses tell you which information is found between those element tags. For example, some elements, like `<book>`, hold other elements, while elements like `<isbn>` hold data.

As you saw in the example, the `<book>` element has a `subject` attribute. Attributes are defined with the `<!ATTLIST>` declaration, which states the element name, the attribute name, and then the acceptable values for the attribute in parentheses. You can see in the DTD in the previous code that the `subject` attribute has been listed as required. In other words, if someone entered a `<book>` element but didn't have the `subject` attribute defined, the document would not be valid.

DTDs can be linked to the XML document, or they can be contained within it. For example, the basic syntax for such a document looks something like this:

```
<?xml version="1.0"?>
<!DOCTYPE book [

<!ELEMENT book ( book.title, author+, pub, isbn, pages, list.price ) >
<!ELEMENT book.title ( #PCDATA ) >
<!ELEMENT author ( firstname, lastname ) >
<!ELEMENT firstname ( #PCDATA ) >
<!ELEMENT lastname ( #PCDATA ) >
<!ELEMENT pub ( #PCDATA ) >
<!ELEMENT isbn ( #PCDATA ) >
<!ELEMENT pages ( #PCDATA ) >
<!ELEMENT list.price ( #PCDATA ) >
<!ATTLIST book subject (computer|fiction|nonfiction) #REQUIRED >
]
>
<!-- The DOCTYPE declaration can either list the element and entity decla-
rations, or accept the URL of the document containing the DTD, for example
"books.dtd" -->
```

```
<store.inventory>
  <title>Inventory of SuperBooks Megastore</title>
  <book subject="computer">
    <book.title>HTML Virtual Classroom</book.title>
    <author>
      <firstname>Robert</firstname>
      <lastname>Fuller</lastname>
    </author>
    <pub>McGraw-Hill</pub>
    <isbn>0072192569</isbn>
    <pages>300</pages>
    <list.price>$29.99</list.price>
  </book>
</store.inventory>
```

The very first line, `<?xml version="1.0"?>`, declares which type of document this is (an XML document) and references the version of the language. This declaration is not an element or a tag, but a processing instruction for the application reading the data. This line is followed by the DTD, which, in this case, is embedded within the XML file. The `<!DOCTYPE>` tag could also have the URL of the external DTD file, which would be a file with a .dtd extension. The next element is the all-encompassing *root element,* in this case, `<inventory.books>`, inside of which is a `<title>` element, followed in this case by as many `<book>` elements as there are books in inventory.

> **TIP** If you're curious, you might try typing this code into your text editor and saving it with an .xml extension, and then try opening it in a browser or two. Internet Explorer 5.0 and later will display an XML document as a tree of elements (nodes) that expand and collapse when you click a plus or minus (+/−) sign beside them. Netscape Navigator 6.0 ignores the tags and simply prints the contents of the tags to the screen.

Granted, what I've laid out here is only the tip of the XML iceberg. XML is compatible with CSS, so it's possible to create style sheets for XML elements and then have a browser display the content. XML also has a native style sheet language called, appropriately, the eXtensible Stylesheet Language (XSL), which is as far beyond CSS as XML is beyond HTML. I simply wanted to give you a basic understanding of what XML is so the next section will make more sense.

XML + HTML = XHTML

So, as the W3C saw it, HTML was in danger of becoming this cobbled, Frankenstein's monster of a markup language. But how to stop it from spinning out of control, bring it back in line with the tenets of SGML, and also make it something that could grow? Reinterpret it as an XML application, of course! Which is just what the W3C did. On January 26, 2000, they released the eXtensible Hypertext Markup Language (XHTML) 1.0 recommendation, and from here on out, you won't see an HTML specification without that *X* in front of it.

The W3C essentially created a DTD that defined the existing HTML tags and their attributes, and firmly removed those tags and attributes that had been deprecated in favor of CSS in the previous versions of the HTML standard. And because XHTML is an XML application, it inherits XML's syntax and the ability to define new tags. That's right—you need a new tag? Just write a DTD and reference it in your XHTML document, create a style rule for your new tag in your CSS file, and away you go.

Now it's safe to say that HTML isn't really going anywhere. Again, think of all the web sites that would have to retool to be XHTML-compliant. In all likelihood, web browsers will continue to support the HTML standard. Presently, the XHTML 1.0 standard is not widely supported, but you can rest assured that as the major browser manufacturers produce new versions of their software, each release will be more and more compliant.

SYNTAX: XHTML VS. HTML

Generally, HTML and XHTML share a common syntax. In places where browsers let you play fast and loose, I have always favored a strict interpretation of the HTML standard in my examples to get you used to what lies ahead. The following sections describe the major syntactic differences between XHTML and HTML.

CASE SENSITIVITY

I'm sure you've noticed that every example in this book has been lowercase, and that I've strongly encouraged you to write all your HTML this way. Why?

XHTML is case sensitive, requiring all tags and attributes, as well as CSS style rules, to be lowercase. This means `<p>` and `<P>` are *not* the same tag, and `width` and `WIDTH` are not the same attribute as far as XHTML is concerned.

CLOSING TAGS

XHTML also requires the use of all closing tags. Unlike HTML, which allows you to omit closing tags where their position can be easily deduced by the browser, XHTML throws up its arms at a document that fails to include the appropriate closing tags.

EMPTY TAGS

XHTML's preference for closing tags goes a step further. Every empty tag is rendered with a forward slash just before the end bracket, like in this example:

```
<base attribute="value"/>
<basefont attribute="value"/>
<br attribute="value"/>
<frame attribute="value"/>
<hr attribute="value"/>
<img attribute="value"/>
<input attribute="value"/>
<link attribute="value"/>
```

Of course, you'll face a small problem when a non-XHTML-compliant browser encounters a tag like this. It has no idea what the tag is or how to deal with it, thus wreaking havoc on your page. The solution is to include a space between the tag and the `/>`, for example, `<br />`, `<hr />`, and `<img src="monkey.gif" alt="Chimpanzee" />`.

ATTRIBUTE QUOTATION MARKS

In XHTML, all attribute values must be placed between quotes. Presently, HTML allows certain numeric attribute values to be rendered without quotation marks. For example, the following code is perfectly valid HTML:

```
<img src="images/monkey.gif" width=50 height=100 border=0>
```

XML, on the other hand, would not be amused, requiring this code instead:

```
<img src="images/monkey.gif" width="50" height="100" border="0" />
```

Again, in the examples in this book, I've placed quotation marks around all attribute values for a number of reasons: it makes for a consistent approach, and if I choose to further convert a document to proper XHTML syntax later on, there's that much less work to do!

SINGLE-WORD ATTRIBUTE VALUES

HTML has a number of attributes that don't require a value. Instead, their inclusion within the tag acts to toggle a specific behavior: for example, the `noshade` attribute of the `<hr>` tag, or the `selected` attribute used in the `<input>` tag to make radio buttons and check boxes prechosen. In XHTML, all attributes must follow the `attribute="value"` syntax, so for example, the `noshade` attribute is defined like this: `<hr noshade="noshade">`.

SPECIAL CHARACTERS

Basically, the ampersand (`&`) and HTML comment tags (`<!-- -->`) present certain problems for XHTML. This predicament really isn't hard to solve, however. As far as ampersands go, they're just fine out in the middle of an element like a paragraph or table cell; they just can't stand alone in an attribute value. For example, an `alt` attribute rendered `alt="Jack & Jill"` would be a problem. The solution is to use the special character entity for the ampersand, `&amp;`. Granted, it has an ampersand in it, but it isn't a lone character like it is in `"Jack & Jill"`.

As for comment tags, they pose a problem for embedded style sheets that use comment tags to hide the contents of the style tag from older browsers, like in this example:

```
<style type="text/css">
<!--
p { margin-left: 2em;
    font-family: Arial, Helvetica, sans-serif;
    color: #ff0000 }
-->
</style>
```

The easiest solution to this problem is simply to use linked style sheets instead of embedded ones, referencing your style sheet with the `<link>` tag, like so:

```
<link rel="stylesheet" type="text/css"
href="http://www.site.com/my_styles.css">
```

THE id ATTRIBUTE

In Chapter 4 on hyperlinks, I discussed using the `id` attribute in place of the `name` attribute when working with anchors. The `name` attribute is also integral to form controls, like the `<input>` tag covered in Chapter 8. HTML 4.0 saw the inclusion of the `id` attribute, which provides the same functionality as the `name` attribute. XHTML 1.0 has deprecated the `name` attribute, preferring the use of the `id` attribute instead.

SUGGESTED READING AND RESOURCES

I highly recommend investigating the path HTML has taken and learning about the emerging technologies of XML and XHTML. Of course, the place to get the first word on each of these subjects is the W3C's home page, at http://w3c.org.

▶ XHTML home page
http://www.w3c.org/MarkUp

▶ XML home page
http://www.w3c.org/XML

HTML Tag and Special Character Reference

HTML Tags and Attributes

This table is a general reference to HTML common tags and attributes, including a description of what they do. A page number is noted for those tags and attributes discussed in this book.

TAGS		ATTRIBUTES	DESCRIPTION	PAGE
`<!--`	`-->`		Creates a comment hidden from the browser.	17
`<a>`	`</a>`		Creates anchors and hyperlinks.	60–61
		href	Defines the URL of the hyperlink.	60–61
		name	Designates a named anchor.	67, 193
		target	Indicates in which window or frame a hyperlink will be displayed.	140
`<address>`	`</address>`		Formats a text address. Typically results in the text being italicized.	
`<b>`	`</b>`		Formats text as boldface.	33, 34
`<basefont>`	`</basefont>`		Sets the default font for text in the document.	30
		color	Sets the default color for text.	32
		size	Sets the default size for text.	30
`<big>`	`</big>`		Increases the size of text, usually by one size value.	33, 34
`<blockquote>`	`</blockquote>`		Turns the text between these tags into an indented block, visually set off from any adjacent text.	36–38
`<body>`	`</body>`		Defines the body element of the document. Encapsulates all other visible markup.	14

Continued

HTML Tags and Attributes

TAGS		ATTRIBUTES	DESCRIPTION	PAGE
		alink	Indicates the color of an active link.	66
		link	Indicates the color of an untouched link.	66
		vlink	Indicates the color of a visited link.	66
		background	Indicates the name of the image file that will serve as the document background image.	
		bgcolor	Indicates the solid color background of the page.	32
		leftmargin	Sets the left margin of the document.	
		topmargin	Sets the top margin of the document.	
		text	Sets the default text color of the document.	32
 	None		Inserts a line break.	24–25
		clear	Prevents text from wrapping after the break.	
<caption>	</caption>		Designates a table caption.	
		align	Indicates the location of the caption, above or below the table.	
<center>	</center>		Centers any content between each tag.	50
<cite>	</cite>		Designates text as a citation. Typically results in the text being italicized.	33, 34
<code>	</code>		Designates text as computer code. Typically results in the text being monospaced.	33, 34
<dd>	</dd>		Designates a definition in a list.	82–83

Continued

HTML TAGS AND ATTRIBUTES

TAGS		ATTRIBUTES	DESCRIPTION	PAGE
`<div>`	`</div>`		Creates a logical division of page content. Typically used to align elements and define positionable content. (A generic tag.)	50, 174
		align	Applies alignment (center, left, or right) to page content.	50
		id	Defines a unique identifier for the division.	175
`<dl>`	`</dl>`		Marks the beginning and end of a definition list.	81–83
`<dt>`	`</dt>`		Designates the terms in the definition list.	82–83
`<em>`	`</em>`		Indicates emphasis. Typically results in the text being italicized.	33, 34
`<font>`	`</font>`		Applies text formatting.	27
		color	Sets the text color.	31
		face	Sets the font.	27–29
		size	Establishes text size.	29–31
`<form>`	`</form>`		Indicates the presence of a form on the web page.	113
		action	Designates the URL for the CGI script to be used for the form.	113
		method	Indicates the way the form data will be processed—as a get or a post.	113–114
`<frame>`	`</frame>`		Establishes the presence of a frame.	130–131
		border	Sets border thickness.	136

Continued

HTML TAGS AND ATTRIBUTES

TAGS		ATTRIBUTES	DESCRIPTION	PAGE
		bordercolor	Sets the color of a border.	138
		frameborder	Determines whether a frame will have a visible border.	135–136
		name	Applies a name to the frame.	140
		noresize	Prevents page visitors from resizing a frame.	137
		marginwidth	Sets a frame's margins on the left and right.	138–140
		marginheight	Sets a frame's margins on the top and bottom.	138–140
		scrolling	Determines the presence of scroll bars on a frame.	138
		src	Designates the URL of a page to be displayed in the frame.	131
		target	Establishes in which frame a link should be opened.	140–141
<frameset>	</frameset>		Defines a frameset.	130–131
		border	Sets the thickness of borders for frames within the frameset.	136–137
		bordercolor	Sets the color of frame borders.	138
		cols	Establishes the size and number of columns in the frameset.	132–134
		frameborder	Determines whether frame borders will be visible.	135–136
		rows	Establishes the size and number of rows in the frameset.	132–134

Continued

HTML TAGS AND ATTRIBUTES

TAGS		ATTRIBUTES	DESCRIPTION	PAGE
`<h1>` through `<h6>`	`</h1>` through `</h6>`		Designates text as a heading, h1 being the largest, and h6 the smallest.	25–26
		align	Sets the alignment of heading text.	27
`<head>`	`</head>`		Marks the head section of a web page.	13–14, 17
`<hr>`	None		Inserts a horizontal rule on the page.	53
		align	Establishes the alignment of the rule.	54–55
		noshade	Turns rule shading off.	56-57
		size	Sets the height (thickness) of the rule.	55–56
		width	Determines the width of the rule.	53–54
`<html>`	`</html>`		Designates a text document as an HTML file.	13
`<i>`	`</i>`		Applies italics to text within the tags.	33, 34
`<img>`	None		Inserts an image on a web page.	43–44
		align	Sets the alignment of the image.	46–50
		alt	Sets text to be displayed when a visitor mouses over an image, or images are turned off in the visitor's browser.	51–52
		border	Sets the thickness of the border around the image.	46
		hspace	Defines the amount of white space to the sides of the image.	50–52

Continued

HTML TAGS AND ATTRIBUTES

TAGS		ATTRIBUTES	DESCRIPTION	PAGE
		vspace	Defines the amount of white space above and below the image.	50–52
		src	Designates the file location where the image can be found.	44–45
		width, height	Sets the dimensions of the image.	45
<input>	</input>		Creates a form control element.	114–115
		checked	Makes a radio button or check box selected by default.	122
		maxlength	Sets the amount of text that can be entered into a form field.	117–118
		name	Designates a label for the data that is entered into a form control element.	115–116
		size	Sets the width of a text box.	117–118
		src	Establishes the file location for an image.	44–45
		type	Sets the type of form element, such as "check box."	114–115, 121
		value	Sets the value that appears in a form element by default.	118
<kbd>	</kbd>		Marks keyboard text. Typically results in text appearing monospaced.	33, 34
<li>	</li>		Designates a list item in an ordered or unordered list.	72
		type	Sets the type of symbol that will precede items in a list.	73–74

Continued

HTML TAGS AND ATTRIBUTES

TAGS		ATTRIBUTES	DESCRIPTION	PAGE
		value	Sets the starting value of the first item in a list.	78
<meta>	</meta>		Identifies properties of a document (e.g., author, expiration date, a list of key words, etc.) and assigns values to those properties.	14
		name	Identifies a property name.	
		content	Specifies a property's value.	
<noframes>	</noframes>		Designates the content to be displayed if frames are not supported by a visitor's browser.	142
<ol>	</ol>		Designates an ordered list.	74
		type	Establishes the character that will precede the first item in the list (such as "1").	73–74
		start	Sets the value of the first item in the list.	76–77
<option>	</option>		Defines menu and list form control selections.	115
		selected	Establishes the default choice in a list of options.	123
		value	Establishes the starting value for a menu.	123
<p>	</p>		Creates a paragraph.	22–23
		align	Sets the alignment of a paragraph.	23–24
<pre>	</pre>		Preserves the white space of the HTML document text in the browser window. Typically displays text with a monospaced font.	36

Continued

HTML TAGS AND ATTRIBUTES

TAGS		ATTRIBUTES	DESCRIPTION	PAGE
<samp>	</samp>		Displays sample text in monotype.	33, 34
<select>	</select>		Establishes a menu or list form control element.	115, 122–124
		name	Creates an ID for the data collected through the form.	115–116, 123
		multiple	Makes it possible to choose more than one item in a menu.	124
		size	Determines how many items are visible in the menu without scrolling.	124
<small>	</small>		Reduces the size of text by one size value.	33, 34
<span>	</span>		Typically applies inline styles to a short text string. (Generic tag.)	174
		class	Applies a name to a custom character style.	
		id	Identifies HTML elements.	68–69
<strike>	</strike>		Applies a strikethrough to text between these tags.	33, 34
<strong>	</strong>		Applies emphasis to text. Typically results in text being made boldface.	33, 34
<style>	</style>		Defines embedded style rules.	151–152
_			Designates text that should be subscript (below the baseline).	33, 34
[	]		Designates text that should be superscript (above the baseline).	33, 34
<table>	</table>		Establishes the presence of a table on the page.	86–87
		bgcolor	Sets the table background color.	87, 93

Continued

HTML TAGS AND ATTRIBUTES

TAGS		ATTRIBUTES	DESCRIPTION	PAGE
		border	Sets the table border thickness.	87–88
		bordercolor	Sets the table border color.	88
		cellpadding	Sets the space between the cell wall and the cell content.	91–92
		cellspacing	Sets spacing between adjacent cells.	91–92
		height	Sets the table height.	90
		width	Sets the table width.	90
`<td>`	`</td>`		Designates a data cell.	86
`<th>`	`</th>`		Designates a header cell.	94, 95
These attributes can be used with both the `<td>` and `<th>` tags.		align	Sets the horizontal alignment of cell content.	95–96
		valign	Sets the vertical alignment of cell content.	96
		bgcolor	Sets a cell's background color.	93
		colspan	Establishes a single cell that spans several cells below it.	98–99
		nowrap	Prevents word wrap within a cell.	97
		rowspan	Allows a single cell to span multiple rows.	98–99
		width, height	Sets the dimensions of a cell.	97
	`<textarea>`	`</textarea>`	Creates a multiline text field within a form.	115, 117, 119–120

Continued

HTML Tags and Attributes

TAGS		ATTRIBUTES	DESCRIPTION	PAGE
		name	Identifies the data gathered through the text area on the form.	115–117
		rows, cols	Establishes how many rows and columns are in the text area.	119–120
<title>	</title>		Defines the document title, displaying the text on either the title bar (Windows) or menu bar (Mac) of the browser.	14
<tr>	</tr>		Designates a table row.	95–96
		align	Sets the horizontal alignment of row content.	95–96
		valign	Sets the vertical alignment of row content.	96
		bgcolor	Sets the background color for a row.	87
<tt>	</tt>		Stands for "typewriter text," meaning monotype, and applies that format to text within the tags.	33, 34
<u>	</u>		Applies an underline to text within these tags.	33, 34
<ul>	</ul>		Sets up an unordered (bulleted) list.	72–73
		type	Sets the symbol to precede items in the list.	72–73

HTML SPECIAL CHARACTERS

This table provides a list of the ISO 8859-1 (Latin-1) characters. Numerous other character entities are available as well. For more information, check out the following URL: http://www.w3c.org/TR/html4/sgml/entities.html.

ENTITY NAME	NUMERIC CODE	DESCRIPTIVE CODE	CHARACTER
Quotation mark	&#34;	&quot;	"
Ampersand	&#38;	&amp;	&
Less-than sign	&#60;	&lt;	<
Greater-than sign	&#62;	&gt;	>
Nonbreaking space			
Inverted exclamation	&#161;	&iexcl;	¡
Cent sign	&#162;	&cent;	¢
Pound sterling	&#163;	&pound;	£
General currency sign	&#164;	&curren;	¤
Yen sign	&#165;	&yen;	¥
Broken vertical bar	&#166;	&brvbar;	¦
Section sign	&#167;	&sect;	§
Umlaut (dieresis)	&#168;	&uml;	¨
Copyright	&#169;	&copy;	©
Feminine ordinal	&#170;	&ordf;	ª
Left angle quote, guillemotleft	&#171;	&laquo;	«
Not sign	&#172;	&not;	¬

Continued

HTML Special Characters

ENTITY NAME	NUMERIC CODE	DESCRIPTIVE CODE	CHARACTER
Soft hyphen	&#173;	&shy;	-
Registered trademark	&#174;	&reg;	®
Macron accent	&#175;	&macr;	¯
Degree sign	&#176;	&deg;	°
Plus or minus	&#177;	&plusmn;	±
Superscript two	&#178;	&sup2;	²
Superscript three	&#179;	&sup3;	³
Acute accent	&#180;	&acute;	´
Micro sign (Mu)	&#181;	&micro;	µ
Paragraph sign	&#182;	&para;	¶
Middle dot	&#183;	&middot;	·
Cedilla	&#184;	&cedil;	¸
Superscript one	&#185;	&sup1;	¹
Masculine ordinal	&#186;	&ordm;	º
Right angle quote, guillemotright	&#187;	&raquo;	>>
Fraction one-fourth	&#188;	&frac14;	¼
Fraction one-half	&#189;	&frac12;	½
Fraction three-fourths	&#190;	&frac34;	¾
Inverted question mark	&#191;	&iquest;	¿
Capital A, accent grave	&#192;	&agrave;	À
Capital A, accent acute	&#193;	&aacute;	Á

Continued

HTML SPECIAL CHARACTERS

ENTITY NAME	NUMERIC CODE	DESCRIPTIVE CODE	CHARACTER
Capital A, accent circumflex	&#194;	&acirc;	Â
Capital A, tilde	&#195;	&atilde;	Ã
Capital A, umlaut mark	&#196;	&auml;	Ä
Capital A, ring (Angstrom)	&#197;	&aring;	Å
Capital AE diphthong (ligature)	&#198;	&aelig;	Æ
Capital C, cedilla	&#199;	&ccedil;	Ç
Capital E, accent grave	&#200;	&egrave;	È
Capital E, accent acute	&#201;	&eacute;	É
Capital E, accent circumflex	&#202;	&ecirc;	Ê
Capital E, umlaut mark	&#203;	&euml;	Ë
Capital I, accent grave	&#204;	&igrave;	Ì
Capital I, accent acute	&#205;	&iacute;	Í
Capital I, accent circumflex	&#206;	&icirc;	Î
Capital I, umlaut mark	&#207;	&iuml;	Ï
Capital Eth, Icelandic	&#208;	&eth;	Ð
Capital N, tilde	&#209;	&ntilde;	Ñ
Capital O, accent grave	&#210;	&ograve;	Ò
Capital O, accent acute	&#211;	&oacute;	Ó
Capital O, accent circumflex	&#212;	&ocirc;	Ô
Capital O, tilde	&#213;	&otilde;	Õ

Continued

HTML Special Characters

ENTITY NAME	NUMERIC CODE	DESCRIPTIVE CODE	CHARACTER
Capital O, umlaut mark	&#214;	&ouml;	Ö
Multiply sign	&#215;	&times;	×
Capital O, slash	&#216;	&oslash;	Ø
Capital U, accent grave	&#217;	&ugrave;	Ù
Capital U, accent acute	&#218;	&uacute;	Ú
Capital U, accent circumflex	&#219;	&ucirc;	Û
Capital U, umlaut mark	&#220;	&uuml;	Ü
Capital Y, accent acute	&#221;	&yacute;	Ý
Capital THORN, Icelandic	&#222;	&thorn;	þ
Small sharp s, German (sz) ligature)	&#223;	&szlig;	ß
Small a, accent grave	&#224;	&agrave;	à
Small a, accent acute	&#225;	&aacute;	á
Small a, accent circumflex	&#226;	&acirc;	â
Small a, tilde	&#227;	&atilde;	ã
Small a, umlaut mark	&#228;	&auml;	ä
Small a, ring	&#229;	&aring;	å
Small ae diphthong (ligature)	&#230;	&aelig;	æ
Small c, cedilla	&#231;	&ccedil;	ç
Small e, accent grave	&#232;	&egrave;	è
Small e, accent acute	&#233;	&eacute;	é

Continued

HTML SPECIAL CHARACTERS

ENTITY NAME	NUMERIC CODE	DESCRIPTIVE CODE	CHARACTER
Small e, accent circumflex	&#234;	&ecirc;	ê
Small e, umlaut mark	&#235;	&euml;	ë
Small i, accent grave	&#236;	&igrave;	ì
Small i, accent acute	&#237;	&iacute;	í
Small i, accent circumflex	&#238;	&icirc;	î
Small i, umlaut mark	&#239;	&iuml;	ï
Small eth, Icelandic	&#240;	&eth;	ð
Small n, tilde	&#241;	&ntilde;	ñ
Small o, accent grave	&#242;	&ograve;	ò
Small o, accent acute	&#243;	&oacute;	ó
Small o, accent circumflex	&#244;	&ocirc;	ô
Small o, tilde	&#245;	&otilde;	õ
Small o, umlaut mark	&#246;	&ouml;	ö
Division sign	&#247;	&divide;	÷
Small o, slash	&#248;	&oslash;	ø
Small u, accent grave	&#249;	&ugrave;	ù
Small u, accent acute	&#250;	&uacute;	ú
Small u, accent circumflex	&#251;	&ucirc;	û
Small u, umlaut mark	&#252;	&uuml;	ü
Small y, accent acute	&#253;	&yacute;	ý
Small thorn, Icelandic	&#254;	&thorn;	þ
Small y, umlaut mark	&#255;	&yuml;	ÿ

Coloring the Web

It goes without saying that all computers are not created equal. Between hardware configurations and operating systems, the endless permutations guarantee that no two visitors to a site will experience it in *exactly* the same way. Some will hit your site on a Mac, others on a PC, and some on a UNIX machine. Many visitors will browse your site using Internet Explorer, while others will use Netscape Navigator. Others still may have more exotic browsers like Opera, Amaya, or Omniweb. With all this variation, you need to create as uniform a user experience as possible. By using the truly websafe color palette when defining the various color-controlling HTML attributes, you ensure that every visitor experiences your color scheme in a similar way, if not in an identical way.

Adding color to the Web is an essential component of web design and development. It helps set the tone for the entire web site and can often provide useful navigation assistance. Adding colors that stay the same on all your users' computers, however, is trickier than it may appear. For one, you have to practically learn a whole new language called *hexadecimal* to designate colors within your HTML. And then you are limited—some would say *severely* limited—in exactly which colors you can use to guarantee that the web site will appear in a similar fashion on all of your users' computers.

HEXADECIWHAT? LEARNING HOW TO SPEAK COLOR FOR THE WEB

It's not enough just to learn one foreign language in this book (Hypertext Markup Language). If you want to use color on your web sites, you also need to learn how to speak in the Web's unique language for color. In fact, you actually need to learn three dialects, so to speak, to be able to communicate effectively:

▶ Red-green-blue (RGB)

▶ Hexadecimal

▶ Common names

RGB

Monitors define color using the RGB color model. RGB color values are actually three separate values, one each for the red, green, and blue component of a color. Operating systems like Windows and the Mac OS each have a palette of 256 colors. Each component's value is defined using a scale from 0 to 255. For example, the RGB value for black, which is the absence of color, is written 0, 0, 0 (Red = 0, Green = 0, Blue = 0), whereas the value for white is written 255, 255, 255 (Red = 255, Green = 255, Blue = 255).

If you're familiar with the printing process, it might help to compare and contrast the printing system **c**yan-**m**agenta-**y**ellow-blac**K** (CMYK) with the computer system RGB. In the CMYK printing process, you start with a white sheet of paper and add each of the four colors. If you keep adding colors, eventually, you lose all distinction between them and the whole sheet appears black. On computer monitors, you start with black (the absence of light), and you add light. When all three spigots add the maximum amount of light, you get white.

To express an RGB value for a particular shade of green, you could thus write 51, 255, 102. This approach makes perfect sense to a number of graphics programs, such as Photoshop's Color Picker in the following illustration. As if that isn't complicated enough, the web browsers don't speak straight RGB. They have their own *dialect,* so to speak, called hexadecimal. It's the same information, just presented in a different way. You can see it in the box beneath the RGB values.

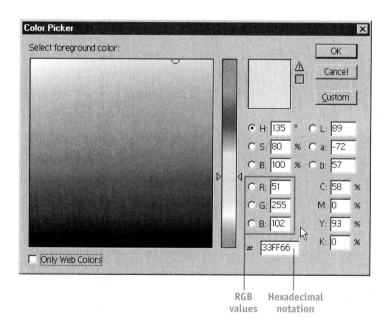

RGB values

Hexadecimal notation

HEXADECIMAL VALUES

If the previous section wasn't confusing enough, wait until you read this. The standard method of counting we are taught in elementary school is the decimal system, which is base ten. In other words, we count ten digits (0 through 9) before we roll over to the next decimal position (10 through 19).

Now, if you know any Latin, you'll recall that the prefix "dec" stands for ten. The prefix "hex" stands for six, so the word "hexadecimal" indicates six plus ten, or base sixteen. To further complicate matters, in hexadecimal notation, two digits are always used, and instead of using 10 through 15, you use the letters A through F, as the following table shows.

Base Ten	0	1	2	3	4	5	6	7	8	9	10	11	12	13	14	15
Hexadecimal	00	01	02	03	04	05	06	07	08	09	0A	0B	0C	0D	0E	0F

When you reach the sixteenth position, it's time to roll over, so you start off with a 1, just like you do after you reach 9 in regular base ten. For example:

Base Ten	16	17	18	19	20	21	22	23	24	25	26	27	28	29	30	31
Hexadecimal	10	11	12	13	14	15	16	17	18	19	1A	1B	1C	1D	1E	1F

Now, you try the next set. When you reach the thirty-second position, it's time to roll over again, so you start off with a 2, just like you do after you reach 19 in regular base ten. Complete the following table:

Base Ten	32	33	34	35	36	37	38	39	40	41	42	43	44	45	46	47
Hexadecimal																

Check your answers against this table:

Base Ten	32	33	34	35	36	37	38	39	40	41	42	43	44	45	46	47
Hexadecimal	20	21	22	23	24	25	26	27	28	29	2A	2B	2C	2D	2E	2F

These examples give you a taste of what hexadecimal notation is all about. Table B-1 is a complete listing of hexadecimal notation corresponding to the base ten digits of 0 through 255. Note that the boldfaced numbers, starting with 0, are in base ten, and the normal type starting with 00 is base sixteen. The highlighted numbers (0, 51, 102, 153, 204, and 255) and their hexadecimal equivalents formed the basis for the original websafe palette, which I'll discuss in a moment.

TABLE B-1 DECIMAL AND HEXADECIMAL NOTATION

0	1	2	3	4	5	6	7	8	9	10	11	12	13	14	15
00	01	02	03	04	05	06	07	08	09	0A	0B	0C	0D	0E	0F
16	17	18	19	20	21	22	23	24	25	26	27	28	29	30	31
10	11	12	13	14	15	16	17	18	19	1A	1B	1C	1D	1E	1F
32	33	34	35	36	37	38	39	40	41	42	43	44	45	46	47
20	21	22	23	24	25	26	27	28	29	2A	2B	2C	2D	2E	2F
48	49	50	51	52	53	54	55	56	57	58	59	60	61	62	63
30	31	32	33	34	35	36	37	38	39	3A	3B	3C	3D	3E	3F
64	65	66	67	68	69	70	71	72	73	74	75	76	77	78	79
40	41	42	43	44	45	46	47	48	49	4A	4B	4C	4D	4E	4F
80	81	82	83	84	85	86	87	88	89	90	91	92	93	94	95
50	51	52	53	54	55	56	57	58	59	5A	5B	5C	5D5	5E	5F
96	97	98	99	100	101	102	103	104	105	106	107	108	109	110	111
60	61	62	63	64	65	66	67	68	69	6A	6B	6C	6D	6E	6F
112	113	114	115	116	117	118	119	120	121	122	123	124	125	126	127
70	71	72	73	74	75	76	77	78	79	7A	7B	7C	7D	7E	7F
128	129	130	131	132	133	134	135	136	137	138	139	140	141	142	143
80	81	82	83	84	85	86	87	88	89	8A	8B	8C	8D	8E	8F
144	145	146	147	148	149	150	151	152	153	154	155	156	157	158	159
90	91	92	93	94	95	96	97	98	99	9A	9B	9C	9D	9E	9F
160	161	162	163	164	165	166	167	168	169	170	171	172	173	174	175
A0	A1	A2	A3	A4	A5	A6	A7	A8	A9	AA	AB	AC	AD	AE	AF

Continued

TABLE B-1 CONTINUED

176	177	178	179	180	181	182	183	184	185	186	187	188	189	190	191
B0	B1	B2	B3	B4	B5	B6	B7	B8	B9	BA	BB	BC	BD	BE	BF
192	193	194	195	196	197	198	199	200	201	202	203	204	205	206	207
C0	C1	C2	C3	C4	C5	C6	C7	C8	C9	CA	CB	CC	CD	CE	CF
208	209	210	211	212	213	214	215	216	217	218	219	220	221	222	223
D0	D1	D2	D3	D4	D5	D6	D7	D8	D9	DA	DB	DC	DD	DE	DF
224	225	226	227	228	229	230	231	232	233	234	235	236	237	238	239
E0	E1	E2	E3	E4	E5	E6	E7	E8	E9	EA	EB	EC	ED	EE	EF
240	241	242	243	244	245	246	247	248	249	250	251	252	253	254	255
F0	F1	F2	F3	F4	F5	F6	F7	F8	F9	FA	FB	FC	FD	FE	FF

You can use this table as a translation guide to communicate RGB values to a web browser via hexadecimal notation. To translate the RGB values for that shade of green discussed earlier, for example, just substitute the hexadecimal equivalents: 51 translates to 33, 255 translates to FF, and 102 translates to 66. Whenever you enter a hexadecimal value in HTML, you always precede it with the pound (#) sign, so this gives you a hexadecimal value of #33FF66.

That's all there is to it. That's not so bad, is it?

COMMON COLOR NAMES

Oh, and did I forget to mention that there's a much easier way of referencing colors in HTML—by their common name, such as black, white, red, etc?

Ah, yes, but all your hard work in learning RGB- and hexadecimal-speak isn't wasted. You *can* reference colors by name, but only 16 of them are likely to work like you intend, and even then, only some browsers will understand you. Like using common names for plants instead of their proper Latin names at a nursery, you may find it *easier* to use the common names of colors, but this approach is not as guaranteed to communicate your meaning. Thus, using common color names in HTML is *not* a practice that I recommend, but you are likely to come across it in the wide world of the Web, so you may find it helpful to understand the process.

As you can imagine, many designers have found that describing colors in RGB and hexadecimal notation is a cumbersome process, so they have translated them back into English in the form of common color names, also sometimes called *predefined color names*. Unfortunately, most predefined color names are not considered to be websafe. In other words, they will not appear consistently on different platforms and browsers, but will likely have color shifts. Table B-2 represents the 16 predefined colors that have commonly been considered to be websafe. As you will see in a minute, though, only six of these colors are truly websafe; they are indicated by boldface.

> **NOTE** Some additional names are recognized by Netscape Navigator but not Windows Explorer, and vice versa, so if you are going to use common names, stick to just these 16. But remember that most browsers other than Netscape Navigator and Internet Explorer don't recognize common names at all, so it's better to use hexadecimal notation.

TABLE B-2 THE 16 RECOGNIZED COLOR NAMES

COMMON NAME	HEXADECIMAL VALUE	COMMON NAME	HEXADECIMAL VALUE
black	#000000	**yellow**	#FFFF00
white	#FFFFFF	fuchsia	#FF00FF
gray	#808080	olive	#808000
red	#FF0000	teal	#008080
green	#008000	navy	#000080
blue	#0000FF	maroon	#800000
purple	#8000080	silver	#C0C0C0
aqua	#00FFFF	**lime**	#00FF00

WHICH COLORS CAN YOU USE? DEFINING WEBSAFE COLORS

How many of the millions of colors available on your computer can you use to develop successful web sites? Until recently, the answer to that question was a mere 216. These 216 colors were grouped together in what was commonly called the *websafe palette* or *browsersafe palette*. This is what I now call the *mythical websafe palette*, however, because most of those colors have been proven *not* to be websafe for a group of users who have their monitors set to display different bit depths of 256 colors, thousands of colors, and millions of colors. A miniscule subset of only 22 colors are considered to be truly websafe.

There's one bit of good news, however. You *can* create the illusion of more websafe colors by creating *hybrid websafe colors*. This tactic is possible only in the creation of web graphics, not in straight HTML, but it's worth mentioning, so I'll discuss it briefly in a moment.

THE MYTHICAL WEBSAFE PALETTE

The original websafe palette was composed of the 216 colors shared in common by the Macintosh and Windows 256-color operating systems. You can see this palette in color at Lynda Weinman's site at http://www.lynda.com or in a number of graphics and web development applications such as Photoshop, Fireworks, Dreamweaver, and GoLive. The colors are sometimes arranged differently but are, indeed, the same 216 colors. Lynda Weinman's site, for example, includes a palette arranged by hue at http://www.lynda.com/hexh.html and one arranged by value at http://www.lynda.com/hexv.html.

This original websafe palette was created using 20 percent increments of the RGB 0 through 255 scale. For example, 20 percent of 255 is 51, add another 20 percent and you get 102, then 153, 204, and finally, 255. (Note that these numbers are all multiples of 51, making them easy to recognize.) Starting with 0 gives you six possible values for each component in the RGB model, which gives you the 216 permutations (6x6x6). These numbers and their corresponding hex values are highlighted in Table B-1. Thus, most combinations of FF, 00, 33, 66, 99, and CC result in websafe colors from the original palette. If you see a color that has a 41 in it, for example, that's a strong clue that it is not websafe.

The palette was created with the intention of stabilizing the display of web colors on every user's system. This strategy still works for the most part when users have their monitors set to display either 256 colors (8-bit) or millions of colors (24-bit). It does not work, however, when users have their monitors set to thousands of colors (15-bit or 16-bit). None of the 216 original websafe colors are included in these sets of thousands of colors.

What happens when you specify a color that is not available?

▶ The browser picks the next closest color in its palette, which may not look anything at all like your original color.

▶ The browser dithers the color in an attempt to approximate the color. Browser *dithering* involves placing two or more colors side by side to try to give the illusion of a third color. Unfortunately, it often results in a speckled or dirty appearance.

Of the original 216 colors, 194 colors fail to shift consistently to an appropriate color. David Lehn and Hadley Stern can be credited with discovering these failings of the original websafe palette. See their full discussion of their research and experiments on WebMonkey at http://www.hotwired.lycos.com/webmonkey/00/37/index2a.html.

THE TRUE WEBSAFE PALETTE

David Lehn and Hadley Stern narrowed down the original websafe palette to a truly websafe palette of 22 colors. The colors are listed in Table B-3. To see them in color, visit http://www.hotwired.lycos.com/webmonkey/00/37/stuff2a/complete_websafe_216/reallysafe_palette.html.

Having a palette limited to 22 rather randomly selected colors, with a decided leaning toward green, makes it a bit difficult to design unique, attractive, compelling screens, doesn't it? Well, right in line with so many other web "solutions," you have a few options if you're willing to bend a little. Mind you, designers usually have no problem bending the rules, but realize that what's at stake here is the consistency of how your web site will be presented on your users' systems. Thus, it is inherently a usability issue, so be cautious about bending too easily—or too far.

TABLE B-3 THE TRULY WEBSAFE PALETTE

FFFFFF	FF00FF	00FFCC
FFFF33	FF0000	33FF33
CCFF66	000033	00FF00
66FF33	FFFF66	FF0033
33FFFF	FFFF00	0000FF
33FF66	66FFFF	000000
00FFFF	66FF00	
00FF66	33FFCC	

First off, understand that the key problem with the original websafe palette is that it does not display the colors properly on operating systems set to thousands of colors (16-bit). Ironically, the original websafe colors display correctly for the most part on both 256 color displays (8-bit) and millions of color displays (32-bit), catching the lowest and highest technology users. Unfortunately, however, at the time Lehn and Stern wrote their article and probably for some time to come, the lion's share of users (56 percent) had systems set to display thousands of colors. This spread makes it very difficult to ignore any one group.

In the rare cases when you are working with a controlled user base, such as developing a corporate intranet for a company that automatically sets all of its employees' monitors to 24-bit, you can design a site using that palette. In most cases, however, the user base encompasses all three levels of technology. So what can you do? I can think of only three viable solutions.

CAUTION At the time of this writing, most of the image-editing programs and web development applications are still built around the original websafe palette, so be wary of many of their devices that aim to guarantee you that a color you have chosen is websafe. Instead, build your own palette out of the 22 truly websafe colors. Their indicators that a color is not websafe, however, are still valid, because the truly websafe colors are a subset of the original websafe palette.

▶ Stick to the true websafe palette of 22 colors.

▶ Add to the true websafe palette by creating hybrid colors for graphics. (See the next section.)

▶ Design to the majority of your user base and test like crazy on the other systems to ensure that the results are acceptable. Modify them as needed.

HYBRID WEBSAFE COLORS

Hybrid colors are essentially controlled dithers. By strategically placing two or more colors next to each other, you can create the illusion of a third color. Instead of letting the browser haphazardly place swathes of colors next to each other, however, you can control this process on the pixel level within an image-editing program such as Photoshop or Fireworks. The trick is to create a pattern that looks like your desired color, as in Figure B-1, and then to fill part or all of your graphic with it. This technique works only within graphic images such as illustrations; you cannot specify a hybrid color within HTML.

> TIP **The colors in photographic images generally exceed the colors in any websafe palette, so it is best to save them as JPEG files, which rely on browser dithering.**

IN PRACTICE: USABILITY GUIDELINES FOR COLOR ON THE WEB

Most people think about color as something pretty that contributes to the aesthetic appeal of a design. The use of color in web design, however, also has some

FIGURE B-1

A 2-pixel by 2-pixel base for a hybrid color, shown at 1600 percent enlargement. When a graphic is filled with this pattern and viewed without magnification, the human eye is tricked into seeing what appears to be a third color—a blend of these two colors.

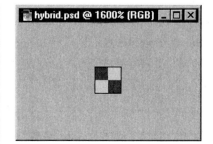

significant usability components. Generally, the easiest place to recognize this, of course, is when color is used poorly.

The use of glaring, jarring colors in bad combinations, for instance, can elicit almost a physical revulsion. If you see users pull back from looking at a screen as though trying to put as much physical distance between themselves and the web site as possible, then you have a pretty strong usability clue—unless, of course, that's the goal of the particular web site.

Conversely, if you observe users leaning in more closely to the screen with a pursed brow, squinting as they try to make out the words, you also have a usability clue. In this case, you likely have a readability problem, which may be caused by poor use of color (particularly low contrast between the text and background) or a number of other factors.

In between these extremes, however, very fine gradations exist between the effective use of color. This list provides some guidelines to follow when establishing color schemes for web sites:

▶ Use appropriate colors for the audience and the site goals.

▶ Use colors within the navigation to support the information architecture.

▶ Avoid unnecessary busyness through the over-use of color.

▶ Don't rely exclusively on color.

> **TIP** I highly recommend that you take this book with you to your computer and check out some of the web sites while reading this section. We, umm, have a little usability problem here in discussing color in a book that uses color sparingly.

USE APPROPRIATE COLORS FOR THE AUDIENCE AND THE SITE GOALS

Take advantage of some common divisions in the use of color throughout our culture, such as the use of primary colors (bright reds, blues, greens, and yellows) for kids. These colors are bright, happy, and playful. Take a look at the logo for Toys Я Us at http://www.toysrus.com for one example. Or scan a number of other kids' sites such as the following:

▶ http://www.lego.com

▶ http://www.mattel.com

▶ http://www.boowakwala.com

▶ http://www.bbc.co.uk/littlekids/

▶ http://www.barneyonline.com

The IBM shade of blue is a cultural hallmark for business, particularly professional, somewhat conservative businesses that want to elicit a sense of security. Banks, management firms, and professional services firms fall into this category. Try searching on any general business subject and glance at the home pages of the first ten entries. You might be surprised by just how many of them use predominantly blue in their design. Here are a few examples as well:

▶ http://www.ibm.com

▶ http://www.uofcfcu.com

▶ http://www.bankofamerica.com

▶ http://www.sba.gov

▶ http://www.prosavvy.com

▶ http://www.pmsinc.com

Of course, you don't need to use predominantly blue in all business web sites. This audience can also be comfortable with other sedate, harmonizing colors. Review some of these women's business sites for their use of slightly more innovative color:

▶ http://www.womensbusinesscenter.org

▶ http://www.sbaonline.sba.gov/womeninbusiness

▶ http://www.cdnbizwomen.com

▶ http://www.wyomingwomen.org

▶ http://www.graspnet.org/women.html

High-contrasting colors may be targeted at youth or young adults and can convey a jazzy sense of energy. They may also certainly target other adults, even the same ones who use the more conservative business sites. Just like there are divisions within our own lives between business and pleasure or daytime activities and nightlife, there can be divisions between color schemes that may appeal to users at different times in their day. Also, note how a number of "younger" companies or even whole industries, such as the dot-com industry, also sometimes take advantage of the energy conveyed by high-contrasting colors. *Wired Magazine*, for instance, set the tone in the early 1990s with bright, highly saturated colors. Its web site today is considerably more subdued, but it is still in the same vein. Check out some of these sites:

- http://www.wired.com
- http://www.girlshop.com
- http://forum-snowboards.com
- http://dreamworksrecords.com
- http://www.billabong-usa.com
- http://www.bonesmovie.com

And earth tones—some of my favorite color schemes—convey a much more down-to-earth attitude. As you would expect, they are used more on outdoors sites, gardening sites, environmentalist sites, or sites that convey a relaxed, week-end-like lifestyle. I encourage you to search topics or hobbies that you like to engage in on the middle of a Saturday afternoon to see if any correlations exist in color schemes. Additionally, the following sites make good use of earth-tone color schemes:

- http://www.oneworldjourneys.com
- http://www.arizhwys.com
- http://www.audubon.org
- http://www.rei.com
- http://www.archcrafters.com
- http://www.onedayhikes.com

USE COLORS WITHIN THE NAVIGATION TO SUPPORT THE ORGANIZATION OF YOUR CONTENT

The colors used within the navigation design can be immensely helpful in supporting the information architecture and the organization of the content. Color can be used to guide users around the web site, like the color-coded labels in parking garages. Assigning different colors to different sections of the site, for example, helps users to realize at a glance which section of the site they are in. A number of large retail sites employ this device, such as Amazon.com and Drugstore.com. The latter makes particularly effective use of this scheme. Visit http://www.drugstore.com to see the color at work.

The developers of Drugstore.com, for example, show all of the colors on the home page, but then in every subsection proceed to gray out all colors except the section the user is in. Amazon.com, in contrast, has removed all the section colors from the home page and employs a color only within each respective subsection. They've also run into problems, however, with the repetition of the color blue. At the time of this writing, they use a similar shade of blue for the home page, "Your Store" (the personalized portion of the site), and the electronics, music, and computers sections. Overall, I'd say that the use of color as a navigational aid has been diminished on this site to a minimal level.

Color can also help establish the priority of content on a site and can draw the eye to the most important navigation options. Take a look at the Osborne/McGraw-Hill site, for example, at http://www.osborne.com. Simple color arcs over the primary navigation buttons emphasize the importance of navigating to the books on the web site, as opposed to the less important (and less colorful) "About Us" information.

Hypertext links automatically include navigation aids that indicate with underlines and color that they are, indeed, a functional link. They also automatically change color after having been clicked on, indicating to the users that they have visited that portion of the site. Many designers lately have started changing these colors away from their defaults. This approach can cause havoc, however, with visually impaired users who may wish to have control over these options within their preference settings, so I advise against it.

Don't Overuse Color

This guideline ought to go without saying, but it's surprising how many designers out there go overboard with color on their web sites. Do not add color for color's sake. Just like all the other elements of design, each introduction of a new element should have a justifiable rationale for how it will help the user better understand a message.

DON'T RELY EXCLUSIVELY ON COLOR

This area is where print design must by necessity vary a bit from web design. In print design, you can rely exclusively on a color to impart information—as long as you avoid colors that a significant number of your audience are not color blind to. The Web, however, has a much higher percentage of users who are visually impaired, and thus, rely on elements other than your color scheme or graphics.

Additionally, you cannot control the color that is displayed on a web user's monitor with nearly the same precision as you can in print design. In print design, you can go stand by the printer and conduct press checks to confirm that the colors are exactly what you intended. Not so in web design. Even when using colors from any so-called websafe palette, many factors affect the display of colors on monitors, including the monitor's age, its manufacturer, and any adjustments made by the user.

Planning Your Web Site

A web site is more than a jumble of individual pages that have been linked together. To make a site that works well, you need to put some thought into what you're doing and why you're doing it. Believe it or not, if you've got a good handle on why you're doing something, it's easier to get a handle on what it is you have to do to make it happen.

Every good web designer takes a number of steps to ensure success. Granted, no two people are alike, and working styles vary, but the steps outlined in this appendix are a good starting point.

GROUNDWORK

Before beginning to physically build a site, you'll want to ask some basic questions:

▶ What is your site's objective?

▶ Who is your site's target audience?

▶ Which hardware and software will your visitors use to view your site?

▶ How do you want visitors to navigate your site?

▶ How will your site look?

Regardless of the size of your web site or your level of skill, you'll want to answer these questions so you can lay out a basic strategy before you start building individual pages. By doing so, you'll save a lot of time and anguish over the life of any project. By keeping a written list of your answers, you can help yourself stay focused throughout the development process.

WHAT IS YOUR OBJECTIVE?

Whether you build a site for yourself or for someone else, you'll want to determine what the site is being created for. This is not an exercise in existentialism, but in understanding the site's purpose. Is it gong to be used as an information resource? To entertain? To sell a product? Determining the site's primary objective will help you answer the questions that follow. You'd make very different design choices in creating a site for a client that sells handmade button-down Oxford shirts than you would for a site that promotes an alternative rock band.

WHO IS YOUR AUDIENCE?

As I said before, answering the previous question will certainly help in answering the rest. If you know what your site is meant to do, it isn't too hard to figure out who your audience will be, or who you'd like it to be. A site geared toward skateboarding will have a pretty specific audience, whereas a site that sells sports-wear will probably aim at a wider group of prospective visitors.

WHICH HARDWARE AND SOFTWARE WILL YOUR VISITORS BE USING?

When considering your audience, there's a lot more to think about than just who you would like to come to your site, however. You also want to know *how* they're coming to your site. Are they mostly Windows users? Mac users? Maybe Linux users? Are they likely to have really big monitors, say 19 inches or better, or 17 inches or less? Are they more likely to be using Internet Explorer or Netscape Navigator? Or are you specifically targeting Opera users? What is their average modem speed? Are you looking to attract big business users who are probably connecting from work on superfast T1 lines, or home users who might have modem speeds as slow as 28.8 Kbps?

All these issues play a role in your design decisions. Ultimately, you'll want a site that looks good to a user of any of these hardware and software configurations, but knowing these details about your audience can help you to make choices about design and what sacrifices, if any, you may have to make to deliver a site that looks good to a variety of users.

You also need to consider web browsers. The two most popular browsers on the market are Internet Explorer and Netscape Navigator, each of which has had over five different versions, and for each version, new functionality has been intro-duced. Consequently, something Internet Explorer 5.5 can do may not be possible in Internet Explorer 2.0. And you can be assured that something Netscape can do may not be possible with Internet Explorer! These inconsistencies are the bane of the web designer. Optimally, you want a site that behaves much the same way across both browsers and across multiple versions of the same browser. Because neither browser supports each new Internet technology exactly the same way, you will end up making compromises.

If you design a site that relies heavily on new technologies, like dynamic HTML, certain kinds of animation, multimedia content, or complex interactivity, chances are, you'll have trouble making your site work the way you want it to across a number of browsers. You will want to find a middle ground that provides greater accessibility to your target audience.

HOW DO YOU WANT VISITORS TO NAVIGATE YOUR SITE?

Now you want to decide if you're going to create some kind of repeated graphic navigation bar, use frames with targeted links, or use another option. Remember that a web site isn't a static object and has to do more than just be pretty. You want to make the process of finding information within your site as painless as possible.

Think about how your visitors will experience your site and how they will flow through it, moving from one piece of information to the next. The navigational elements should be easy to use and consistently placed, and content (as well as navigational elements) should provide visitors with a clear indication of where they are in your site.

HOW WILL YOUR SITE LOOK?

OK, you've figured out what this site is meant to do, you've got a handle on who your potential audience is, you know which hardware and software considerations you'll have to take into account, and you've set aside a little real estate on your PC for a local site folder and possibly even made a few folders inside it to better organize your content. Now comes the fun part: designing what the site will look like.

This step is usually referred to as creating *mock-up* pages, and these mock-ups don't have to be anything more elaborate than a drawing of what you want the various pages of your site to look like before you go and start building elements. You can lay something out on paper, or you can use your favorite graphics software to create your mock-up. The choice is yours. The object is to have a visual representation of your layout so you have something to refer to as you move through the development process. The main reason for doing this step is to help you maintain a level of consistency throughout your site. Users will tend to get confused if the look and feel of your site changes radically page by page, or if key elements like navigation links are in different locations in every page.

STORYBOARDING YOUR SITE

Before you sit down in front of the computer and start designing your pages, you need to take your visions of your individual pages and how they work together as a cohesive site, and put them on paper or onscreen so that you can review and revamp them. A good technique for performing this task is called *storyboarding*: drawing pictures that illustrate the way the site you have in mind will look and function.

You may have seen storyboards for television shows and movies. When a program is storyboarded, each scene is depicted to show where the actors will be, which camera angles will be used, even the general lighting and set design that will be used. Your web site storyboard should indicate what your pages will look like— where the text and graphics will be placed, the colors and layout you envision, etc. You should also include any notes about each page's functionality or effects you want to achieve.

Even if you're the only person involved in the design, storyboarding is still a valuable process. The storyboard lets you see, and then fix, any flaws in your overall design strategy before you've built them in HTML, which is always preferable to backing up from a problem after you've devoted considerable resources to a bad idea.

SKETCHING YOUR IDEAS

A storyboard is, traditionally, drawings or sketches of a process, whether they are on paper or in your favorite graphics program. There's no need for works of art at this stage, which is evident in Figure C-1. Now is the time to scribble, jot, or

FIGURE C-1

Choose your weapons: graph paper, index cards, computer, or cocktail napkin.

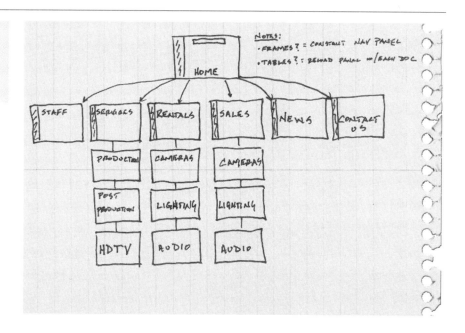

doodle, as long as you commit your ideas to writing and have something you can work from. You're developing an idea, not finishing the blueprints for the Eiffel Tower.

Once you have the basic sketches of your pages worked out, just draw lines connecting the pages, to show how each page will be linked to the rest of the site. You can indicate links to pages outside your site by simply writing the URLs of the sites that these external links will point to.

CHOOSING A STORYBOARDING MEDIUM

To create your storyboard, use any method that works for you. You can work with the traditional pen or pencil, or use your favorite graphics program. Whether you choose a default painting program that comes with your operating system or a more powerful program doesn't really matter, as seen in Figure C-2. What's important is that you do it. If you don't start with a drawing board, there's no drawing board to go back to, if you take my meaning.

I'm a big fan of pencil and paper. I can erase pencil without having to remember a menu command or keyboard shortcut, and there's no real danger that the paper

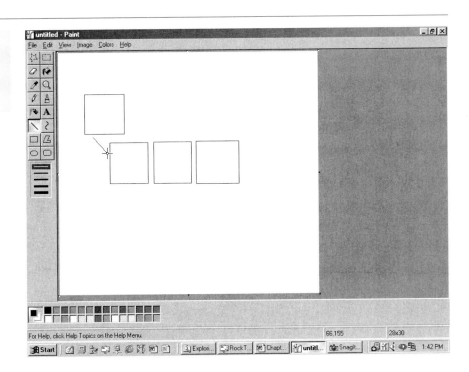

FIGURE C-2

You can use something as simple as Microsoft Paint to make a storyboard.

medium I choose will crash right when I get a brainstorm. I like to use note cards; I can jot down the basic content of a page along with any technical notes about widgets I want in the page, and I can sketch out the look of the page on the other side. Then, when I want to plan my site's navigation, I can stick the pages on a bulletin board or lay them on the coffee table in the order I envision. If something doesn't flow right, I can push the pages around until I'm satisfied.

BUILDING THE LEVEL OF STORYBOARD DETAIL

Whether you use my method or draw out a bunch of boxes all on the same sheet of paper doesn't really matter. This storyboard is yours, and you should do what works for you. Just be sure that you have enough information available to work from. You certainly don't need to write out all the text you expect to be in a particular page, but at the very least, include the name of the page and a list of its basic contents. You might sketch the basic layout, including the location of text and graphics, possibly mentioning the names of any graphics files you have in hand already, or where you're getting the text content from, as seen in Figure C-3.

This part of the storyboarding process is a precursor to the next step in the design process, which is gathering your content: that is, getting any images and text you're going to need for your site all in one place, so when you actually start building pages, you aren't scrambling for them. Storyboarding gets you thinking

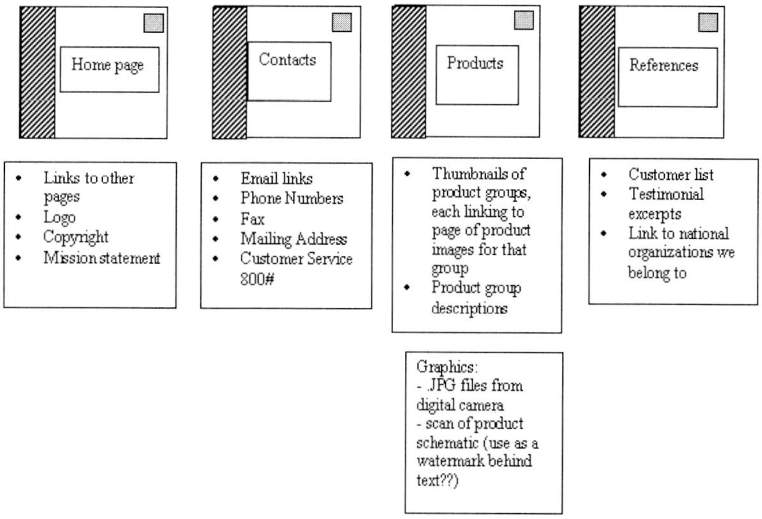

FIGURE C-3
Using the computer for your storyboard makes it easy to keep lists of topics and to insert notes as reminders.

Home page
- Links to other pages
- Logo
- Copyright
- Mission statement

Contacts
- Email links
- Phone Numbers
- Fax
- Mailing Address
- Customer Service 800#

Products
- Thumbnails of product groups, each linking to page of product images for that group
- Product group descriptions

Graphics:
- JPG files from digital camera
- scan of product schematic (use as a watermark behind text??)

References
- Customer list
- Testimonial excerpts
- Link to national organizations we belong to

about where you're going to find the content or how you're going to create the content you have in mind.

As you begin to put your ideas on paper or onscreen, the level of detail will certainly increase. By the time your storyboard is finished, a complete stranger, with no prior sense of your web site vision, should be able to see where you're going and what your site will look like, just by looking at the storyboard.

GATHERING YOUR ASSETS

After you've mocked up your basic design and know where you're going to need artwork or graphics buttons, you should create or find these elements and have them ready to go before you start building your pages.

I tend to create all of my own graphic art. My tools of choice are Adobe's Photoshop and Illustrator. If you're into graphic design, you're probably quite familiar with both packages. Lots of other tools are on the market, for example, Macromedia Fireworks, CorelDraw, or GIMP (a UNIX application). If you have any of these tools and/or you want to learn more about them, I suggest these web sites.

Manufacturers web sites include the following:

▶ http://www.adobe.com The Abobe home page, makers of Photoshop, ImageReady, Illustrator, GoLive, and Live Motion

▶ http://www.macromedia.com The Macromedia home page, makers of Dreamweaver, Flash, and Fireworks

▶ http://www.corel.com The Corel home page, makers of CorelDraw and WordPerfect

▶ http://www.gimp.org The GIMP home page

And check out these web-based tutorials:

▶ http://www.phong.com Provides some very good Photoshop tutorials

▶ http://www.fwzone.net Provides Fireworks discussions, news, and tutorials

▶ http://www.grafx-design.com/coreltut.html Provides CorelDraw tutorials

▶ http://empyrean.lib.ndsu.nodak.edu/~nem/gimp/tuts Links to the best GIMP tutorials on the Web

Sometimes I need things I can't produce. That's when I turn to these web sites:

▶ **www.eyewire.com** EyeWire

▶ **www.corbis.com** Corbis

▶ **www.photodisc.com** PhotoDisc

Each company has a vast amount of images, graphics, and fonts—both for sale as well as for free, depending on how you intend to use them.

STRUCTURING YOUR LOCAL SITE FILES

Once you're ready to sit down and start building pages, you want that computer-based work area to be well organized too. The best approach is to create one main folder in which to store all your associated files. This folder acts like a local version of your web server's root folder.

I like to keep all my HTML documents and CSS files in this root folder, and then create another folder for my image files, and then others for each different type of media I might be working with: for example, sound and video clips, as shown in Figure C-4. This way, I know where all my files are, and I don't have to think

FIGURE C-4

Make your computer mimic the web server by creating a logical file structure.

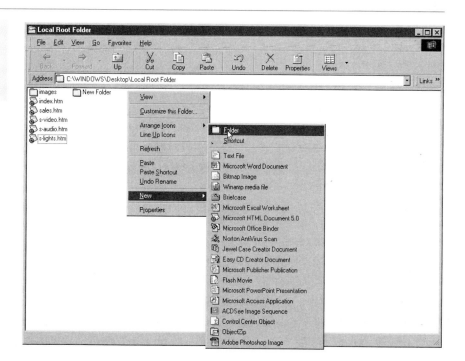

too hard when I need to create links or other references in my pages. By using document-relative pathnames for all my hyperlinks and other file references, I create a fully functioning version of the web site right on my PC that I can then transfer as a working whole straight onto the web server.

Well then, now you know what you should be thinking about before you actually start building a web site, you know how to organize the structure of the site by using a storyboard, and you know how to structure your computer to start building the site. Now all you need to do is go forth and create!

Appendix D

Uploading and Testing

Your pages are beautiful, informative, and compelling. All of your links work. Your graphic images display quickly and cleanly, and you couldn't be happier with the way your site turned out. Now what? Well, unless you want to be the only one admiring your web design handiwork, it's time to upload your site to your web server and launch into the next phase of the development process: testing.

POSTING PAGES TO THE WEB

So how do you actually get your files uploaded to your web server? In most cases, the answer is FTP software. Some great FTP programs are available as *freeware*, meaning that you can download and use them at no cost. Some are *shareware*, meaning that you can download and test them for free, but you must buy them (usually at a very low price) when the evaluation period is over. Some of the shareware programs stop working when the evaluation period is over; others keep working indefinitely. In either case, it's stealing if you keep using the shareware without paying for it.

Where do you find these programs? The Web, of course! You can go to sites like http://www.hotfiles.com or http://www.tucows.com and do a search for "FTP software," or simply search through a site like http://www.google.com or http://www.yahoo.com and use the same search criteria. The benefit of using a site like http://www.tucows.com is that you can usually get product ratings supplied by people who have already downloaded and used the software.

Once you've searched for and found a list of FTP products, pick one and click the link(s) to download it. Typically, you're downloading a self-extracting zip file or an installation/setup file that you double-click after the download is complete, at which time, the installation process begins automatically. Don't worry that you'll need any special skills to download this software—the installation process is automated, and at most, you'll be asked to enter your name and/or company name and then have to choose or approve a folder into which the program files will be copied. The questions you're asked will be clear, and when the software is installed and ready for use, you'll see a prompt telling you that.

USING FTP SOFTWARE

FTP software works by connecting you to a web server via the File Transfer Protocol. Once you've uploaded your site files to the server, your pages are available to the browsing public.

To connect to an FTP site, you need three pieces of information:

▶ The FTP site name/location, such as ftp.hostname.com. Your FTP hostname and web site hostname are usually the same.

▶ A user ID. This ID is assigned by the site administrator. If you have your own web server, you can create user IDs for anyone who needs access to the FTP site. Most user IDs are from four to eight characters long, with no punctuation or spaces.

▶ A password. The password is associated with the user ID and works only for that ID. A password makes it possible for different people to maintain different sites on the same server, and/or to maintain different parts of the same site. Passwords should be at least four characters long, and they should be something that only the user knows. Security for web servers is very important, especially if you're tracking visitor data, selling products directly through your web site, or storing potentially sensitive information in a database that your site accesses.

Once you have these three pieces of information, you can set up an FTP connection through the software. As shown in Figure D-1, you'll fill out a simple form that contains all the information needed about the FTP connection and your access to it.

After you've defined the required information, you can then connect to the server. Of course, you must be online before you can do this. Assuming you're online, in most cases, you'll simply double-click an icon representing the FTP site you want to connect to, or you'll click once on the site by name and click a Connect button. Figure D-2 shows a connection being made.

As the connection is being made, you'll see a progress report of sorts—the status of each part of the connection process is documented in the window. When a

FIGURE D-1

Tell the FTP software all about your intended FTP connection.

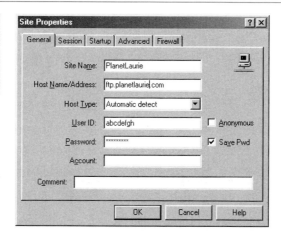

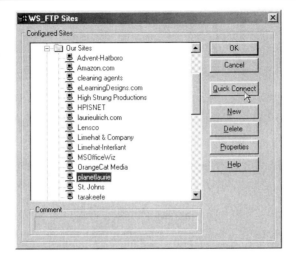

connection is completed, the word "Connected" or something similar (it varies by application) appears, and you know you're connected to the FTP site.

Most FTP applications offer a two-sided window. One side displays the folders and files that are on your local hard disk, and the other side displays the folders and files on the web server. To use the window, click files on your local drive and either drag them over to the FTP site side of the window, or click a button to indicate that the selected local files need to be copied to the remote FTP location. Of course, you can also go the other way—copy files from the web server down to your local drive. Figure D-3 shows a group of selected web page files ready for copying to the FTP site.

FIGURE D-3

Press and hold the CTRL key as you select multiple files to be uploaded.

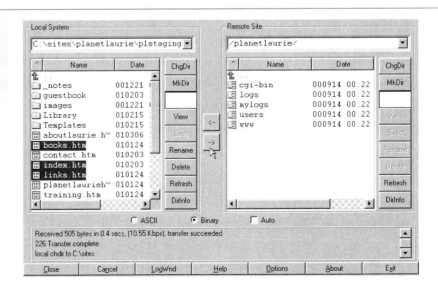

ORGANIZING YOUR FILES ON THE WEB SERVER

When you upload your files, be sure to maintain the same folder structure you have on your local drive. In other words, if you have page files in the site's root folder and graphics in an images folder, you should make sure the page files are in the site root folder and the graphics are in an images folder on the server, too. Why is this important? Because you need to maintain the same path relationships between your files. If the files are not in the same relative places on the server, the paths are invalidated, and the browser won't find linked pages and graphics where it's told to look for them.

The process of establishing identical folder hierarchies on both your local drive and the web server is not complex or difficult. When I connect to the web server for the first time and the root directory is completely empty, I select the entire contents of the folder I have acting as my local root directory and transfer it in a single shot. This way, the whole site is copied at once to the web server, preserving all my link relationships.

Sometimes, however, trying to move a big site over a slow connection prevents me from being able to accomplish this task. Not to worry. FTP software offers tools for creating folders, so you can create the appropriate folders on your web server and then transfer your local site files over in manageable chunks. Figure D-4 shows the Windows Explorer view of a site's folders and files.

FIGURE D-4

A site's folders as stored on the local drive.

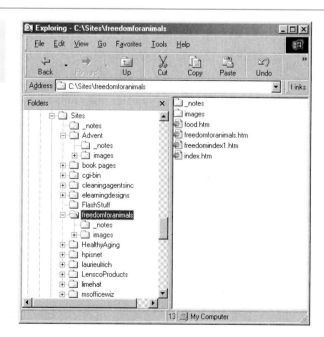

This structure is the same one that exists in the view of a web server shown in
Figure D-5.

Extra files or folders may exist on either the local drive or on the web server for
a variety of reasons. The key is to make sure that if your page files are in the site
root folder on the local drive, they're in the site root folder on the web server; and
that if you store your pictures in an images folder inside your local root folder, you
copy them to an images folder in the root directory of the web server.

TESTING YOUR WEB SITE

Once you've uploaded your web site to a server, do you think you're done with
the project? Not on your life. Before you announce the launch of your web site to
the entire world, I highly recommend testing it—thoroughly. And I recommend
testing it for two purposes: to make sure that everything is working technically, as
well as to make sure that the final product actually meets your planning goals.

Testing is not a task that you should leave entirely to the end of the project. As is the
case for much of web development, testing is an iterative process. You test a little
here, a little there, make some changes, and test again; you then conduct one final,
big test at the very end of development, prior to launching the site. Large web teams
even have dedicated testing staff, but this fact never takes the HTML developer off

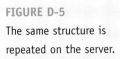

FIGURE D-5
The same structure is
repeated on the server.

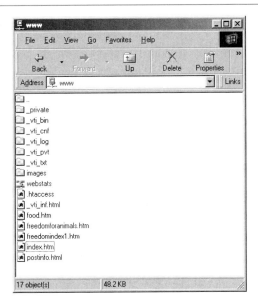

the hook. Each member of the team is responsible for conducting preliminary tests of his or her pages to make sure that they work like they're supposed to.

In general, you should start every testing session with broad, sitewide issues and then narrow your focus down to the nitty-gritty details on each page. It's far too easy to get caught up in the little details and miss something big—far too easy—and the consequences can be far too serious as well. Most project managers don't like to hear excuses along the lines of "Oops, wasn't that content supposed to be on this page?" Yet, stupid mistakes such as mixing the content up or using old versions of documents happen far too frequently.

TESTING EQUIPMENT

Keep in mind that your typical work computer may well not be what the web site visitors will be using to view your site. Ideally, you should test on all the browsers, operating systems, screen resolutions, and bandwidths that your visitors are likely to have. Now, you may not just happen to have that full range of equipment on hand, unless you're a very rare bird. Some web development companies have testing rooms set up for this purpose with a broad range of computer hardware and software or even rent such facilities on an as-needed basis.

If you're on your own, however, or with a very small team, you may need to scrounge around a bit. Some good places to look for this variety of equipment include your friends and family, of course—don't you just love them?!—as well as public Internet access points such as libraries, Internet cafes, and sometimes even shopping malls. And then, of course, a really valuable source is your users themselves. This way, you can combine user feedback with the technical side of testing.

With every testing situation, however, follow the pattern of testing from broad to specific issues.

TESTING TOOLS

You may be glad to hear that you don't need to conduct *all* of the web site testing by hand. A number of free services exist, as well as some fee-based services, that can do a lot of the legwork for you. Code validators, for example, have saved millions of hours of tedious review and probably caught more mistakes than most human effort, especially those little mistakes that actually may not cause a problem in some browsers, such as no closing tags. The validators are designed in such a way that they can identify any aspect of your code that does not fully comply with the latest standard. A number of web authoring tools have built-in validators. The World Wide Web Consortium (W3C) also offers two key validators for free:

▶ HTML validator at http://validator.w3.org

▶ CSS validator at http://jigsaw.w3.org/css-validator

A number of web development tools, such as Macromedia's Dreamweaver, offer a browser check as well, which checks your site performance on whichever browsers (and versions of browsers) you specify that your target audience will be using. Take advantage of these tools. They can provide very valuable information and help you considerably in spotting trouble areas for your site. However, do not exclusively rely on them. They are still no substitute for actually testing on the operating systems and platforms of your intended audience.

SITEWIDE TESTING ISSUES

Some key areas to test for on a sitewide basis are consistency and performance. Ask yourself the questions in the following sections.

DOES THE SITE APPEAR CONSISTENTLY IN TARGET BROWSERS AND OPERATING SYSTEMS?

Sometimes, if you've developed a site exclusively in one browser such as Internet Explorer, it will look terrific in that browser and just awful in another, such as Netscape Navigator. This problem can occur in part because the browsers' vendors have frequently developed *proprietary* tags—tags that will work only in their browser and that have not been adopted by other browsers or included in the HTML standards issued by the W3C. Fortunately, this problem is decreasing as the W3C standards are becoming stronger and the competing browser companies are agreeing to increase their support of those standards with each new release. This solution does not solve the problem for older browsers, however, which are still commonplace among users.

A few web authoring tools are also biased toward one browser over another. This fact has been particularly true in the past for Microsoft products, such as FrontPage and Word, being biased in favor of Microsoft's Internet Explorer.

If you run into this problem, follow these guidelines:

▶ Determine whether the web site features that you want are supported by all targeted browsers. In general, avoid any markup that is not cross-browser compatible. In some cases, however, you may decide to leave the feature in for users with one browser if it will not hurt the display for other browsers.

▶ Check the code for browser proprietary tags, and delete them or replace them with fully supported tags whenever possible.

▶ Confirm that your code conforms to the latest standard: for example, with the eXtensible Hypertext Markup Language (XHTML) 1.1 standard, all tags need to be closed. Don't be sloppy; stay up to date with the latest standards. Adhering to them will ensure that the web sites you build today will still work tomorrow.

IS THE NAVIGATION CONSISTENT THROUGHOUT THE SITE?

A web site's navigation design should have logic and structure that is upheld throughout the site so that at any point, users can identify where they are on the site and what their options are. If you have global navigation (such as a nav bar with links to each of the major sections of the web site) on some pages but not on others, or if you change the global navigation options available to the users, you will be bound to confuse and frustrate the user. Having to use the browser's Back button or go to the home page every time you want to explore a new area is a sign of poor navigation.

Subsections of the site, however, may certainly add a secondary navigation scheme so that users can easily decide between the options available to them in that section. This design should not, however, replace the global scheme.

Another tip is to develop HTML templates for coding each page, which can be very helpful even on small sites—and is fairly essential on large sites. *HTML templates* are similar to word processing or spreadsheet templates. If you are going to write a bunch of letters, for example, you would save time by creating a word processing template that included your company logo and return address so that you would not have to retype that information in each new letter.

In the same vein, when you are creating a web site, often many elements are shared in common on each page, such as the global navigation bar. Thus, you can save a lot of time if you create a template with those elements already in place, which you then use to build out each page. On large sites with a number of different sections, you may also benefit from creating a new template for each section: for example, a blue one for the section that has a blue tab, a red one for the section with a red tab, etc.

In addition to streamlining the production, templates help you build the web site correctly in the first place because they ensure consistency. Additionally, however, they give you a standard to check against during the testing phase. In that case, you need to follow these guidelines:

▶ Confirm that each section follows the site template.

▶ Confirm that each page follows the section template.

IS THE LOOK AND FEEL CONSISTENT AND APPROPRIATE FOR THE AUDIENCE?

No matter how large a web site is, it should have a consistent look and feel throughout all its sections if it is to establish a strong identity. Although each sub-section can also have distinct identifiers, such as the use of colors or icons that are unique to that section, they should be integrated with the overall site design. You can conform to this rule by creating HTML templates and writing down a set of design guidelines for the site, often called a *style guide,* before the HTML development process begins. The style guide may include such elements as the typefaces, sizes, and styles to be used in the heads, the colors chosen for each section, and specifications about how the company logo can or cannot be used. By spelling out the details of the design ahead of time, all members of the web development team can refer to it and check their work against it throughout the production process.

The look and feel of a site also needs to be appropriate for the content and audience. A conservative business such as a bank, for instance, that needs to convey a sense of trustworthiness and security to its consumers, would not be served very well by highly saturated neon colors with fast-moving animations that promote excitement and surprise. Those design elements might be more appropriate for an adventure sports site targeted at youth. (See Appendix B for more information about the use of color.)

Thus, the first step of this review stage is to confirm that each page conforms to the style guide and templates. If variations in the site's look and feel exist between testing systems, use the following guidelines:

▶ Check the monitor bit depth or color settings to confirm that it matches your target audience. For example, in designing a site for users who have their monitors set to thousands of colors, the colors may appear differently on monitors set to 256 colors or millions of colors.

▶ Confirm that you are using only truly websafe colors, particularly if your site needs to appear the same at all three common bit depths.

IS THE BACKGROUND COLOR CONSISTENT?

If the background color in particular varies between testing machines, check the following:

▶ Confirm that the background color is specified in the HTML. Relying on the browsers' default background colors may produce variations. For example, Internet Explorer's typical default for the background color is white, while Netscape Navigator's is gray.

▶ Confirm that the code is correct and that all tags have been closed.

DOES EACH SECTION CONTAIN THE CORRECT CONTENT?

Step back from the close work you have been doing in programming the pages and look at each one from a user's perspective to make sure the right material actually appears under the right heads:

▶ Review the content list to confirm that each page has the correct information in the correct places.

▶ Verify that nothing is missing altogether from the web site.

DOES THE SITE MAP CORRECTLY REFLECT THE STRUCTURE OF THE SITE?

Site maps, which give a visual overview of the entire site, can change a lot during the course of production. Before launching a site, it's essential to confirm that the final, published site map does indeed correctly reflect the structure of the final version of the site and all documentation. Thus, you must follow these guidelines at this stage:

▶ Check the site map against the actual site.

▶ Check the site map against the final information architecture plans or flowcharts, just in case the site has been built incorrectly.

> **TIP** See Appendix C on web site planning for more information on the creation and use of site maps.

DO ALL PAGES LOAD?

This test is good to conduct while you are confirming the site map because it involves clicking through to every single page:

▶ Confirm that the links to each page work.

▶ Confirm that the pages are in the intended locations as per the information architecture and site plan.

▶ Confirm that no pages are missing.

SPECIFIC PAGE TESTING

To test for some key areas on a page-by-page basis, ask yourself the questions in the following sections.

DO THE TITLES APPEAR CORRECTLY AT THE TOP OF THE BROWSER?

Titles are an often-overlooked piece of the coding, especially the deeper you go into a site. But titles are one of the very first elements that users see in the browser. Users rely on titles to provide valuable information about where they are in a site, so be sure to check the following three aspects.

▶ Confirm that the title tag is completed for each page.

▶ Confirm that the code is correct so that the title displays properly.

▶ Confirm that the text for each title accurately and succinctly describes the contents of the page.

ARE THE meta TAGS COMPLETE?

Unlike titles, users never even see the meta tags, but they can be inadvertently influenced by them nonetheless. Whenever a user conducts a search on the Web, many search engines use whatever you include in your meta tags to determine whether to recommend that site to the user and how high to rank it. Many developers include appropriate meta tags on the home page document but then forget to include them when new material is introduced on subsequent pages. You don't want to make that mistake, so make sure you follow these guidelines:

▶ Confirm that the code is present.

▶ Confirm that the code is correct.

▶ Confirm that the key words are an accurate reflection of the web site content.

DOES THE PAGE DOWNLOAD QUICKLY?

Ideally, each page should download in *less* than ten seconds on your target users' systems. Any longer, and you risk losing the users' attention and causing frustration. (Ten seconds gives users a lot of opportunity to click away to another site.) Too often, web site developers conduct all their work on computers that have high-bandwidth connections, so they may never even notice if particular pages are performing sluggishly. There's nothing quite like actually trying to use your own site on the lowest bandwidth that your users will have to drive home what that actual experience of the web site will be like.

If you find that any pages are loading slowly, take care of the following three items:

▶ Minimize the size of graphics and other media.

▶ Clean up the code.

▶ Optimize the server. Sometimes, the problem is not with the web site at all, but with the server. You may need to discuss this possibility and its solutions with the system administrator.

> **TIP** For more information and guidance on optimizing your web site, see Jason Cook's "Site Optimization Tutorial" on the WebMonkey site at http://hotwired.lycos.com/webmonkey/design/site_building/tutorials/tutorial2.html.

ARE THE MOST IMPORTANT ELEMENTS ON EACH PAGE VISIBLE BEFORE SCROLLING?

Test this guideline on the lowest screen resolution that your userbase will have, commonly 640 × 480 or 800 × 600, with the browsers set to their default preference settings. All of the primary navigation and content of your web page should be readily visible at this setting. Users tend not to scroll to see which other information or options may be available on a page, particularly the home page. They strongly prefer to be able to assess the site and make their decision about where they'd like to go at a glance.

Consider each of the following guidelines:

▶ Review the layout of elements on each page to ensure optimum presentation.

▶ Confirm that the table widths accommodate this lowest common denominator.

▶ Confirm that the image heights and widths are appropriate for this page size.

▶ Replace fixed-width tables with relative-width ones whenever possible, to provide maximum flexibility for users who drag the corners of their browser windows to make them even smaller than the default settings.

DOES RESIZING THE BROWSER WINDOW ADVERSELY AFFECT THE PAGE OR INDIVIDUAL ELEMENTS?

Have you ever been looking at a web site and decided to resize the window on your desktop, only to find that the page goes haywire? That's what this check is for. This medium is interactive, and users may do all sorts of things to your site that you haven't planned for, like resizing the browser window. Fortunately, for the most part, this problem does not occur with HTML-only pages. It occurs more frequently with pages that use the positioning capabilities of cascading style sheets (CSS) coupled with JavaScript to create dynamic content, also referred to as dynamic HTML (DHTML). Therefore, you need to test for this problem only on sites that use more advanced technologies.

DOES THE CORRECT VERSION OF THE PAGE DISPLAY IN THE BROWSER?

Ah, this is the dreaded "version control" monster. Web pages go through many iterations during the development process, and, if you're not careful, you can easily lose track of which version is, indeed, the most current one. This issue is largely about management, and you just need to cross-check files.

Sometimes, however, you can make changes to a file, and then look at it again in the browser and find yourself staring at an old version. If you run into this problem, take the following steps:

► Double-check that you saved the corrected file.

► Try reloading the file into the browser using the Browser button.

► If that does not work, clear the browser cache and reload the page or even just restart the browser.

DOES UNWANTED CONTENT (SUCH AS CODE) APPEAR ON ANY PAGE?

"@o!pfthhhth!!!" Have you ever seen bizarre bits of text appear on your web page that you just wanted to curse back at? It happens to the best of us, but of course, the very best of us make sure that it is eliminated before the web page goes live. To find and destroy such invaders, do the following:

► For whole pages that have gone nuts, confirm that the document has been saved with an .htm or .html extension.

► Confirm that the document is saved as text-only. Some programs that can nominally convert files to HTML, such as Word, save all sorts of other strange directions within the file, which can be the source of all sorts of problems, including this one. You can get rid of all that information just by saving the file as text-only.

► Check for unclosed tags, which is probably the source of the problem if the previous two guidelines are met. In particular, watch out for tags that appear to be closed but that are missing the final backslash, such as `<p> <p>` instead of `<p> </p>`.

IS THE SOURCE CODE WELL COMMENTED IN PREPARATION FOR MAINTENANCE?

This aspect of web development may not impact the user experience, but maintenance can strongly impact the maintenance and revision of a web site. If you have well-commented code, you can save hours of tedious, eyestraining labor trying to find which bit of code needs to be updated. This fact is particularly true of complex tables or frames. If nothing else, label all your tables and frames with descriptive titles such as "main navigation" or "lower right-hand frame."

Even if you will be the one doing all the maintenance on a site, you may forget over time just how you set something up. That's how our memories work. A detail may be crystal clear one day, and then need to be completely rediscovered another.

You need do only two checks:

▶ Confirm that comments are present.

▶ Confirm that comments are informative and correct.

IS THE TEXT CONTENT READABLE?

This aspect is a major usability issue for the Web. Requiring users to read off monitors is already a liability because it can induce such eyestrain. Presenting users with unreadable type, however, can be a sure way to lose them. You must design the site so that the text will be readable. Designating all the type, for example, to be 6 point Times may look cool, but many of your users will just not be able to read the words. See what I mean? It's essential to design the site from the ground up to be easily readable.

If the site is fully readable on one system but not on another, however, follow these guidelines:

▶ Check the monitor bit depth. A shift in colors between, say, using 256 colors or thousands of colors may reduce the contrast between the type and its backgrounds, making it hard to distinguish the letters.

▶ Check the monitor gamma settings. Gamma controls the range of midtones on a monitor, so different gamma settings can alter the contrast, making grays fade into blacks, etc., and thus making it hard to distinguish the letters. Unfortunately, Macintosh monitors out of the box typically have a darker gamma setting (1.8) than Windows and UNIX machines (2.2 to 2.5), so if possible, you should design your site to work within a gamma range of 1.8 to 2.5. Some image-editing programs such as Photoshop include a gamma control panel and enable you to toggle between Mac and PC gamma settings. Alternatively, you can reset the monitor to its default settings, which will reset a Mac monitor to 1.8 and a PC to somewhere in the range of 2.2 to 2.5. Check your monitor reference guide for individual instructions.

▶ Check the browser's font settings. Some users change the default font preferences in their browsers. In general, you should test each site using default settings because most users do *not* alter them.

▶ Check the specified font settings in the web page. When designating any font other than the fonts automatically installed with an operating system, you can't confirm that every user will have your preferred fonts installed on his or her system. Therefore, you should always include one of the default fonts in your list of font choices and test the appearance of the site with each font you've suggested.

DOES TEXT APPEAR IN THE DESIRED FONT?

If you know that the computer you are testing on has your designated font installed but that the web page is still not using it, check the following:

▶ Confirm that the code is correct.

▶ Confirm that the font name is spelled correctly.

DO ALL SPECIAL CHARACTERS APPEAR?

If you've specified a special character such as a copyright symbol or accent, but it is not appearing correctly on the page, check the following:

▶ Confirm that the entity begins with an ampersand (&) and ends with a semicolon (;).

▶ Confirm the browser support. See Appendix A for a list of commonly supported special characters.

DO ANY UNWANTED CHARACTERS APPEAR IN THE TEXT?

Unwanted characters (such as □ or Ü) often appear in the text if you have typed a special character into the code, such as ©, without coding it as a special character. Check the following:

▶ Confirm that the desired special characters are designated correctly in the code.

▶ Confirm that the document has an .html or .htm extension.

▶ Confirm that the document is saved as text-only.

Do All Page Elements Load?

Broken image icons never add much beauty to a page. If graphic or multimedia files fail to load properly, look into the following:

▶ Confirm that the code is correct.

▶ Confirm that the links are correct.

▶ Confirm that the files are in the correct place.

▶ Confirm that filenames are consistent.

▶ Confirm that the file types are web viewable (e.g., GIF, JPEG).

▶ Confirm that the necessary plug-ins are installed.

Do Page Elements Load in the Appropriate Order?

One sure way to slow down the performance of a web page is to have each of the elements load inconsistently so that the browser has to load all the pieces and then redraw the page to fit. This problem is what is happening when you think a web page has loaded but suddenly, the whole page disappears and then eventually reappears. There's one key guideline for this problem:

▶ Verify that all element sizes are specified in HTML. If you omit the height and width attributes, the browser does not know how much space to reserve on the page for that element, so it has to load everything, analyze the dimensions of the file, and then redraw the page accordingly, slowing the process way down.

Do Unwanted Dashes Appear by Linked Images?

This problem is simple and has a simple fix:

▶ Delete all the carriage returns within image tags so that the code is on a single line. For some unknown reason, the carriage returns cause unwanted dashes in some browsers.

Are the alt Attributes for Each Element Working?

The chief culprit for this problem is usually that the developer forgot to code alternative text for each graphic or media element. Providing alternative text is becoming increasingly important. Visually impaired users, in particular, rely on these descriptions (which are often read to them through smart browsers) to understand what is included on a page. But they are not the only ones; anyone who has graphics turned off can also at least read the text so they know what is supposed to be in that spot. And, of course, if there are ever any problems with a file, alternative text provides any user with that information. Use these guidelines:

▶ Confirm that the code is present.

▶ Confirm that the code is correct.

ARE ALL THE LINKS WORKING PROPERLY?

You must constantly check this area even *after* you launch your web site. A web site's internal links are unlikely to change unless someone on your team intentionally changes them while updating a site, but external links can frequently change. You have no control over web sites other than your own, but you do have an obligation to your users to make sure that your links stay current. Occasionally, of course, a server will go down, and a web site will disappear for a period of hours or even days, so you may not be able to avoid having a deadend link for that period. However, to have a page full of deadend links simply because you have not maintained your site will detract from the sense of reliability for the whole web site. Fortunately, much of this task can be automated, at least the identification of broken links. However, you do need to supply the information to correct any broken links:

▶ Confirm that the code is correct.

▶ Confirm that linked pages exist in the place where you have linked to.

DO ALL SCRIPTS WORK?

Finally, if your site includes scripts such as rollovers or scripts to process forms, you must confirm that each one of them works as intended. Programming such scripts is certainly beyond the HTML you have learned in this book, but you can still help determine whether they are working properly:

▶ Check the browser settings to confirm that the scripting language has been enabled.

▶ Confirm that the script works as intended.

TESTING CHECKLIST

Use the following testing checklist whenever you get to the testing stage of the web site development process. Feel free to photocopy it and keep a stack handy for your personal use.

TABLE D-1 WEB SITE TESTING CHECKLIST

		TESTING SYSTEM SPECS. OPERATING SYSTEM: _____ BROWSER: _____ SCREEN RESOLUTION: _____ BANDWIDTH: _____	TESTING SYSTEM SPECS. OPERATING SYSTEM: _____ BROWSER: _____ SCREEN RESOLUTION: _____ BANDWIDTH: _____
Sitewide Checks	Does the site appear consistently in target browsers and operating systems?		
	Is the navigation consistent throughout the site?		
	Is the look and feel consistent and appropriate for the audience?		
	Is the background color consistent?		
	Does each section contain the correct content?		
	Does the site map correctly reflect the structure of the site?		
	Do all pages load?		

Continued

TABLE D-1 WEB SITE TESTING CHECKLIST

		TESTING SYSTEM SPECS. OPERATING SYSTEM: _____ BROWSER: _____ SCREEN RESOLUTION: _____ BANDWIDTH: _____	TESTING SYSTEM SPECS. OPERATING SYSTEM: _____ BROWSER: _____ SCREEN RESOLUTION: _____ BANDWIDTH: _____
Page-by-Page Checks	Do the titles appear correctly at the top of the browser?		
	Are the meta tags complete?		
	Does the page download quickly? (Ideally in less than ten seconds on your target user's system)		
	Are the most important elements on each page visible before scrolling?		
	Does resizing the browser window adversely affect the page or individual elements?		
	Does the correct version of the page display in the browser?		
	Does unwanted content (such as code) appear on any page?		
	Is the source code well commented in preparation for maintenance?		

Continued

TABLE D-1 WEB SITE TESTING CHECKLIST

		TESTING SYSTEM SPECS. OPERATING SYSTEM: _____ BROWSER: _____ SCREEN RESOLUTION: _____ BANDWIDTH: _____	TESTING SYSTEM SPECS. OPERATING SYSTEM: _____ BROWSER: _____ SCREEN RESOLUTION: _____ BANDWIDTH: _____
Page-by-Page Checks	Is the text content readable?		
	Does text appear in the desired font?		
	Do all special characters appear?		
	Do any unwanted characters appear in the text? (such as □ or Ü)		
	Do all page elements load? (including any multimedia)		
	Do page elements load in the appropriate order?		
	Do unwanted dashes appear by linked images?		
	Are the alt attribute tags working for each element?		
	Are all the links working properly?		
	Do all scripts work?		

Index

SYMBOLS

<!-- --> (comment tags)
   about HTML, 16–17
   problems in XHTML,
      192–193
" (quotation marks)
   including for attributes,
      191–192
   omitting for attributes, 16
(pound sign)
   linking to named
      anchor, 68
   preceding CSS class name
      with, 150
& (ampersand)
   in HTML and XHTML, 192
   preceding character entities
      with, 38
. (period), separating CSS
      selector and class
      name with, 149
.. (dots), in document-relative
      pathname, 64
- (hyphens), adding spaces
      to named anchors
      with, 68
/ (forward slash), in
      pathnames, 65
; (semicolon), following
      character entities
      with, 38
_ (underscore), adding spaces
      to named anchors
      with, 68

A

<a> tags
   hypertext reference (href)
      and, 60–61
   name attribute of, 67–68

absolute bottom, 50
absolute keyword for
      position property,
      175–176
absolute pathnames
   about, 45, 62
   linking files to other servers,
      63, 65
absolute scale for font sizes,
      30, 158
action attribute of <form>
      tag, 113
align attribute
   for <hr> tag, 54–55
   for <img> tag, 46–50
   for <p> tag, 23–24
   for <table> tag, 88–90, 95
   for <tr> and <td> tags, 95
alignment
   baseline, descenders, and
      absolute bottom, 50
   of cells and rows, 95–96
   centering images with <div>
      tag, 50
   horizontal rules, 54–55
   paragraphs, 23
   of text with CSS text-align
      property, 164
alink attribute of <body>
      tag, 66
alphabetical lists, 76
alt attribute for <img> tag, 51,
      52, 53
alternative text for images,
      51–52
ampersand (&)
   in HTML and
      XHTML, 192
   preceding character entities
      with, 38

anchors
   <a> tag and, 60–61
   named, 67–68
Andreessen, Marc, 3, 5
applets, 5
ARPANET, 2, 3–4
attributes
   including quotation marks
      for, 191–192
   omitting quotation marks
      for, 16
   single-word attribute values
      in XHTML and
      HTML, 192
   syntax for, 15–16
   See also specific attributes
auto keyword for overflow
      property, 182

B

background attribute for
      <table> tags, 93
background-attachment
      property, 161
background-color
      property, 160
background-image
      property, 160
background-position property,
      161–162
background-repeat property,
      160–161
backgrounds
   CSS properties for
      background-attachment
         property, 161
      background-color
         property, 160
      background-image
         property, 160

background-position
property, 161–162
background-repeat
property, 160–161
table
setting color setting for, 87
tiling image across, 93–94
base data type, 186–187
<basefont> tag, 30
baseline, 50
BBEdit text editor, 9
Berners-Lee, Tim, 3
bgcolor attribute for <table> tags,
87, 93
<blockquote> tags, 36–38
body element, 14
<body> tags
alink attribute, 66
CSS parent/ child relationship
and, 156–157
link attribute, 66
text attribute of, 32
vlink attribute, 66
border area of box properties,
165, 166
border attribute
for <frameset> tag, 136–137
for <img> tag, 46, 66–67
for <table> tag, 87–88, 92–93
for <tr> and <td> tags, 87–88
border properties
border widths, colors, and
styles, 167
margins, 169
setting width, height, float,
and clear properties,
167–169
border styles, 167
bordercolor attribute
for <frameset> and <frame>
tags, 138
for tables, 88

borders
formatting
frameset document,
135–138
table, 87–88
setting CSS properties for
boxes, 166–169
specifying CSS border
properties of element
box, 166–169
See also border attribute;
border properties
bottom property, 179
box properties, 165–166
about, 165–166
border properties, 166–167
illustrated, 166
padding properties, 166

 tag, 24–25
browsers, 5–8
about frames-based web
pages, 130
accommodating older, 141–142
choosing and downloading,
7–8
defining window by pixel
values, 132
development of, 3, 5–6
how they work, 6–7
importance of closing tags
for, 16
pros and cons of frames,
142–143
providing alternative text for
images, 51–52
setting frames using
percentage values, 13
support of CSS layer content
specifications, 174–175
testing XML code in, 189
tiling image across table
background, 93–94

web addresses and
hyperlinks, 60
See also Microsoft Internet
Explorer; Netscape
Navigator
bullet styles for lists, 73–74

C

capitalization styles, 164
cascading style sheets (CSS),
145–170
about, 146
box properties, 165–166
about, 165–166
border properties, 166–167
illustrated, 166
margin properties, 169
padding properties, 166
classification properties,
169–170
display property, 169–170
list-style-image
property, 170
list-style-position
property, 170
list-style-type property, 170
white-space property, 169
color and background
properties, 159–162
about, 159
background-attachment
property, 161
background-color
property, 160
background-image
property, 160
background-position
property, 161–162
background-repeat
property, 160–161
color property, 159–160

contextual selectors, 148

creating layered content, 174–175

CSS-Positioning properties, 175–182

CSS-Positioning standard, 172–173

declarations, 147–148

font properties, 157–159

  <font> tag and, 157

  font-family property, 157–158

  font-size property, 158

  font-style property, 158–159

  font-variant property, 159

  font-weight property, 159

HTML text formatting vs., 20

ID classes, 149–150

selector classes, 149

standard classes, 149

style classes, 148

style properties, 153–157

  color values, 155–156

  length values, 154–155

  parents and children, 156–157

  percentage values, 155

  units of measure, 153–154

  URLs, 156

syntax for style rules, 147

text properties, 162–165

  about, 162

  letter-spacing property, 163

  line-height property, 165

  text-align property, 164

  text-decoration property, 163

text-indent property, 164–165

  text-transform property, 164

  vertical-align property, 163–164

word-spacing property, 162–163

types of, 150–153

  embedded style sheets, 151–152

  imported style sheets, 153

  inline styles, 151

  linked style sheets, 152

  overview, 150–151

case sensitivity, 16, 190–191

cellpadding attribute, 91–92

cells

  adding spacing to table borders, 92–93

  aligning, 95–96

  nowrap attribute, 97

  padding and spacing of, 91–92

  spanning rows and columns, 98–99

  table headers, 94–95

  vertical alignment, 96

  width and height, 97

cellspacing attribute, 91–92

centering images, 50

CGI (Common Gateway Interface), 108

character entities, 38–39

check boxes, 121

child elements, 156–157

classes. *See* style classes

classification properties, 169–170

  display property, 169–170

  list-style-image property, 170

  list-style-position property, 170

  list-style-type property, 170

  white-space property, 169

clear property, 168–169

client side, 6

client/server relationship, 6–7

clipping area for layers, 183

closing tags

  importance of, 16

  syntax for XHTML and HTML, 191

color

  bgcolor attribute for <table> tags, 87, 93–94

  CSS color values, 155–156

  CSS properties for background-color property, 160

    color property, 159–160

  default text, 32

  formatting hyperlink, 66

  setting for borders

    CSS, 167

    HTML tables, 88

color attribute

  for <font> tag, 31

  Internet Explorer proprietary, 56

cols attribute

  for <frameset> tags, 132

  for text areas, 119–120

colspan attribute, 98–99

columns in frameset documents, 132

comment tags (<!-- -->)

  about HTML, 16–17

  problems in XHTML, 192–193

Common Gateway Interface (CGI), 108

container tags, 15

content area of box properties, 165, 166

contextual selectors, 148

coordinate properties for CSS-Positioning, 177–188

copyright insignia, 38, 39

creating
    e-mail links, 69
    layered content, 174–175
    named anchors, 67–68
CSS. *See* cascading style sheets
.css file extension, 152
CSS-Positioning properties,
    175–182
    about, 175
    coordinate, 177–188
    defining layer dimensions, 180
    overflow, 182
    position, 175–177
    visibility, 181
    z-index, 181–182
CSS-Positioning standard,
    172–173

D

<dd> tag for definitions in list,
    72, 82–83
declarations
    as part of CSS style rule, 147
    syntax and function of,
        147–148
    XML element and entity, 187
default text color, 32
definition lists, 81–83
    <dd> and <dt> tags with, 72,
        82–83
    <dl> tags for, 72
    illustrated, 72
    uses for, 82
descenders, 50
DHTML (dynamic HTML), 181
dimensions
    defining layer, 180
    values for setting frame and
        frameset, 133–134
directory name in URLs, 61–62
display property, 169–170

<div> tags
    <span> and, 174
    centering images with, 50
<dl> tags, 72, 82–83
    <dd> and <dt> tags with, 72,
        82–83
    illustrated, 72
    uses for, 82
document header, 13–14
document type definitions
    (DTDs), 187–189
document-relative pathnames, 45,
    63–65
documents, 12–18
    body element, 14
    case sensitivity, 16
    closing tags, 16
    comment tags, 16–17
    embedding CSS style sheets in
        HTML, 151–152
    example of simple, 12–13
    frameset, 130–140
        defining columns and
            rows, 132
        defining pixel values,
            132–133
        formatting borders,
            135–138
        illustrated, 130
        mixed value settings for
            frame dimensions, 134
        nesting framesets, 134–135
        percentage values for
            setting frame
            dimensions, 133
        relative values for frame
            dimensions, 133–134
        setting frame margins,
            138–140
        setting scroll bar
            properties, 138

head element, 13–14
<html> tags, 13
recognizing XML, 189
style sheet, 152
syntax
    for HTML, 14–15
    for XML, 188–189
    tags and attributes, 15–16
    <title> tags, 14
dots (..) in document-relative
    pathname, 64
downloading browsers, 7–8
drop-down menus, 122–124
<dt> tag for definition list terms,
    72, 82–83
DTDs (document type
    definitions), 187–189
dynamic HTML (DHTML), 181

E

element declarations, 187
elements, 15
Emacs text editor, 9
e-mail links, 69
embedded style sheets, 151–152
empty tags
    defined, 15
    <img> tag, 43
    syntax for XHTML and
        HTML, 191
entity declarations, 187
evolution of, 190
eXtensible Hypertext
    Markup Language.
    See XHTML
eXtensible Markup Language.
    See XML

F

face attribute of <font> tag,
    27–29, 157

fields
  file, 124–125
  hidden, 125
  password, 119
  text
    size and maxlength
      attributes for,
      117–118
    value attributes for, 118
file field form control, 124–125
file structure, 44
filenames in URLs, 61, 62
files
  .css, 152
  linking to other servers, 63, 65
  structure of, 44
float property, 168
font properties, 157–159
  <font> tag and, 157
  font-family property, 157–158
  font-size property, 158
  font-style property, 158–159
  font-variant property, 159
  font-weight property, 159
<font> tag, 27
  font properties for CSS and, 157
  See also fonts
font-family property, 157–158
fonts
  absolute and relative scale for
    sizes, 30
  color attribute for, 31
  controlling default text
    color, 32
  face attribute, 27–29
  <font> tag, 27, 157
  overview, 27
  properties for cascading style
    sheets, 157–159
    font-family property,
      157–158

font-size property, 158
font-style property,
  158–159
font-variant property, 159
font-weight property, 159
serif and sans-serif, 28
setting page base, 30
size attribute, 29–31
font-size property, 158
font-style property, 158–159
font-variant property, 159
font-weight property, 159
form controls, 114–116
  defined, 112
  file field, 124–125
  hidden fields, 125
  name attribute for,
    115–116
  for text boxes, 116–120
  type attributes for,
    114–115
<form> tag, 113–114
  action attribute, 113
  method attribute,
    113–114
formatting
  check boxes, 121
  file fields, 124–125
  hidden fields, 125
  hyperlinks, 65–67
    controlling image-link
      borders, 66–67
    examples of, 65–66
    link colors, 66
  menus and lists, 122–124
  precedence of in style sheets,
    150–151
  radio buttons, 121–122
  submit and reset buttons, 126
  tables, 87–99
    alignment, 88–90

background colors and
  images, 93–94
borders and border colors,
  87–88
cell and row width and
  height, 97
cell padding and cell
  spacing, 91–92
cell spacing and borders,
  92–93
dimensions of, 90
headers, 94–95
hierarchy of formatting, 87
nowrap attribute, 97
row and cell alignment,
  95–96
spanning rows and
  columns, 98–99
vertical alignment, 96
text, 21–39
  block quotes, 36–38
  CSS vs. HTML, 20
  example for, 20–22
  <font> tag, 27
  headings, 25–27
  nesting tags, 34–35
  overview, 19
  paragraphs, 22–25
  physical and logical styles,
    32–34
  preformatted text, 35–36
  special characters, 38–39
text boxes, 116–120
  overview, 116–117
  password fields, 119
  text areas, 119–120
  text fields, 117–118
forms, 107–127
  coding example for,
    108–112
  form controls, 114–116

defining type attribute,
114–115
name attribute, 115–116
<form> tag, 113–114
action attribute, 113
method attribute, 113–114
formatting
check boxes, 121
file fields, 124–125
hidden fields, 125
menus and lists, 122–124
radio buttons, 121–122
submit and reset
buttons, 126
text boxes, 116–120
graphic images for submit
buttons, 126–127
overview, 108
forward slash (/) in pathnames, 65
frame margins, 138–140
<frame> tags
bordercolor attribute for, 138
frameborder attribute for,
135–136
marginwidth and
marginheight attributes
for, 138–140
noresize attribute for, 137
scrolling attribute for, 138
using, 130–131
frameborder attribute for
<frameset> and <frame>
tags, 135–136
frames, 129–143
about frames-based web
pages, 130
accommodating older
browsers, 141–142
frameset documents, 130–140
defining columns and
rows, 132

defining pixel values,
132–133
formatting borders, 135–138
<frameset> and <frame>
tags, 130–131
mixed value settings for
frame dimensions, 134
nesting framesets, 134–135
percentage values, 133
relative values for frame
dimensions, 133–134
setting frame margins,
138–140
setting scroll bar
properties, 138
illustrated, 130
linking between, 140–141
setting base target, 141
special target names, 141
targeting frames, 140
overview, 129
pros and cons of, 142–143
frameset documents, 130–140
defining
columns and rows, 132
pixel values, 132–133
formatting borders, 135–138
illustrated, 130
mixed value settings for frame
dimensions, 134
nesting framesets, 134–135
percentage values for setting
frame dimensions, 133
relative values for frame
dimensions, 133–134
setting
frame margins, 138–140
scroll bar properties, 138
<frameset> tags
border attribute for, 136–137
bordercolor attribute for, 138

cols and rows attributes of, 132
frameborder attribute for,
135–136
using, 130–131
FTP sites for browser software,
7–8
future of HTML, 185–193
common syntax of XHTML
and HTML, 190–193
last version of, 185–186
XHTML, 190
XML and, 186–189

G

GIF image format, 42–43
graphic images for submit
buttons, 126–127

H

<h1> through <h6> tags
defined, 25–26
using id attribute with, 68–69
hanging indents, 164–165
head element, 13–14
headings
<h1> through <h6> tags for,
25–26
using id attribute with, 68–69
height attribute
for <img> tag, 45
for <table> tag, 90
for <td> tag, 97
height property for CSS element
box, 168
hidden fields, 125
hidden keyword for overflow
property, 182
horizontal rules, 53–57
about, 53
adjusting width, 53–54
aligning, 54–55

<hr> tag for, 53
noshade attribute, 56–57
setting size, 55–56
hostname, 61
<hr> tag, 53–57
    about horizontal rules, 53
    align attribute for, 54–55
    noshade attribute for, 56–57
    size attribute for, 55–56
    width attribute for, 53–54
href attribute
    of <a> tag, 60–61
    of <link> tag, 152
hspace attribute for <img> tag,
        50–51, 52
HTML (Hypertext Markup
        Language), 2–10,
        185–193
    browsers and, 3, 5–8
    cascading style sheets, 145–146
    common syntax of XHTML
        and, 190–193
        attribute quotation marks,
            191–192
        case sensitivity, 16,
            190–191
        closing tags, 191
        empty tags, 191
        id attribute, 193
        single-word attribute
            values, 192
        special characters, 192–193
    documents, 12–18
        <title> tags, 14
        body element, 14
        case sensitivity, 16
        closing tags, 16
        comment tags, 16–17
        example of simple, 12–13
        head element, 13–14
        <html> tags, 13

    syntax for, 14–15
    tags and attributes, 15–16
    evolution of Web, 2–4
    history of Internet, 2
    hyperlinks and, 60
    last version of, 185–186
    markup and markup
        languages, 4–5
    text editors and, 8–10
    text formatting vs. cascading
        style sheets, 20
    XHTML, 190
    XML and, 186–189
<html> tags, 13
hyperlinks, 59–69
    <a> tags and hypertext
        reference, 60–61
    about, 60
    creating e-mail links, 69
    formatting, 65–67
        controlling image-link
            borders, 66–67
        examples of, 65–66
        link colors, 66
    named anchors, 67–68
        about, 67
        creating, 67–68
        linking to, 68
        using id attribute, 68–69
    overview, 59–60
    parts of URLs, 61–62
    pathnames, 62–65
        absolute, 62–63
        relative, 45, 63–65
Hypertext Markup Language. *See*
        HTML
hypertext reference (href), 60–61
Hypertext Transfer Protocol
        (HTTP), 3
hyphens (-), adding spaces to
        named anchors with, 68

I

id attribute
    for <h1> through <h6> tags,
        68–69
    syntax for XHTML and
        HTML, 193
ID classes, 149–150
<img> tag
    about, 43–44
    align attribute for, 46–50
    alt attribute, 51–52
    border attribute for, 46, 66–67
    centering images, 50
    hspace and vspace attributes
        for, 50–51, 52
    src attribute, 44–45
    width and height attributes
        for, 45
imported style sheets, 153
inheritance of styles, 156–157
inline styles
    applying to tags, 151
    positioning with <div> tag, 175
inserting images, 43–53
    adjusting vertical and
        horizontal spacing,
        50–51, 52
    alternative text, 51–52
    attributes for aligning images,
        46–50
    centering images, 50
    defining source of image,
        44–45
    GIF and JPEG image formats,
        42–43
    <img> tag, 43–44
    setting image width and height
        attributes, 45
    specifying border width, 46
    as table backgrounds,
        93–94

Internet, 2–4
  evolution of Web, 2–4
  FTP and FTP sites, 8
  history of, 2
  Web vs., 3
  See also web sites; WWW
Internet Explorer. *See* Microsoft
      Internet Explorer
ISO-Latin-1 code, 38

J

JavaScript
  evolution of, 5
  resources on, 181
JPEG image format, 42–43

K

keywords
  absolute, 175–176
  auto, 182
  defined, 155
  hidden, 182
  relative, 176
  scroll, 182
  static, 177
  visible, 182
  See also CSS-Positioning
      properties

L

layers, 171–183
  <div> and <span> tags, 174
  controlling overflow of, 182
  creating layered content,
      174–175
  CSS-Positioning, 172–173
  defining clipping area for, 183
  overview, 171–172
  positioning elements, 175–182
    about, 175

coordinate, 177–188
defining layer
    dimensions, 180
position, 175–177
visibility, 181
z-index, 181–182
leading, 165
left property, 177–178
length values, 154–155
letter-spacing property, 163
<li> tags
  for list items, 72
  modifying bullet style for,
      73–74
  value attribute for ordered
      lists, 78
line breaks, 24–25
line-height property, 165
link attribute of <body> tag, 66
<link> tag, 152
linked style sheets, 152
linking
  files to other servers, 63
  between frames, 140–141
    setting base target, 141
    special target names, 141
    targeting frames, 140
  to named anchors, 68
  See also hyperlinks
lists, 71–83
  definition, 81–83
    <dd> and <dt> tags with,
      72, 82–83
    <dl> tags for, 72
    illustrated, 72
    uses for, 82
  general uses for types of, 82
  nesting, 79–81
    ordered, 80–81
    unordered, 79–80

ordered, 74–78
  illustrated, 72
  start attribute for, 76–77
  value attribute for, 78
  types of, 72
  unordered, 72–74
list-style-image property, 170
list-style-position property, 170
list-style-type property, 170
logical styles
  defined, 32–33
  physical vs., 34
  tags for, 33
lossless and lossy compression
      methods, 42
lowercase alphabetical lists, 76
lowercase Roman numeral lists,
      75

M

mailto: protocol, 69
marginheight attribute for
      <frame> tags, 138–140
margins
  frame, 138–140
  margin area of box properties,
      165, 166
  setting for border of element
      box, 169
marginwidth attribute for
      <frame> tags, 138–140
markup and markup languages,
      4–5
  See also HTML; XHTML;
      XML
maxlength attribute for text field
      form control, 117–118
menus and lists, 122–124
<meta> tag, 14
metalanguages, 186

method attribute of <form> tag,
113–114
Microsoft Internet Explorer
development of, 5–6
downloading, 8
proprietary color attribute
of, 56
single version installations
for, 7
support of CSS layer content
specifications, 174–175
testing XML code in, 189
tiling image across table
background, 93–94
mixed value settings for frame
dimensions, 134
Mosaic, 5

N

name attribute
of <a> tag, 67–68
for form controls, 115–116
named anchors, 67–68
about, 67
creating, 67–68
linking to, 68
using id attribute, 68–69
Navigator. *See* Netscape Navigator
NCSA (National Center for
Supercomputing
Applications), 3
nesting
framesets, 134–135
lists, 79–81
ordered, 80–81
unordered, 79–80
tables, 99–105
tags for text formatting, 34–35
Netscape Navigator
downloading, 8
evolution of, 5

having multiple versions of, 7
support of CSS layer content
specifications, 174–175
testing XML code in, 189
tiling images for, 94
no frames content concept,
141–142
noresize attribute for <frame>
tag, 137
noshade attribute for <hr> tag,
56–57
Notepad text editor, 8
nowrap attribute, 97
numbered lists. *See* ordered lists

O

<ol> tags, 72, 74–78
example of coding for, 74
illustrated, 72
modifying numbering styles
for, 74–76
start attribute, 76–77
value attribute for, 78
ordered lists, 74–78
coding example for <ol>
tags, 74
illustrated, 72
modifying numbering styles
for, 74–76
nesting, 80–81
start attribute, 76–77
uses for, 82
value attribute for, 78
overflow property, 182

P

<p> tags, 22–23
padding
of cells, 91–92
padding area of box
properties, 165, 166

paragraphs, 22–25
adding <p> tags, 22–23
aligning, 23
line breaks, 24–25
parent/child relationship in
cascading style sheets,
156–157
password fields, 119
pathnames, 62–65
absolute
about, 45, 62
linking files to other
servers, 63
defined, 44
relative
about, 45, 63
document-relative
pathnames, 45, 63–65
site root-relative
pathnames, 45, 65
percentage values
as CSS style property, 155
for frame dimensions, 133
period (.), separating CSS selector
and class name with, 149
physical styles
defined, 32
listing of, 33
logical vs., 34
pixel values, 132–133
position property, 175–177
pound sign (#)
linking to named anchor, 68
preceding CSS class name
with, 150
<pre> tag
avoiding tab spaces inside, 36
preformatted text with, 35–36
preformatted text, 35–36
properties of cascading style sheets
classification, 169–170

color and background,
159–162
CSS-Positioning, 175–182
about, 175
coordinate, 177–188
defining layer
dimensions, 180
overflow, 182
position, 175–177
visibility, 181
z-index, 181–182
defined, 147–148
font, 157–159
style, 153–157
text, 162–165

Q

quotation marks (")
including for attributes,
191–192
omitting for attributes, 16

R

radio buttons, 121–122
rel attribute of <link> tag, 152
relative keyword for position
property, 176
relative pathnames
about, 63
document-relative pathnames,
45, 63–65
site-root relative pathnames,
45, 65
using within own web site, 65
relative scale for font sizes, 30
relative values for frame
dimensions, 133–134
reset buttons, 126
right property, 179–180
Roman numeral lists, 75

rows, 94–99
aligning, 95–96
defining for frameset
documents, 132
formatting cells to span
columns and, 98–99
nowrap attribute, 97
table headers, 94–95
vertical alignment, 96
width and height, 97
rows attribute
for <frameset> tags, 132
for text areas, 119–120
rowspan attribute, 98–99
rules. *See* horizontal rules;
style rules

S

sans-serif, 28
scroll bar properties, 138
scroll keyword for overflow
property, 182
scrolling attribute for <frame>
tags, 138
selector, 147
selector classes, 149
semicolon (;), following character
entities with, 38
serif, 28
server side, 6
servers, linking files to other, 63
SGML (Standard Generalized
Markup Language), 186
shareware, 9
SimpleText text editor, 9
site-root relative pathnames, 45, 65
size attribute
absolute and relative scale for
font sizes, 30
of <font> tag, 29–31

for <hr> tag, 55–56
for text field form control,
117–118
spaces
adding to named anchors, 68
avoiding tab spaces inside
<pre> tags, 36
<span> tags, 174
special characters in XHTML
and HTML, 192–193
src attribute for <img> tag, 44–45
stacking order, 181
standard classes, 149
Standard Generalized Markup
Language (SGML), 186
start attribute for <ol> tags,
76–77
static keyword for position
property, 177
strings, 15
style classes
defined, 148
ID, 149–150
selector, 149
standard, 149
style properties, 153–157
color values, 155–156
length values, 154–155
parents and children, 156–157
percentage values, 155
units of measure, 153–154
URLs, 156
style rules
defined, 147
style classes, 148–150
style sheets
defined, 147
types of, 150–153
See also cascading style sheets
<style> tag, 152

submit buttons
    formatting, 126
    graphic images for, 126–127
syntax
    for CSS style rules, 147
    declarations in cascading style
        sheets, 147–148
    document, 14–15
    e-mail links, 69
    example of simple document,
        12–13
    named anchor, 67
    nesting tags for text
        formatting, 34–35
    tag and attribute, 15–16
    XHTML and HTML,
        190–193
        attribute quotation marks,
            191–192
        case sensitivity, 16,
            190–191
        closing tags, 191
        empty tags, 191
        id attribute, 193
        single-word attribute
            values, 192
        special characters, 192–193
    XML document, 188–189

T

table data (<td>) tags, 86–87
table header (<th>) tags, 94–95
table row (<tr>) tags, 86
<table> tags
    align attribute for, 88–90, 95
    border attribute for, 87–88,
        92–93
    cellpadding attribute, 91–92
    cellspacing attribute, 91–92
    height and width attributes
        for, 90

using, 86–87
valign attribute for, 96
tables, 85–105
    formatting row and cell
        properties, 94–99
        nowrap attribute, 97
        row and cell alignment,
            95–96
        spanning rows and
            columns, 98–99
        table headers, 94–95
        vertical alignment, 96
        width and height, 97
    formatting table properties,
        87–94
        background colors and
            images, 93–94
        cell padding and cell
            spacing, 91–92
        cell spacing and borders,
            92–93
        hierarchy of formatting, 87
        setting border colors, 88
        table alignment, 88–90
        table borders, 87–88
        table dimensions, 90
    nesting, 99–105
    overview, 85–86
    <table>, <tr>, and <td> tags
        for, 86–87
tags
    <a>, 60–61
    applying inline styles to, 151
    attributes, 15–16
    <blockquote>, 36–38
    <body>, 32

, 24–25
    closing, 16, 191
    comment, 16–17, 192–193
    container, 15

contextual selectors within
    cascading style
    sheets, 148
<dd>, 72, 82–83
defined, 4–5
<div>, 174
<dl>, 72, 82–83
<dt>, 72, 82–83
empty, 15
<font>, 27
<form>, 113–114
<frame>, 130–131
<frameset>, 130–131
<h1> through <h6>, 25–26
<html>, 13
<img> tag, 43–52
<li>, 72
<link>, 152
logical style, 33
<meta>, 14
nesting, 34–35
<ol>, 72, 74–78
<p>, 22–23
physical style, 33
<pre>, 35–36
<span>, 174
<style>, 152
<table>, 86–87
<td>, 86
<th>, 94–95
<title>, 14
<tr>, 86
<ul>, 72–74
targeting
    defined, 140
    setting base target, 141
    special target names, 141
<td> tag, 86
    align attribute for, 95–96
    border attribute for, 87–88
    colspan attribute, 98–99

nowrap attribute, 97
rowspan attribute, 98–99
valign attribute for, 96
width and height attributes
    for, 97
terminal interfaces, 2
text, 21–39
    block quotes, 36–38
    cascading style sheets vs.
        HTML text
        formatting, 20
    creating bulleted lists, 73–74
    example for formatted, 20–22
    fonts
        color attribute for, 31
        controlling default text
          color, 32
        face attribute, 27–29
        <font> tag, 27
        overview, 27
        setting page base, 30
        size attribute, 29–31
    foreground color for, 159
    headings, 25–27
    nesting tags, 34–35
    numbered lists, 72, 74–78
    overview, 19
    paragraphs, 22–25
        adding <p> tags, 22–23
        aligning, 23
        line breaks, 24–25
    physical and logical styles,
        32–34
    preformatted, 35–36
    special characters, 38–39
text attribute for <body> tag, 32
text boxes, 116–120
    overview, 116–117
    password fields, 119

text areas, 119–120
text fields, 117–118
text editors, 8–10
    BBEdit, 9
    Emacs, 9
    Notepad, 8
    SimpleText, 9
    TextPad, 8–9
    vi, 9
text fields
    size and maxlength attributes
        for, 117–118
    value attributes for, 118
text properties, 162–165
    about, 162
    letter-spacing property, 163
    line-height property, 165
    text-align property, 164
    text-decoration property, 163
    text-indent property, 164–165
    text-transform property, 164
    vertical-align property, 163–164
    word-spacing property,
        162–163
text-align property, 164
text-decoration property, 163
text-indent property, 164–165
TextPad text editor, 8–9
text-transform property, 164
<th> tags, 94–95
tiling image across table
        background, 93–94
<title> tags, 14
tokens, 15
top property, 178
<tr> tags, 86
    align attribute for, 95–96
    border attribute for, 87–88
    valign attribute for, 96
trademark symbol, 38

type attribute
    for <style> and <link> tags,
        152
    defining form controls with,
        114–115
    modifying
        bullet style with, 73–74
        numbers for ordered
          lists, 74–76

U

<ul> tags, 72–74
underscore (_), adding spaces
        to named anchors
        with, 68
uniform resource locators.
        See URLs
units of measure, 153–154
UNIX text editors, 9
unordered lists, 72–74
    <ul> tag for, 72
    modifying bullet style in,
        73–74
    nesting, 79–80
    uses for, 82
uppercase alphabetical lists, 76
uppercase Roman numeral
        lists, 75
URLs (uniform resource locators)
    CSS style properties for, 156
    defined, 44
    directory name in, 61–62
    filenames in, 61, 62
    hostname in, 61
    parts of, 61–62
    placing in anchors, 60–61

V

valign attribute for <table>, <td>,
        and <tr> tags, 96

value attribute
    for <ol> tags, 78
    for text areas, 120
    for text field control, 118
values for CSS, 147–148
vertical alignment for rows
        and columns, 96
vertical-align property,
    163–164
vi text editor, 9
visibility property, 181
visible keyword for overflow
        property, 182
vlink attribute of <body> tag, 66
vspace attribute for <img> tag,
    50–51, 52

W

web address. *See* URLs
web server, 6
web sites
    about frames-based pages, 130
    accommodating older
        browsers, 141–142
    downloading browsers
        from, 7–8
    evolution of WWW, 2–4
    for JavaScript and
        DHTML, 181
    pros and cons of frames,
        142–143
    See also browsers

white space
    controlling amount of, 50–51
    CSS white-space property, 169
width attribute
    for <hr> tag, 53–54
    for <img> tag, 45
    for <table> tag, 90
    for <td> tag, 97
width property, 168
word-spacing property, 162–163
World Wide Web. *See* WWW
wrap attribute for text areas, 120
WSYIWYG (What You See Is
        What You Get)
        editors, 10
WWW (World Wide Web)
    about frames-based web
        pages, 130
    accommodating older
        browsers, 141–142
    development of browsers, 3,
        5–6
    evolution of, 2–4
    Internet vs., 3
    See also browsers; web sites

X

x-axis
    defined, 172
    illustrated, 173
XHTML (eXtensible Hypertext
        Markup Language)
    about, 190

common syntax of HTML
    and, 190–193
    attribute quotation marks,
        191–192
    case sensitivity, 16,
        190–191
    closing tags, 191
    empty tags, 191
    id attribute, 193
    single-word attribute
        values, 192
    special characters, 192–193
XML (eXtensible Markup
        Language)
    about, 190
    case sensitivity in, 16
    document type definitions
        (DTDs), 187–189
    evolution of XHTML, 190
    improvements on HTML,
        186–189
    recognizing documents, 189

Y

y-axis
    defined, 172
    illustrated, 173

Z

z-axis
    defined, 172
    illustrated, 173
z-index property, 181–182

INTERNATIONAL CONTACT INFORMATION

AUSTRALIA
McGraw-Hill Book Company Australia Pty. Ltd.
TEL +61-2-9417-9899
FAX +61-2-9417-5687
http://www.mcgraw-hill.com.au
books-it_sydney@mcgraw-hill.com

CANADA
McGraw-Hill Ryerson Ltd.
TEL +905-430-5000
FAX +905-430-5020
http://www.mcgrawhill.ca

GREECE, MIDDLE EAST,
NORTHERN AFRICA
McGraw-Hill Hellas
TEL +30-1-656-0990-3-4
FAX +30-1-654-5525

MEXICO (Also serving Latin America)
McGraw-Hill Interamericana Editores S.A. de C.V.
TEL +525-117-1583
FAX +525-117-1589
http://www.mcgraw-hill.com.mx
fernando_castellanos@mcgraw-hill.com

SINGAPORE (Serving Asia)
McGraw-Hill Book Company
TEL +65-863-1580
FAX +65-862-3354
http://www.mcgraw-hill.com.sg
mghasia@mcgraw-hill.com

SOUTH AFRICA
McGraw-Hill South Africa
TEL +27-11-622-7512
FAX +27-11-622-9045
robyn_swanepoel@mcgraw-hill.com

UNITED KINGDOM & EUROPE
(Excluding Southern Europe)
McGraw-Hill Publishing Company
TEL +44-1-628-502500
FAX +44-1-628-770224
http://www.mcgraw-hill.co.uk
computing_neurope@mcgraw-hill.com

ALL OTHER INQUIRIES Contact:
Osborne/McGraw-Hill
TEL +1-510-549-6600
FAX +1-510-883-7600
http://www.osborne.com
omg_international@mcgraw-hill.com

WARNING: BEFORE OPENING THE DISC PACKAGE, CAREFULLY READ THE TERMS AND CONDITIONS OF THE FOLLOWING COPYRIGHT STATEMENT AND LIMITED CD-ROM WARRANTY.

Copyright Statement

This software is protected by both United States copyright law and international copyright treaty provision. Except as noted in the contents of the CD-ROM, you must treat this software just like a book. However, you may copy it into a computer to be used and you may make archival copies of the software for the sole purpose of backing up the software and protecting your investment from loss. By saying, "just like a book," The McGraw-Hill Companies, Inc. ("Osborne/McGraw-Hill") means, for example, that this software may be used by any number of people and may be freely moved from one computer location to another, so long as there is no possibility of its being used at one location or on one computer while it is being used at another. Just as a book cannot be read by two different people in two different places at the same time, neither can the software be used by two different people in two different places at the same time.

Limited Warranty

Osborne/McGraw-Hill warrants the physical compact disc enclosed herein to be free of defects in materials and workmanship for a period of 60 days from the purchase date. If you live in the U.S. and the CD included in your book has defects in materials or workmanship, please call McGraw-Hill at 1-800-217-0059, 9 A.M. to 5 P.M., Monday through Friday, Eastern Standard Time, and McGraw-Hill will replace the defective disc. If you live outside the U.S., please contact your local McGraw-Hill office. You can find contact information for most offices on the International Contact Information page immediately following the index of this book, or send an e-mail to omg_international@mcgraw-hill.com.

The entire and exclusive liability and remedy for breach of this Limited Warranty shall be limited to replacement of the defective disc, and shall not include or extend to any claim for or right to cover any other damages, including but not limited to, loss of profit, data, or use of the software, or special incidental, or consequential damages or other similar claims, even if Osborne/McGraw-Hill has been specifically advised of the possibility of such damages. In no event will Osborne/McGraw-Hill's liability for any damages to you or any other person ever exceed the lower of the suggested list price or actual price paid for the license to use the software, regardless of any form of the claim.

OSBORNE/McGRAW-HILL SPECIFICALLY DISCLAIMS ALL OTHER WARRANTIES, EXPRESS OR IMPLIED, INCLUDING BUT NOT LIMITED TO, ANY IMPLIED WARRANTY OF MERCHANTABILITY OR FITNESS FOR A PARTICULAR PURPOSE. Specifically, Osborne/McGraw-Hill makes no representation or warranty that the software is fit for any particular purpose, and any implied warranty of merchantability is limited to the 60 days duration of the Limited Warranty covering the physical disc only (and not the software), and is otherwise expressly and specifically disclaimed.

This limited warranty gives you specific legal rights; you may have others which may vary from state to state. Some states do not allow the exclusion of incidental or consequential damages, or the limitation on how long an implied warranty lasts, so some of the above may not apply to you.

This agreement constitutes the entire agreement between the parties relating to use of the Product. The terms of any purchase order shall have no effect on the terms of this Agreement. Failure of Osborne/McGraw-Hill to insist at any time on strict compliance with this Agreement shall not constitute a waiver of any rights under this Agreement. This Agreement shall be construed and governed in accordance with the laws of New York. If any provision of this Agreement is held to be contrary to law, that provision will be enforced to the maximum extent permissible, and the remaining provisions will remain in force and effect.

NO TECHNICAL SUPPORT IS PROVIDED WITH THIS CD-ROM.

LEARN DREAMWEAVER EASILY!
MORE VIDEO LESSONS
FROM ROBERT FULLER AND BRAINSVILLE.COM

Dear Friend,

Thank you for buying this book. I hope that you found it useful and enjoyed the CD-ROM full of video lessons.

Now that you are learning HTML, you may also be interested in the video CD I've created about Dreamweaver, the **Dreamweaver CD Extra**. It covers key areas like these:

Creating Flash Elements
Use Dreamweaver to produce eye-catching Flash animations

Text and Links
Format these essential Web site elements swiftly and easily

Styles and Tables
Tools and techniques for making your pages look the way you want

Easy Access to HTML
Work "under the hood" with the language of the Web

Extending Dreamweaver
Go beyond the basics and improve Dreamweaver's capabilities

...And more! The complete contents are listed at www.Brainsville.com.

The lessons on the **Dreamweaver CD Extra** use the same easy-to-follow video presentation style as the CD you already have. I'm right there on your screen, talking to you about Dreamweaver in the same practical, understandable way.

The **Dreamweaver CD Extra** is an essential tool for learning Dreamweaver. Check it out at www.Brainsville.com.

Best Wishes,

Robert Fuller

CD-Extras

USE THE SAME EASY-TO-FOLLOW
VIDEO PRESENTATION STYLE AS THE
CD INCLUDED WITH THIS BOOK

Check it out @
Brainsville.com

Name: Robert Fuller
Project: Dreamweaver CD Ext

ORDER THE DREAMWEAVER CD-EXTRA AT
Brainsville.com™
The better way to learn™